Date Du

THE ANTHROPOLOGY OF ANGER

The Anthropology of Anger

Civil Society and Democracy in Africa

Célestin Monga

translated by

Linda L. Fleck & Célestin Monga

BOULDER
LONDON

For Kephren and Yvette

Published in the United States of America in 1996 by
Lynne Rienner Publishers, Inc.
1800 30th Street, Boulder, Colorado 80301

and in the United Kingdom by
Lynne Rienner Publishers, Inc.
3 Henrietta Street, Covent Garden, London WC2E 8LU

An earlier version of this book was published as *Anthropologie de la Colère*
(Paris: L'Harmattan 1994; © in 1994 by L'Harmattan)

Library of Congress Cataloging-in-Publication Data
Monga, Célestin.
[Anthropologie de la colère. English]
The anthropology of anger : civil society and democracy in Africa /
by Célestin Monga.
p. cm.
Includes bibliographical references and index.
ISBN 1-55587-644-7
1. Democracy—Africa, Sub-Saharan. 2. Civil society—Africa, Sub-Saharan. 3. Representative government and representation—Africa, Sub-Saharan. 4. Africa, Sub-Saharan—Politics and government—1960– 5. Africa, Sub-Saharan—Social conditions—1960– I. Title.
JQ1879.A15M6613 1996
320.96'09'045--dc20 96-7588
CIP

British Cataloguing in Publication Data
A Cataloguing in Publication record for this book
is available from the British Library.

This book was typeset by Letra Libre
1705 Fourteenth Street, Suite 391, Boulder, Colorado 80302.

Printed and bound in the United States of America

The paper used in this publication meets the requirements
of the American National Standard for Permanence of
Paper for Printed Library Materials Z39.48-1984.

5 4 3 2 1

Contents

Preface

As I begin to write this preface to the expanded, English-language edition of this book, Lokua Kanza is singing on my CD player. His music sounds simple, yet it is so profound: a crystal-clear, breathy, melancholic voice, whispering some fresh words in Lingala, and following a circular melodic line that seems to express the quintessential magic of his guitar. His singing has a cosmic dimension, reverberating the rising and insistent scream of human loneliness on each vibrato—a scream tragic, but not desperate.

As the lyrics flow, expressing the sensation of a fissure in the soul—the original feeling of an age-old, open wound with which any African is familiar—in my apartment in Somerville, Massachusetts, I recognize the main features of what was a few years ago the sonorous ambience of my daily life in Douala, Cameroon. I can hear all the delicious noises, smell the heady fragrances, and recall the spicy memories of the African *quotidienneté* I know. Through the song, which alternates yearning and anger, which evokes at once the frustration of sorrow and the pleasure of uncertainty, I can feel the subtle and harmonious hubbub of everyday life in sub-Saharan Africa.

Lokua Kanza lives in Paris, but his voice and style express—perhaps better than anything else does—what I have observed in his fellow citizens in Zaire: the consciousness of pain and suffering, the desire to survive madness, the quest for another, better world, and the confidence that the worst is never inevitable. Yes, I am aware of the conceptual dangers of associating too quickly the work of an artist with the prevailing historical and social narrative. Nevertheless, I strongly believe that creators of African music like Lokua Kanza do not conceive the beauty of their art to be the full sum of it. Even if we acknowledge, as Jean-François Lyotard suggests (1993:111), that there is an intrinsic freedom to any given artistic product that transcends any historical determinism, we must also agree that "no art exists in a vacuum" (Carruth, 1993:24)—and certainly not that which, roughly speaking, we can label today's African art.

Why is it that so many experts on Africa seem almost impervious to what I consider the best in African music? Why is so little consideration given to Lokua Kanza's work, and to many other powerful pieces, in the traditional analysis of contemporary African art? Why is it that whenever a West-based scholar (whether African, American, or European) undertakes a study of the discourse of African music, he or she never mentions the existence of artists who try to express an alternative way of thinking? And to draw a parallel with the social sciences, why do we always read and hear accounts of everyday life in Mobutu Sese Seko's Zaire with no reference whatsoever to Lokua Kanza's version of the story? In other words, why is the everyday-life approach, the grassroots perspective, so consistently absent from the literature on social change in Africa? Here is an artist with all the credentials usually required for success and international recognition: his work is highly original, substantial, technically sophisticated, and properly packaged and marketed by a respected French producer. Yet, because he does not represent what is considered to be the mainstream of African music, because his records do not sound like those that, according to critics, the public is used to listening to, he is not taken seriously. At best, he is seen as another Francis Bebey, or another Pierre Akendengue—that is, an artist for a limited audience, a singer for a minority of embittered intellectuals—which means he will probably be the victim of his talent.

This brings me to the point of this book. Not only are African artists treated this way by the so-called experts (academics and journalists, for example), all African social actors who happen to be different, whether in the nature of their message or in the way they act, are ignored by those who influence public perception of the continent. This has been true for decades, in literature, in the movie industry, in painting, and it seems to be true today in politics as well. Most of the political science literature devoted to the continent is full of predominant paradigms and reductionist stereotypes, not only of African politicians but also of African peoples' behavior in politics—or, more precisely, their lack of political behavior. And these paradigms and stereotypes are used to explain the economic misery and democratic ineptitude that characterize the continent in the eyes of the average Western citizen.

Having been brutally involved in sociopolitical turmoil in my country, Cameroon, and having worked and traveled extensively in various other African countries, where I became connected to different social networks, I felt frustrated by most of the literature on the determinants of a successful process of democratization, the exact role of civil society in the current changes, and the political behavior of African people. The more I read, the more frustrated I became, because I could perceive in the political historiography of Africa the same contempt and disconnection I described with regard to Lokua Kanza. I was most irritated by the fact that neither the academics nor the journalists were able (or willing) to capture what was the very essence of the social phenomena and the political movements that I had witnessed for years: the determination of people at the grassroots level to engage in the political arena, at any cost, in order to bring about some positive changes in the way they had been ruled for several centuries.

Working as chief economist for a commercial bank, I did not expect to write a political analysis of the events. But, as I said, I did become involved in the struggle for democracy in Cameroon. In late December 1990, four years after I had come back from Europe, I was fed up with the political monolithism that was destroying the economy. I wrote a small piece for a private local paper, criticizing the government. In early January, I was arrested, held without charge until my release (a few days later), and was not permitted any visitors. Charges were subsequently brought against me, notably for contempt of the president of the republic. The first session of my trial took place on January 10 in Douala. More than two hundred lawyers from the Cameroonian Bar Association joined to act as the defense counsel. Several thousand people showed up to manifest publicly their opposition to the government. It was the first time since the early 1960s that popular demonstrations against the government had taken place in the country. Everyone (including myself) was surprised. The trial was adjourned until the following week. On January 17, when the second session of the trial was set to begin, demonstrations took place in a number of cities. In the northern city of Garoua, troops fired on a demonstration supporting me and calling for democratization (the country was still under a single-party regime). Several people were killed, dozens were wounded, and many were beaten by the police or jailed without any specific charges.

Such an event is banal under *monocracy,* to use Ambroise Kom's word (1991b). I was lucky that a popular uprising and international pressure prevented the Cameroonian regime from using against me some of its usual repressive tactics (such as secret trials and executions). But the fact that some people who did not even know me had been killed shook me profoundly. I visited their families, but did not know what to say to weeping mothers, tearful fathers, suspicious friends and cousins. I decided to step back momentarily from my economic writings and to record my thoughts on the political transformations I was part of. I wanted to tell the story of the variety of ways in which people in Cameroon and elsewhere stood up—despite their fears, their material poverty, and the very real danger they faced—in order to defy humiliation and to live their humanity. I had completed a degree in political science at the Sorbonne, and I hoped that I could recall the rudiments of political anthropology I was taught by Professor Maurice Duverger and use them as a framework for analyzing what was going on in my country and in many others. (I was subsequently encouraged by my feeling that most of what was published did not properly reflect the real logic behind the new wave of social changes in Africa.)

Thus, I wrote to describe and to analyze our collective anger, mostly for conferences I was invited to attend between 1991 and 1993. I was concerned about my capacity to explore a field that was outside my area of professional specialization; furthermore, I was angry myself, and I knew that anger has its risks, chief among which is its impediment to clear-sightedness. But my good friends Paul Dakeyo and Ambroise Kom convinced me that some anger is healthy and that the only relevant question is what you do with it. This was enough to stimulate in me what Léon Poliakov once called the "Sorbonic vanity" (1981:104) to describe the inherent self-confidence of any graduate of the Sorbonne.

In carrying out this task, I tried not to be naive about the magnitude of the phenomena I was describing, nor about the chances of success. I also struggled not to be part of the game—I tried to remain "positively neutral," to maintain the critical distance of a "*spectateur impur*" or "*spectateur engagé*," as Raymond Aron used to say about himself (1972). I have every reason to fear that this book will strike some readers as "very African." This would not be a compliment. African it is, of course, by virtue of its empirical focus. It would, however, be a mistake to regard all that is said here about different techniques of rebellious behavior in the arts, culture, politics, and everyday life as a collection of exotic curiosities and frivolities. My guess is that most of these patterns of behavior can be found in many parts of the developing world and even used for an ambitious, universal theory of sociopolitical change.

That there is an exciting political life in Africa is an idea unfamiliar to many people; the intellectual sterility of the continent's leaders and people is too often taken for granted, and the intellectual achievements of its societies too often overlooked. I suggest here some ways of looking differently at Africa's sociopolitical dynamics and also present a few tools for adjusting political science theories to the African context.

*

* *

There have been substantial changes between the French and the present version of this book. First, I have added Chapter 2, to situate my work in the theoretical frameworks available in recent literature on political issues in Africa. Second, I have taken into account some of the relevant findings in the North American literature, to which I did not have access previously. I have also updated the empirical evidence, using the latest available information on the democratic experience in such countries as Senegal, Benin, Kenya, and Zambia.

I have been fortunate to live in the Boston area over the past several years and to work in one of the best academic environments in the world. Being affiliated with M.I.T. and Harvard University and holding visiting professorships at Boston University and the University of Bordeaux has given me the chance to use some of the finest research facilities and also to meet many wonderful people, some of whom have contributed—whether consciously or unwittingly—to this book. I am grateful to my friends, colleagues, and mentors at Harvard (Kathryn Dominguez, Kalypso Nicolaidis); M.I.T. (Willard Johnson, Olivier Blanchard, Rudi Dornbusch, Susan Lowance, Glen Urban); Boston University (Edouard Bustin, Bill Bicknell); the University of Bordeaux (Daniel C. Bach, Jean-François Médart); the University of Pau (Thiérry Michalon); Stanford University (Larry Diamond); the University of Rochester (Cilas Kemedjo); the University of Yaounde (Ambrose Kom); Editions Nouvelles du Sud (Paul Dakeyo); CODESTRIA (Achille Mbembe); the World Bank (Eric Chinje); and also Augustin Nya, Jean-Pierre Kakmani, Martin Jumbam, Jean-Marc Sika, Richard Nouni, Benjamin Zebaze, Pius Njawe, Severin Tchounkeu, and Charles Tchoungang. Some of them will probably wonder why on earth I made such a great leap from international monetary issues, which is my main area of academic specialization, into the study of political behavior. I do hope that after shaking their heads doubtfully they will dismiss the most obvious motivations (intellectual dilettantism of a trapezist, unchecked egotism) and understand the real reason for this book: the need to acknowledge a moral debt to those who paid with their lives for my innocence and, beyond them, the need to pay tribute to all the ordinary African men and women who struggle every day, in a variety of silent ways, to escape political cannibalism.

1

The Need for Some Alternative Ideas

I am the product of the anger of the people, which means they are active and no longer spectators.

—Jerry Rawlings,
president of Ghana

In Abidjan, the large boulevard that links the airport and downtown and runs through the popular residential areas of Koumassi, Marcory, and Treichville is called Boulevard Giscard d'Estaing. It obviously is a name that is not indigenous. Having had to get used to it, however, and having learned to pronounce it, the inhabitants of this prestigious lagoon city quickly found a way to integrate such a barbarous surname into their imagination. When the boulevard was first built, there were no sidewalks, and the population in that area was not used to traffic lights. As a result, dozens of pedestrians were hit by speeding cars every month. For the most part, these accidents were caused by the nouveaux riches, for whom the car had become the ultimate symbol of social success. The Boulevard Giscard d'Estaing became a frontier the ordinary people of Treichville could not cross—or could cross only by putting their lives on the line. Getting safely from one side to the other amounted almost to a miracle. In the popular mind, the Boulevard Giscard d'Estaing was thus renamed the Boulevard du Destin (the Boulevard of Fate).

*
* *

This book seeks to propose some alternative approaches to the study of sociopolitical change in Africa. It is important to explore the determinants of collective creativity—to grasp the meaning of small, ordinary things and to understand, via an examination of phenomena generally overlooked by social scientists and policymakers, the dynamics of the social structure. In this work, therefore, I will opt for an approach informed by commonplace phenomena. My aim is to decipher events and cast light on much that is usually left unsaid or that is stated inexplicitly. Since Veyne's seminal work on how history is written (1984), we have learned that there can be neither guilt nor shame in probing into our daily experiences.

Analytical Matters

Many scholars have argued that the ongoing democratization process in Africa is doomed to fail because of insufficient internal demand for political reforms—the underlying assumption being that democratization is a consequence of conditionality imposed by external donors. Others have challenged the very roots of the current changes, alleging some kind of determinism as prerequisite; that is, Africa needs cultural and economic adjustments before it is ready for sustainable democracy. In this book I argue that both views are wrong. Indeed, African peoples have been trying for decades to challenge authoritarianism, but their patterns of behavior could not be captured by the classical tools used by social scientists. I also argue that it was the upsurge of popular protest in African countries that forced African regimes and the international community to reconsider the way in which the political process operates. For several decades, the rules of the political game and the social game (concerning power, status, wealth, and domination) were unilaterally determined by Africa's authoritarian states, and people feigned to accept those rules when in fact they constantly adjusted their behavior to escape domination and to circumvent the most coercive strictures.

Proposing an outline of what can be called a political anthropology of anger, I will shed some light on the continent's long tradition of an indigenous form of activism—through culture, arts, social organizations, individual and collective behavior within the public sphere, etc. By analyzing social changes from a grassroots perspective, I will show that the quest for freedom in Africa is deeply entrenched and that the most noticeable thing about the continent is that the recent sociopolitical events—successes or failures—are simply the natural (and somewhat predictable) results of the dynamics of political markets with highly creative political entrepreneurs. Finally, I argue that collective resistance to authoritarianism and collective willingness and commitment to build new and more effective political systems are functions of the development of civil society.

Such a statement needs clear definition of the main concepts.

Political Markets

Markets used to be institutions where buyers and sellers came together to exchange goods. "Today, the concept of markets is used to include any situation where exchange takes place" (Stiglitz 1993:13). I borrow this concept from economics to illustrate the dynamics of the ongoing democratization process in Africa. Applying tools from economics to the anthropology of African politics, I focus on four basic questions that economists tend to pose when analyzing any market—what is produced, how it is produced, how these decisions are made, and for whom political goods (ideas) are produced—and on the whole, the answers reflect the efficiency of these political markets.

In political markets with competition, citizens make choices that reflect their needs. And political actors (parties, civil society) make choices that maximize their gains (in terms of power and influence); to do so, they must produce the ideas that citizens want, and they must produce and implement them at a lower cost than do other political actors. As they compete against one another in the quest for power and influence, citizens benefit, both in the kind of ideas produced and the cost at which they are implemented. Political markets allocate ideas to those who are willing (or able) to "buy" them, that is, to participate in the political game. Images used by Stiglitz to describe market economies can be used here to present my conception of African political markets. Like bidders at an auction, the market participants willing to pay the highest price (defined in any terms) take home the goods, in the sense that their willingness legitimizes the supplier of those political goods. But what people are willing or able to accept depends on the quality of information they have about the game and the actors and also on their level of trust in the whole system. That is why many people are kept out of the market.

Such an analysis leads to the idea of political entrepreneurship as a key concept for understanding how African political systems work. A successful political entrepreneur is someone who can not only compete within the existing boundaries of the market but also increase the number of potential consumers by drawing new citizens into the game—this is called *participation,* in democratic theory (see, for instance, Schneider and Teske 1992). There is a strong tendency among those who dominate the game to eliminate competition or to maintain a limited number of participants, since any enlargement is likely to disturb the prevailing equilibrium and to force all the actors into new struggles. One has to think about the challenges facing African authoritarian regimes as a situation of monopoly, in which the dominant player is unwilling to accept new entrants. The discussion of the democratization process can be analyzed using this simple and basic framework.

In spite of the monopolistic resistance of governments, African peoples have always tried to enter political markets. Although governments have often succeeded in maintaining a limited level of competition in political arenas, political participation has always existed, but in a form different from what can be captured by the classical tools of analysis available in political science. By taking a grassroots approach to the study of the democratization process, I try to substantiate that statement. Furthermore, I argue that the numerous techniques invented to escape enslavement over several decades of dictatorship eventually led to the emergence of an informal civil society that cannot be observed and analyzed the same way that societies are in other parts of the world. It follows that the "success" of the current social changes taking place in all African countries will be a function of the cohesiveness of civil society and its ability to come out of the closet and occupy the public sphere in a positive way.

My central assertion is not far from the observation made by de Tocqueville (1945): The strength of civil society will strongly affect the industrial and the democratic structure of African countries over the next decades. But contrary to Putnam (1992), whose ideas are behind much of the current scholarly interest in intermediate institutions, I use a different definition of civil society—a definition that will, I hope, keep me from falling into the trap of naiveté about the virtues of civil society into which most thinkers have fallen, beginning with de Tocqueville himself.

Civil Society

To define civil society is an ambitious task, given the breadth of recent writings on the topic (Gellner 1991; Shils 1991; Seligman 1992; Cohen and Arato 1992; Gautier 1993; Harbeson et al. 1994). As Zakaria puts it, "In the world of ideas, civil society is hot." (1995) In this book, I define it as new spaces for communication and discussion over which the state has no control. For a number of reasons, which are discussed in Chapter 6, I define it as including only those groups, organizations, and personalities that pursue freedom, justice, and the rights of citizenship against authoritarian states. Some scholars may find such a restrictive view problematic, since conceptions of freedom, justice, and the rights of citizenship vary across social groups and it is difficult to find an objective standard for inclusion and exclusion; moreover, some groups pursue these goals without being against the state, while other groups are against the state without pursuing these goals. But I chose a narrow definition because one needs to be careful in grouping under the same label all kinds of organizations. Indeed, the problem with general definitions such as "intermediate institutions" and "private groups that thrive between the realms of the state and the family" is that they include almost everything between the family and the state, which would also include the Mafia! As Zakaria explains:

> The space between the realm of government and that of the family can be filled with all kinds of associations, liberal and illiberal. Historians have

> amply laid out how the Nazi Party made its first inroads through infiltrating local groups. On a less extreme note, many of the small groups that have formed in America over the last two decades have been thoroughly illiberal in spirit: victims' groups that have discouraged individual responsibility, minority clubs that have balkanized the campus and the workplace, pseudoreligious cults with violent agendas (1995:25).

Further, I argue that Africa's social capital is dwindling dangerously in some regions, not because of the declining number of people in charity organizations, choral groups, and soccer associations, or the decreasing membership in Rotary Clubs, as Putnam's model predicts, but because of the absence (or the weakness) of spiritual capital within civil society. That is why I suggest the concept of a *civic deficit,* which is not the consequence of any kind of cultural gap but rather the product of collective anger.[1]

The Anthropology of Anger

The driving force behind my argument is anger. This notion might suggest that this book is primarily addressed to social psychologists, which is not at all the case. Without attempting to provide a full theoretical statement of the anthropology of anger (this book is by no means aimed at launching a school of thought), let me give a straightforward definition of the term: People get angry when they are systematically oppressed, and they develop many ways of escaping repression, some of which may lead to the fragmentation of the most stable countries and the worsening of social conditions; in this new era of democratization, the vicious legacy of anger is a factor of political instability and democratic sustainability. One of the dangers of the new politics is that there may be no rules—perhaps just a generalized anomie. I am aware that this is a strong statement, with important ramifications. Indeed, by so defining the *problématique,* I can foresee some criticism: not everyone in society is oppressed, and not everyone is oppressed in the same way; how, then, do collective dreams and fears take shape, and what mechanisms finally convert anger into a political attitude (action or withdrawal from the political market)?

There are at least two bodies of literature that can help explain why I confer an analytical status to the term *indiscipline.* First, Ted Gurr's reflections on "relative deprivation" and "potential for action" (1970, 1985) are very useful in understanding how frustration can propel individuals to participate in some kind of political protest. As Gurr argued (somewhat solemnly): "The basic relationship is as fundamental to understanding civil strife as the law of gravity is to atmospheric physics: relative deprivation … is a necessary precondition for civil strife of any kind. The greater the deprivation an individual perceives relative to his expectations, the greater his discontent; the more widespread and intense is discontent among members of a society, the more likely and severe is civil strife" (1970:596). Those who are familiar with the numerous forms of political protest in Africa will agree that Gurr's conceptualization of what he calls "relative deprivation" is only a rough approximation of what is really going on today. Gurr has subsequently adjusted his analysis to take into account some of the criticism, giving more importance to factors that he initially neglected: the "cultural" prerequisites for violent forms of protest and some other rational calculations (Gurr and Duvall 1976). I shall not discuss his culturalistic approach to politics at this point; I will move beyond his cynical view of the determinants of political protest. My arguments in this book are substantially different—they may sound far more idealistic in some sense.

The second group of thinkers that I found useful to engage are those working on everyday forms of resistance, such as James Scott and the so-called Subaltern Studies School. They are much more appealing to me, since they adopt a grassroots perspective of analysis. They start from the observation that historical records and archives never mention peasantry, for instance, except when their activity is menacing. This observation confirms that "most subordinate classes throughout most of history have rarely been afforded the luxury of open, organized, political activity. Or, better stated, such activity was dangerous, if not suicidal. Even when the option did exist, it is not clear that the same objectives might not also be pursued by other stratagems" (Scott 1985:xv). That is why it is important to understand everyday forms of peasant resistance, defined by Scott as "the prosaic but constant struggle between the peasantry and those who seek to extract labor, food, taxes, rents, and interest from them. Most forms of this struggle stop well short of outright collective defiance. Here I have in mind the ordinary weapons of relatively powerless groups: foot dragging, dissimulation, desertion, false compliance, pilfering, feigned ignorance, slander, arson, sabotage, and so on" (1985:xvi). In fact, many historians have argued that such informal methods of protest are eventually what really pushes history. As Bloch put it in his study of feudalism, the great millennial movements were "flashes in the pan" compared with what he called the "patient, silent struggles stubbornly carried on by rural communities" to resist oppression and injustice (1970:170).

While this second approach seems to capture the type of social dynamics that I will describe and analyze in the context of the current sociopolitical changes in Africa, I must emphasize that I disagree with one of Scott's assumptions; that is, the idea that "most subordinate classes are … far less interested in changing the large structures of the state and the law than in what Hobsbawm has appropriately called 'working the system … to their minimum disadvantage'" (1985:xv). Peasants in Africa and, more generally, people living in rural areas had no such limited views on the significance of their citizenship during the first phase of the democratic liberalization that occurred between 1989 and 1993: like other social groups, they wanted the quest for dignity to be a top priority on the national agenda. The claim for a national conference, for instance, in order to "fix" the government, was as strong in rural areas as in major cities.[2] In fact, the strong belief in the necessity to change the way the state functions has always been a characteristic of African peasantry, as Ela has shown (1982, 1990).

For these reasons, I would rather follow de Certeau's dilettantism in investigating the behavior of ordinary people—peasants or others—commonly assumed to be passive and manipulated by corrupted elites or governments (1984). This book is aimed at exploring the ambiguity behind the enforcement of social rules. Apparently submissive and even consenting to their subjection, African peoples nevertheless often transformed the laws imposed on them into something quite different from what their leaders had in mind. They subverted the rules not by confronting them directly, but by circumventing them very carefully, or even by using them to achieve objectives contrary to the system that they had no choice but to accept. They were *other* within the authoritarian regimes that outwardly assimilated them. To use de Certeau's words, "Their use of the dominant social order deflected its power, which they lacked the means to challenge" (1984:xiii). The strength of their difference lay in their use of subversive tactics, which are worth examining, since they reveal the amazing existence of what can be called a collective consciousness.

Theoretical and Conceptual Issues

Observing the widening gap between theory and research, Coleman highlighted the fundamental contradiction confronting social scientists today: "Social theory continues to be about the functioning of social systems and behavior, but empirical research is often concerned with explaining individual behavior" (1990:1). Indeed, a key issue that is not always fully addressed by Africanists is that of accounting for the functioning of the political system: They tend to draw general conclusions on the system as a whole from uncertain anecdotes about individual cases. Of course, this is not specific to African studies. However, whereas researchers in other fields of knowledge usually acknowledge the existence of the problem and try to solve it by using quantitative methods, Africanists tend to avoid it. Their work is rarely scrutinized by the academic community in the same manner as other publications are, and their "empirical evidence" is generally limited to some administrative data or a few patterns of behavior they noticed during their short trips to the field—both of which are highly unreliable. Since this book has been written from the perspective of my personal involvement in the struggle for freedom in my own country, I will not tackle this issue here. However, I will briefly mention the various options available to anyone dealing with it, and I will clearly present where I stand.

Broadly speaking, there are two methods of explanation in the literature devoted to individuals: One focuses on individual behavior, using principally factors external to the individual or factors characterizing him or her as a whole (let's call this approach A_1). Another examines processes internal to the individual, focusing on processes through which these internal changes lead to a specific behavior (A_2). Both approaches have their advantages and disavantages, whether one undertakes qualitative or quantitative research (see Coleman). But the theoretical difficulties are compounded by the fact that many social scientists analyze social systems using data and information collected from individuals. Whether this is supported by methods of statistical association or analyses of processes internal to those individuals does not really matter, since it is very hard to explain the functioning of social systems using (unreliable) information from single individuals. Yet many political scientists working on African issues do this all the time, without recognizing the numerous hidden assumptions sustaining their models.

Yet, even if one follows the second approach—that is, studies social systems, not merely groups of individuals—there are still many difficulties because of the existence of several levels of analysis: One can either focus on a sample of cases of system behavior or observe system behavior as a whole over a period of time; this requires the use of statistical techniques (let's call this approach B_1). A second method is to examine processes internal to the system: component parts at a level below that of the system institutions, individuals in subgroups, etc. (B_2). Each of these four modes of explanation has certain points to recommend it and certain shortcomings that one must acknowledge while using it.

I do not think that there has to be a clear-cut separation among these four approaches, yet, the academic community is generally divided along the lines of Figure 1.1. In order to be considered "scientific," and to benefit from the respect of their peers, Western political scientists studying Africa usually adopt either A_1 or B_1. Otherwise, their work is quickly dismissed as being too subjective and too superficial; in "scientific" terms, it is said to lack quantitative and empirical evidence or no formal model to support the theory. But those working on African issues do not bother to build quantitative models or to back up their observations with empirical evidence. And there is good reason for this: In countries where even the president does not always know how many citizens live in the capital city, it is risky to

Figure 1.1

		Level of analysis	
		Focus on the individual	Focus on the whole system
Analytical method	Statistical association	A_1	B_1
	Examining processes internal to the individual or the system	A_2	B_2

undertake quantitative analysis based solely on statistical techniques. Moreover, almost all the theoretical frameworks used by political scientists cannot be transferred to the very specific sociological environment of African countries; they simply do not support broad and simplistic comparisons. How would one classify Mobutu's regime in Zaire using Robert Dahl's definitions? How would one assess the rigidity of political parties in Tanzania using Maurice Duverger's law? How would one define civil society in Sudan with Gramsci's perception of the state and his concept of hegemonic alliance in mind?

Facing such an unusual environment, where most of their quantitative tools need to be readjusted, many political scientists have chosen the easiest way of dealing with the situation: using an A_2 approach—that is, observing microphenomena from the perspectives of individuals and trying to draw general conclusions as to how the system works simply by interpreting individual behavior. In doing so, they fall into the trap of subjectivism—and their work is rarely perceived as contributing to knowledge in any way.

In this book, I follow the A_2 and B_2 approaches. I could have tried to give a "scientific" flavor to my work by backing it up with some mathematical formulas. But given that these are general reflections concerning many issues and covering a vast geographic area, I chose instead to limit myself to the analysis of phenomena within my main area of interest (mostly western and central Africa), using my personal experience in the field where necessary. As noted by Coleman, "The major problem for explanations of system behavior based on actions and orientations at a level below that of the system is that of moving from the lower level to the system level. This has been called the micro-to-macro problem, and it is pervasive throughout the social sciences" (1990:6). In spite of the considerable body of theoretical work attempting to deal with this problem, I do not think that I could have tackled the issue properly, given the high level of complexity of African social systems. The only way I could honestly address the question was to limit my propensity to generalize about Africa.

I therefore decided to conduct research based on the commonplace attitudes and events of everyday life, that which is beyond the realm of words, in an attempt to uncover the logic that most accurately serves collective ambitions. My observations lead to the conclusion that the democratic project in sub-Saharan Africa has not been perceived by the people as a cultural fetish used to disguise famine, misery, and suffering. Rather, they see it as a means of expressing citizenship, confiscated and perverted by decades of authoritarianism.

Throughout Africa, people are invading the political arena in an (often furious) attempt to get their will finally taken into account by the leaders, and ethical ambition is expressed through explosions of anger. The real issue lies in the fact that these popular movements lack appropriate leadership. Their new "representatives" do not have the competence to build institutions that take into consideration the cultural realities and power relationships among the major social actors. It is these factors that finally determine the dynamics of the democratic project.

Africa in anger offers political scientists new areas of reflection. Avenues, themes, and dimensions of political participation are viewed here from a highly unusual perspective. The range of political activities treated elsewhere—for example, ways of expressing political choices, manifestations of discontent, methods of organizing electoral campaigns—has been considerably enlarged because of the creativity inherited from a long tradition of indiscipline. The feeling of political competence has rapidly become one of the values most common among all groups of the population.

These interesting indications, which are signs of the rebirth of civil society, raise the question of the validity of the analytical tools and frameworks for the interpretation of voter behavior. For instance, the so-called ecological models that are based on theories of human geography appear to be just as inadequate in capturing African realities as the so-called psychosociological ones (see Mayer and Perrineau 1992)—even though the latter theories are more adaptable to the African context, provided that local cultural factors are incorporated into the analysis.

The major problem with Africanists is that they are doggedly trying to make sense—any sense, actually—of African political changes. Thanks to Axelle Kabou's impressive talent, we now have a series of questions that demand the right answers.[3] By studying people's anxieties, by observing the deep ambitions behind their innocuous behavior, I had the feeling that beyond the concerns regarding the uncertainties of current events there was a certain optimism. If complacent optimism is unrealistic, then Afro-pessimism has no basis either. The optimism that underlies the following text has nothing to do with slogans; it is simply a necessity that is fueled by the potential and the will of people encountered in African political markets over the last few years.

The conclusions in this book indicate that, far from rejecting development, Africa is forging new trails toward the affirmation of its dignity. The discrepancy between political supply and social demand summarizes the present difficulties in Africa's democratic process. The populist inflation that seems to pervert the art of politics in some countries accrues in reality because of this gap, and it is amplified by external financial and economic constraints. Since authoritarian regimes have limited the state to a prebendal role (Joseph 1983), communities have reasserted their liberty toward it. Civil disobedience tends to be the order of the day, and public policies are invalidated daily by collective indiscipline.

The question as to what would have to be done to improve the performance of the democratization wave (actors, rules, or the very nature of the game) loses its importance once one ceases to engage in classical political science and undertakes a political anthropology of anger. Actors matter only in as much as they agree to comply with certain rules. The important problem of the ethnogeographic dimension of politics comes afterward. Once Africans and their representatives give priority to the question of institutionalization as opposed to solutions centered on infighting among individuals or on mere leadership, once the organs for managing civil societies are well structured and the ambitions of their proponents become well known because they are widely disseminated and broadly discussed, social balance will be restored and public authority will be reestablished.

The state will then cease to be the battlefield of private interests and will become the place for discussing and stabilizing various types of social organization. The discrepancy between the collective ambitions of social groups and communities on the one hand and the individual expectations of the citizens on the other is not due to a lack of will or to the people's familiarity with the "delights" of authoritarianism, but rather to the shortcomings of methods designed to integrate individuals into the democratic process.[4] At the heart of the present malaise are the issue of the involvement of the majority in building new institutions and the problem of accumulation schemes. The aim of this book is to offer some suggestions to the study of political processes that seem to be nonlinear and to shed some light on ways of analyzing social changes in countries where people are angry.

Chapter 2 presents the main theoretical frameworks political scientists use to assess political changes in sub-Saharan Africa, emphasizing the shortcomings and contradictions of each model, and also underscores the need for another conceptual approach. I suggest a simple model of the first phase of democratic development in Africa (1990–1995).

Chapter 3 focuses on the cultural foundations of social changes. I discuss the psychological and philosophical background of public discourse since independence and some related issues: the politics of culture launched by African governments in the 1960s and 1970s; the ambiguity of being African in today's world; the use of memory, utopia, and myths in politics; the relationship between culture, revolt, and violence in countries where young people seem to have no future; and finally the work of intellectuals and artists who have decided to express another vision of the way their societies should be organized by challenging most of the conventional aesthetic standards.

Chapter 4 identifies the emerging democratic patterns behind the banality of everyday life in Africa. By exploring the language of the ordinary people, and by looking beyond the behavior of all kinds of people, one can perceive a refreshing optimization of disorder. Thus, one needs to reinterpret the people's "natural propensity to indiscipline" and their rejection of official watchwords.

Chapter 5 is devoted to the study of the politics of the sacred. Given the explosion of the quest for God in Africa today, it is important to analyze how collective anger and anxieties are translated into the mechanics of new spiritual habits that seem to influence and, sometimes, to determine the outcome of political battles in many countries.

Chapter 6 explores the role of civil society in the quest for democracy. I underline its key influence in reshaping the emerging political markets in sub-Saharan Africa and its conflicting objectives, as well as the risks of disintegration of countries where some of the most powerful civic organizations are essentially created along "ethnic" or regional lines, or for political purposes only. Finally, I make some policy recommendations aimed at strengthening civil society.

In conclusion, I discuss why people in some countries are still expecting a messiah. I look at the high level of initial expectations and the risks of frustration and downfall. I also analyze how the cynical (mis)management of collective anger by some political entrepreneurs can lead to such tragedies as Rwanda, Burundi, or Liberia.

Notes

1. The logic of the argument may seem somewhat confusing: the anthropology of anger derives from civil society, but civil society is defined by the anthropology of

anger. In fact, one can think about this by understanding the relationships among society, civil society, and personalities, all of which appear to be part of the anthropology of anger. This logic is clarified in Chapter 6.

2. A national conference can be defined as a popular meeting during which all the politically active groups in the country redesign the rules of the political game and elaborate a new electoral agenda. See Robinson (1994).

3. In 1991 Cameroonian sociologist A. Kabou published a provocative best-seller arguing that Africans had decided to reject the very idea of economic and political development.

4. Building on Gabriel Almond and Sidney Verba's idea of the importance of civic culture, various theories have been suggested by those who define some cultural prerequisites to democracy; they consider the "lack" or the "immaturity" of people's political culture is the reason that democratization is "failing" in Africa. This issue is discussed in Chapter 2.

2

How Africa Fits into Democratic Theory

Celui qui parle ne sait pas.
Celui qui sait ne parle pas.

*

He who speaks doesn't know.
He who knows doesn't speak.

—Mosse proverb

In one of his most recent works, Paul Krugman (1995) relates the intriguing paradox of the evolution of the knowledge of European cartographers who charted Africa between the fifteenth and eighteenth centuries. He observes that in theory one would expect knowledge to develop in a linear fashion and maps to become ever more precise as more research was carried out. However, this was not the case.

As Krugman explains, the maps roughly sketched by the first explorers, despite some inaccuracies with respect to distances, the shape of the coastline, and characteristics of the inhabitants, contained a wealth of useful information on the interior of the continent. As time went by and sources of information grew more reliable, the coastline was studied carefully, along with its cities and populations. As early as the eighteenth century, the mapping of the coastline had by and large taken its definitive form. At the same time, however, the interior—most of the continent—became less well known. Fantastic legends concerning the inhabitants' characteristics gradually disappeared, but nothing more was learned about the real locations of towns and rivers. Over time, European cartographers actually became more ignorant of the continent than they were at the time of the first explorers.

What occurred over three centuries to cause such a regression? Krugman's hypothesis, which strikes me as a good one, is that the improvement in mapmaking techniques raised standards with respect to the reliability of data. Secondhand information and intuitive judgments once taken at face value no longer measured up to the academic standards of those working in the discipline. Only data gathered in accordance with the research methodology and theoretical models of the day were considered valid. Although the plotting of the map of Africa benefited in the end from the initial skepticism of researchers—those who relied on data meeting the rigorous standards of present-day cartography—there was a time in which the improvement in scientific methods resulted in a loss of knowledge.

The analogy between the development of mapmaking and the evolution of research on Africa in the social sciences is striking. There was a time when the travel journals of a Ibn Battuta, a Ibn Khaldun, or even a René Caillé provided the West with information on the organization and operation of African societies that was considered generally accurate, if paternalistic and somewhat crude. Then ethnologists landed on the continent equipped with their theories and armed with their subjectivism and arrogance. Whether in good or bad faith, they claimed they were there to make the field of African studies "clear" and "rational" through the application of models that had more to do with the logic of their own mentalities than with the identity and structure of the places they claimed to analyze "scientifically." From Jahn and Hegel to Lévy-Bruhl and Voltaire, the obsessive desire to apply rigid theories to recalcitrant terrain, without always verifying their validity through empirical research, resulted in a literature of dubious worth (Amondji 1993).

The present state of research in Africanist political science confirms that scientific knowledge in this field remains utterly confused. Despite the number of publications and the high methodological standards, the results are rather thin. Despite the repeated use of econometrics and complex models borrowed from game theory (which completely altered research methodology and revolutionized the knowledge of Western political scientists), one has the impression that Africanist political science is still stammering, still sterile, and in general it has yet to be taken seriously within the social sciences. As Sklar bluntly puts it:

> The vast majority of political scientists still classify research on Africa questions as a peripheral "area study" which is not essential to the discipline's scientific progress.... In competitive appointment processes, Africanist scholarship does not enjoy a comparative advantage based on disciplinary contributions of its practitioners. If the question is, "Why do we want an Africanist particularly?" no decisive reason, based on scientific or theoretical necessity, can be adduced. In fact, I cannot think of a widely recognized problem or theory, of concern to political scientists generally, that requires African area expertise to either explore scientifically or explain to students (1993:84).

It is clear that ignorance does not prevent researchers from being arrogant: if nothing has been found in Africa, they conclude, it is because the continent has nothing original to offer political thought. How can one seriously believe that the cradle of civilization, at present an immense territory where all races and cultures coexist, where every type of social organization on the planet is found, has nothing specific to offer political science? How can one believe that the current social transformations are reducible to the level of slight social tremors brought on by the economic crisis? How can one continue to affirm that the existing literature has properly interpreted the complex phenomena that have occurred throughout Africa when the theories and models developed over the past decades were incapable of not only predicting but even explaining the current social changes? It is high time that social scientists abandoned their arrogant attitude toward Africa, for to date very little of their research has helped us decipher its complexity.

That is why it is necessary to take a long, hard look at the basic assumptions that have governed thought in the social sciences up to now. In this chapter, I shall first examine democratic theory as it is used today, then compare and contrast this with African realities so as to measure its effectiveness and underscore its limitations. The first section deals with the polarization of the debate on democracy in Africa and demonstrates how the analytic paradigms that are usually employed to define and measure democratic progress do not properly evaluate what is happening in the African political arena. Epistemological, hermeneutic, and semantic questions, which the very idea of democracy has always raised, have caused Africanist political scientists to adopt divergent viewpoints, reducing their work to a web of contrasting and often incoherent ideas. I analyze the reasons for this confusion and try to shed light on the different ways in which the subject is approached, the conflicting objectives of researchers, the subterranean strategies used by political actors to exploit the nebulousness of the current situation, and especially the two main philosophical anchors that govern or justify the reasoning and arguments of scholars: ethnocentrism and cultural relativism.

The second section of this chapter underscores the need for a new approach to the definition of democracy so that it is not a projection of the values of those performing the analysis but a representation of the values of those experiencing it. This requires above all the adoption of a different conceptual framework for measuring democratic progress, such as the democratization index I have earlier proposed (Monga 1993, 1995b). Unlike other methods available in literature on the subject, it has the advantage of being more "legitimate" and flexible, and it provides for the possibility of both geographic and temporal improvement.

I conclude by calling upon Africanist political scientists both to rid themselves of the straitjacket of models ill adapted to the environment they seek to grasp and to espouse a multiple, imaginative perspective on African politics. Only then will scholars be able to see how old the quest for freedom in Africa truly is and the degree to which democratization is taking hold; only then will they be able to measure the vast riches the continent has to offer the social sciences. I also suggest a simple model of democratization in Africa, emphasizing the importance of the elaboration phase of the rules of the political game.

The Polarization of the Democratic Debate on Africa

One of the paradoxes of current democratic theory is the growing gap between theoretical advances and the practical application of models derived from them. Though questions and disputes about democracy go back to its origins, an examination of the present state of knowledge in the field allows one to better conceptualize its objective and understand the source of disagreement among the different schools of thought. However, applying research results to societies engaged in what Huntington (1991) has termed the Third Wave of democratization results in contradictions that lead one to adopt a skeptical attitude toward the utility of political science.

To begin, it is necessary to put things into their proper perspective and to demonstrate that, despite the debates on the definition of democracy and the conditions for its sustainability, not only do current theories rely on the same paradigm, but the blind application of this paradigm, which is incapable of grasping the dynamics and the meaning of political transformations in Africa, creates confusion.

Theoretical Advances of Democratic Theory

Let us return for a moment to the European cartographers, who, as time went by, knew less and less about their subject. Between the fifteenth and eighteenth centuries, they had so refined their research methodology that they grew more and more ignorant of the continent's geography, because information no longer met their stringent criteria. Their intellectual itinerary is comparable to that of present-day political scientists, who have adopted such high standards for their paradigms of analysis that they are unable to use them to define the current state of African politics. To understand why confusion reigns in the study of African politics, let us begin with a brief discussion of the evolution of democratic theory and the principal issues being debated today.

It is surprising that the extensive literature produced by political scientists tells us little about the origin of democracy. Despite research indicating that the ethical quest at the heart of this idea is practically consubstantial with humanity—compare Snowden (1970) and Bernal (1987) to cite two mainstream publications—political scientists insist that democracy originated somewhere in ancient Greece. However, the definition of the word *democracy* and the implications of the Greek concept of the term call this opinion into question. The very principle of the rule (*kratos*) of the people (*demos*) opens up an infinite number of questions that are generally ignored but nevertheless explain the heart of the debate among various schools of thought. As Held has pointed out with respect to the notion of *rule* alone:

> Definitional problems emerge with each element of the phrase: "rule"?—"rule by"?—"the people"? To begin with "the people": who are to be considered "the people"? What kind of participation is envisaged for them? What conditions are assumed to be conducive to participation? Can the disincentives and incentives, or costs and benefits, of participation be equal?
>
> The idea of "rule" evokes a plethora of issues: how broadly or narrowly is the scope of rule to be construed? Or, what is the appropriate field of democratic activity? If "rule" is to cover "the political" what is meant by this? Does it cover (a) law and order? (b) relations between states? (c) the economy? (d) the domestic or private sphere?
>
> Does "rule by" entail the obligation to obey? Must the rules of "the people" be obeyed? What is the place of obligation and dissent? What mechanisms are created for those who are avowedly and actively "non-participants"? Under what circumstances, if any, are democracies entitled to resort to coercion against some of their own people or against those outside the sphere of legitimate rule (1987:2–3)?

The definition of *the people,* the other component of the word *democracy,* raises at least as many questions, and each carries with it important implications (Held 1987:iii). Far from being a purely philosophical discussion, an interrogation of the idea of democracy must include philosophical, theoretical, and practical dimensions. I shall argue in this chapter that it is because Africanist political scientists have not dealt sufficiently with such fundamental questions that they have had such difficulty in coherently conceptualizing the ways in which Africans conceive of and experience democracy. This opens up a larger debate about the geographic and temporal validity of the models used in the social sciences. One of the advantages of the index of democratization I have proposed is that it is capable of integrating this intrinsically conflictive problematic and capturing not only the specificity but also the range of indigenous perceptions of the idea of democracy without altering its original and "universal" substance.

But above all else, it is useful to look at the evolution and current status of democratic theory. The necessity of distinguishing between different types of approaches to democracy (philosophical, theoretical, conceptual, and practical) is no doubt the source of the debates that have pitted political scientists against one another over the last three centuries. Held (1987) provides an overview of the principal issues disputed in political theory since Plato and an interesting schematic presentation of the intellectual landscape today.

On the one hand, there is the liberal model, derived from the classical Greek model, influenced by the ideas of Hobbes, Locke, Mill, and Montesquieu and synthesized over the course of the twentieth century by Hayek (1960, 1976) and Nozick (1974). This model derives from what is referred to as legal democracy, whose principal justification is as follows: "The majority principle is an effective and desirable way of protecting individuals from arbitrary government and, therefore, of maintaining liberty. For political life, like economic life, to be a matter of individual freedom and initiative, majority rule, in order for it to function justly and wisely, must be circumscribed by the rule of law" (Held 1987:251). The key features of legal democracy are a constitutional state (modeled on features of the Anglo-American political tradition, including the clear separation of powers), the rule of law, minimal state intervention in civil society and private life, and a free-market society given the fullest possible scope. Its general conditions include effective political leadership guided by liberal principles, limitations on bureaucratic regulation, and, if possible, the eradication of the threat of collectivism of any kind.

On the other hand, there is the Marxist model, inspired notably by Rousseau's skepticism regarding the representative structure and codification of the general will. Like all others, this model has evolved considerably throughout history. It is one of the principal sources of inspiration for what is called participatory democracy, which Macpherson (1977) and Pateman (1985) have theorized in recent years. Participatory democracy is defined in the following manner: "An equal right to self-development can only be achieved in a 'participatory society,' a society which fosters a sense of political efficacy, nurtures a concern for collective problems and contributes to the formation of a knowledgeable citizenry capable of taking a sustained interest in the governing process" (Held 1987:262). Its key features are the direct participation of citizens in the regulation of the main institutions of society, including the workplace and the local community; the reorganization of the party system so that political leaders are directly accountable to the membership; a flexible institutional system with political parties much more integrated into the parliamentary structure; the adoption of the principle of better distribution of resources; and an open information system to ensure informed decisions.

These two models evolved from a variety of theoretical approaches to democracy, as shown in Figure 2.1.

Figure 2.1

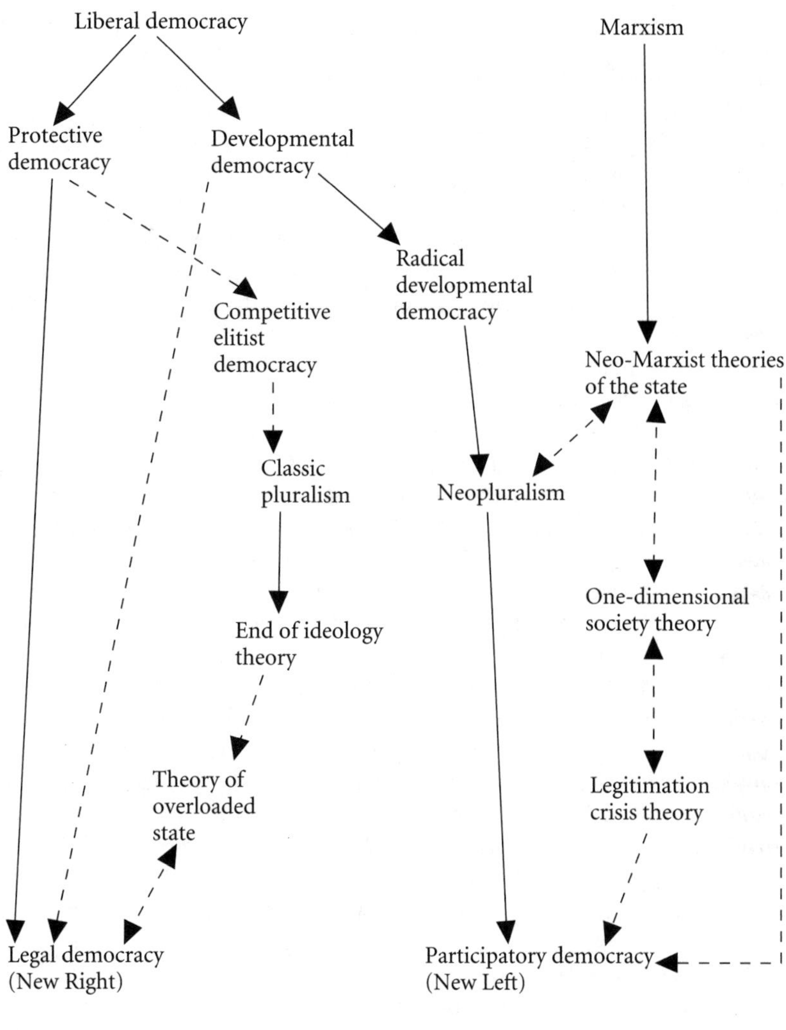

__________ indicates theoretical variants

_ _ _ _ _ _ indicates patterns of influence

Source: David Held (1987), *Models of Democracy* (Stanford: Stanford University Press), p. 224; and Polity Press, Cambridge, United Kingdom. Reprinted with permission.

Held's categories are, of course, subject to critique insofar as they rely on ideological distinctions that are not always as clear-cut as he suggests. That said, I shall maintain his basic definitions all the while broadening them to include extensive French research on the question.[1] I want to distinguish between theorists who think that the idea of democracy should be limited to purely political concepts—that is, to the political rights of the individual and the right to choose those who decide the rules of government (roughly speaking, what Held calls legal democracy)—and those who consider that democracy should apply to all aspects of social life and that individual rights should include economic, social, and cultural dimensions (an extension of participatory democracy as defined by Held and others). We shall later see that, in the case of African countries, it is necessary to use such definitions so that inspired autocrats will not twist too easily the concept of liberal democracy.

Political science has yet to go beyond the dichotomy between these models. Of course, some authors have questioned their validity in today's world, given the implacable logic of the market economy. Revitalizing Rousseau's skepticism regarding all forms of representation, Dahl, for example, has underscored the developmental logic of capitalism, which tends to "produce inequalities in social and economic resources so great as to bring about severe violations of political equality and hence of the democratic process" (1985:60).[2] Other writers have addressed similar concerns. For example, the democratic models Held (1987, 1994) and Gould (1988) have proposed insist on the necessity of extending the democratic agenda beyond government and into the business world and social life. But these ideas have remained theoretical—one can easily imagine how disastrous a practical application of such an approach would be, especially for highly industrialized nations that pride themselves on being the exclusive repositories of freedom, the owners of democratic truth.

In sum, it appears that centuries of heated debates among political scientists have produced works that, however technical and advanced theoretically, are not applicable to the study of African societies. Much remains to be said and done on this subject.

The question is how to use these various models to decipher the sociopolitical transformations that began to take shape in Africa in the early 1990s. The answer, of course, is not an easy one. The syndrome of inefficient overqualification with which Africanist cartographers were stricken comes into full force here: How is one to use the variants of the liberal or Marxist model to measure political development in Zambia, Djibouti, or Mauritania? How can one be sure that the political institutions adopted in Malawi after the fall of the former "president for life," Hastings Kamuzu Banda, are evaluated in the same way as the British institutions on which they are based? Should one believe that the strategies of Congolese politicians can be analyzed through the prism of French political science simply because the system is a replica of France's form of government? Should one think that imported institutional paradigms, which Badie (1992) has denounced, have a concrete impact on the African political landscape, that they really affect the nature and operation of African politics? Should one believe that the fragility of the transition to democracy, which appears to have taken place in Zambia, Madagascar, Niger, and Congo, is a reflection of the low level of political development in these countries and hence of the impossibility of establishing a true democracy in these countries?

No. The practical application of the theoretical advances in political science described earlier has failed by and large, especially when it concerns understanding the actual organization and operation of African politics today. The liberal and Marxist traditions, along with their numerous variants, have produced increasingly sophisticated methods of analysis, but the environment they seek to encompass and interpret remains resistant to their application. Nevertheless, unlike European cartographers of yore, political scientists today insist upon using them in Africa at all costs. As a result, they perceive there only troubling images, signals of a profound disorder. They are nonetheless wrong to interpret this "nebulousness" as proof of Africa's political backwardness.

The Paradigm of African Political Backwardness

This rapid overview of contemporary thought on democracy is necessary, even if its complexity is somewhat daunting. First, it helps one understand why Africanist political scientists are guilty of the crime of which economists are generally accused—as soon as two of them get together, they disagree about everything down to the most elementary conceptual tools. Second, it enables one to pinpoint the technical origin of errors in analysis and judgment that political science "experts" have made with regard to Africa.

Nothing is more enigmatic and confused than current research in Africanist political science. It is enough to read some books and articles on the subject to measure not only their complexity but the poor quality of the findings. Analyses of the sustainability of the democratic process, which were begun in the early 1990s in most African nations, are even more confused—even if one manages to decipher them, the conclusions reached by the various authors are often contradictory. Some view the present state of affairs in a positive light and think that time will improve the performance of local political actors. Others are pessimistic and think that the political, economic, institutional, and cultural prerequisites for democracy do not exist in Africa and are not likely to exist there for at least another generation or so. The only thing upon which everyone appears to agree is the political backwardness of Africa, not in terms of its obvious marginalization in world affairs, but in terms of its present capacity to adopt democratic ways. But they are all wrong and I propose to show how and why.

No encyclopedia is vast enough to cover exhaustively the vast array of incoherent mishmash published recently by the "experts." So let us begin with the university scholars who have studied the political unrest on the continent. So as not to tire the reader, I will confine myself to the main theses advanced by the most renowned scholars, whose work has been published in the most prestigious journals.

The Presumption of Incompetence

Dabezies is a professor at the Sorbonne, an influential man, a former diplomat and military officer; in short, he is the prototypical French Africanist, having spent considerable time as a power broker in both government and research. Stupefied by the fact that "democracy has suddenly reemerged as a sort of panacea," he cannot help wondering, with barely veiled irony, whether it is a "passing fever, an ephemeral illusion or an ersatz remedy" (1992:22). In his view, failure is all the more predictable in that its causes may be traced to decolonialization, for independence was attained before the new local leaders had time to acquire the political training necessary to govern effectively. The constitutional mimetism that determined their choice of governmental models could only lead to the present impasse: "Democracy, let it be said, is a long and difficult path; it is hard to manipulate and brings no miraculous remedy to Africa's ills—notably material ones; it is, moreover, a new idea on the continent, and neither the colonial period nor the era of independence movements saw such a 'bubbling over,' which some have described in lyrical if not demagogic terms" (1992:25). The absence of historical depth—in terms of a democratic tradition and an institutional framework for the ratification of democratic values—is also cited by eminent British and American scholars as one of the causes of Africa's present difficulties. In a recent book, Apter, a professor at Yale, and Rosberg, Berkeley professor emeritus, write that the various European political and administrative traditions of the colonial era "left a legacy of institutional indigestion, insufficiently trained cadres, poorly entrenched but with great power, and a host of developmental problems that quickly overwhelmed nationalist political successors" (1994:17).

Writings by Africanist political scientists are filled with such justifications, whose pertinence is dubious at best. (Though there is a strong body of literature in comparative politics providing evidence of democratic systems designed without any structural prerequisite [Rustow 1970; Karl 1990; Diamond 1992]). Let us skip the paternalistic commentaries on the continent's "structural incapacity" and move on to the soundness of the arguments behind this thesis. Must there be a certain tradition and a group of men "trained" in the conceptualization and management of freedom for the idea of democracy to succeed? History offers few examples of such prerequisites because the quest for freedom is so intimately linked to human life itself that democracy emerges almost ex nihilo. Neither the fathers of the American Revolution nor the French revolutionaries needed prior training in order to construct political systems protecting citizens from arbitrary government!

Indeed, the most intriguing aspect of this argument is the refusal to apply the same presumption of incompetence to politicians in countries in other parts of the world whose political history resembles that of Africa. Eastern Europe, for example, had little experience with democracy before the fall of the Berlin Wall. A study by Stubos concludes: "All Eastern European countries, with the noticeable exception of Czechoslovakia, had no prior tradition of democratic rule before the imposition of communism. In some cases, of course, some sort of limited or guided democratic practices were in place and formal parliamentary institutions were in existence. The fact remains, however, that democratic institutions and practices never acquired deep roots in these countries, neither did they make a dent in their political culture" (1993:31). The presumed absence of a "democratic culture" (I will later return to this notion) did not prevent Eastern bloc countries from implementing a democratic process that scholars regard with interest and optimism. Only Africa is consistently labeled as a place where certain conditions must first be met if its democratic ambitions are to be taken seriously. Moreover, no one would suggest for Eastern Europe, as Collier (1991) did for Africa, the creation of some "external agencies of restraint" to prevent leaders from making "structural" or "natural" political mistakes because of their countries' alleged lack of democratic culture.

The Absence of a Critical Mass of Democrats

Many consider that the threat to the future of African democracies lies in a small number of citizens who "want" democracy. This low demand for political reform is described by Dabezies: "If [democracy] corresponds to a diffuse feeling of freedom, indeed, at a higher level, to a profound desire to liberate the masses, it as yet directly concerns but a minority, intellectuals and civil servants in particular, certain of whom have only recently begun to oppose the regimes they denounce" (1992:25).

Widner is in full agreement: "Pressure for great political competitiveness came from elites who found that public offices they held suddenly stopped yielding the rents they used to supplement their income. Where these elites could organize general strikes, incumbent heads of state often tried to preempt their demonstrations by legalizing such opposition while maintaining control over critical electoral resources" (1994).

Starting from the same assumption, Bates (1994) tries to explain the shift in the position of the elites, advancing a convoluted theory based on the notion of human capital. Bates explains that the growth of certain types of local elites (especially old guard politicians, attorneys, church leaders, and community activists), whose skills are marketable only in their own countries, eventually created a tense political situation in which there was a surplus of this type of labor. The elites could survive and provide for their families only by fighting the regimes in power. They therefore initiated the present democratic process, which remains limited to a few social groups:

> From whom does the reformist impulse emanate? One source is fixed and specific human capital, those people who have invested in skills that are but imperfectly transferable elsewhere. Among these are the old guard politicians and those who people the ranks of local, community-based hierarchies: lawyers, community activists, and church leaders. A lawyer in Ghana, for example, especially one at the peak of his career, is unlikely to find a comparable position in London. Although he might join an international agency, his career path is not international. Unlike finance capital or people with general, as opposed to community-specific, skills, professionals cannot readily defect abroad. Therefore, in the face of declining welfare, rather than exit, they may find it preferable to give voice (1994:21–22).

Médart (1994) is even more blunt when he states that democracy has difficulty taking shape in Africa "because there is no democracy without democrats." The events that led to a softening of authoritarian regimes are reduced to a mere game between elites and stripped of any legitimacy. In short, the quest for democracy in Africa is superficial.

Such arguments are invalid. They demonstrate a profound misunderstanding of what has been happening in Africa over the past few decades. To affirm that the battle for democracy was engaged by African elites (Bates even claims that this is one of the "paradoxes" of democratization in sub-Saharan Africa!) is to ignore the silent struggle by men and women of all social classes from the beginning of the colonial era. Collective insubordination is the oldest watchword in African societies across the board. Accounts by historians (Mbokolo 1992; Roberts 1990) and more general works on arts and literature (Kom 1983; Ngandu Nkashama 1984; Mouralis 1984) bear witness to this.

If Widner's thesis were correct—that is, if civil servants and local elites initiated the democratic process in Africa—then the political system would function beautifully, for this social group is the most homogeneous and has the fewest conflicts of interest. Bates's thesis does not withstand scrutiny, either: it is both an insult and an error to assert that African elites suddenly demanded a better system of government simply because their financial resources had dried up over the years and their skills were not exportable.

How can one claim that a Ghanaian lawyer could not find the same type of position in London that he had in Accra? Or that a Kenyan priest would not be accepted in a New York parish? Or that a Malian volunteer working in the private sector in Bamako could not perform the same service in Paris?

Médart's maxim, "There is no democracy without democrats," is elegant but inaccurate and utopian. Were it true, Italian democracy would not work, and neither would French and U.S. democracies. For democrats exist nowhere—there are only human beings who agree, willingly or by force, to bow to institutions that function in accordance with a set of rules deemed to have been established democratically by the majority of citizens (see again Rustow 1970; Karl 1990).

The Urban-Rural Dichotomy

There is a tendency among some authors, Anglo-Saxon scholars in particular, to cast doubt on the legitimacy of demands for democracy by questioning the prevalence of such demands in the population of the countryside. This idea is based on the urban-bias theory, first advanced by Lipton (1977) and developed notably by Bates (1981). The basic assumption is as follows: "The most important class conflict in the poor countries of the world today is not between labor and capital. Nor is it between foreign and national interests. It is between rural classes and urban classes. The rural sector contains most of the poverty and most of the low-cost sources of potential advance; but the urban sector contains most of the articulateness, organization and power. So the urban classes have been able to win most of the rounds of struggle with the countryside" (Lipton 1977:13).

The apparent dichotomy between urban and rural areas determined public policy and the political economy of sub-Saharan Africa during the 1980s. In the past few years, it appears to have taken over scholarship as well. Political scientists are all too ready to view the democratic process as an exclusively urban phenomenon. The rebellious cities, symbols of the arrogance of the state and the wasteful expenditure of public funds, are pitted against the silent and exploited rural areas, "victims" of the power of civil servants and urban elites. Occasionally the "opposition" between urban and rural areas is technically explained and the well-documented propensity to overvalue African currencies becomes the conceptual justification for the domination of the urban sector over the rural one—an overvalued currency hurts exports and lowers the price of imported goods. In other words, having long accepted uneven exchange rates, African governments have made an essentially political choice that favors the lifestyle of city dwellers, who are more likely to purchase imported luxury items, and reduces the purchasing power of rural inhabitants, who are the exporters of raw materials (Bates 1981). From there it is but a short step—which certain authors do not hesitate to take—to the conclusion that the eruption of demands for democracy in Africa's large urban centers is simply a noisy display by a bunch of hungry city dwellers who suddenly find themselves deprived of their numerous privileges.

Although such analyses are at once superficial and caricatural, they are influential and dominate thought in the academic community (the urban-bias theory has recently been critiqued on economic grounds by Varshney [1993], whose work will not be discussed in detail here). However, the decline of agriculture's contribution to the economy is a normal phenomenon. Studies have shown that industrialization generally occurs at the expense of agriculture inasmuch as agriculture must contribute an increasing share of its revenues to the industrial sector (Timmer 1988, 1992, 1993; Quisumbing and Taylor 1990). Of course, these studies do not answer all the questions raised by the urban-bias theory—notably, whether the democratic movement stems from a loss in purchasing power among city dwellers. But as Bratton and Van de Walle have pointed out, that does not mean a correlation necessarily exists between economic factors and social demands: "It is ultimately misleading to interpret political protest in strictly economic terms ... there is little or no correlation between the intensity of political unrest on the one hand and the severity of economic crisis or austerity measures on the other. Some countries with very deep economic problems, such as Tanzania, Guinea, or Guinea-Bissau, witnessed little or no unrest by 1990, yet riots and strikes shook relatively wealthy countries" (1992:41).

This observation sufficiently invalidates the urban-bias thesis; however, the theory's success in academic circles warrants a few additional remarks. The implicit idea behind the theory of urban bias concerns the political inertia of the bulk of the African population, which is manipulated from time to time by perverted urban elites. Nothing could be farther from the truth. First, one must question the validity of the urban-rural dichotomy given that sub-Saharan Africa is more and more urban and less and less rural. At the very least, it is incongruous to speak of the urban domination of the rural "masses" in such countries as Cameroon, Côte d'Ivoire, and Congo, where the percentage of city dwellers is around 50 percent! What is more, it is erroneous to view social groups as political monoliths, even in the Sahel countries, where the rural population is quite large. Conflicts of interest and ideological differences in rural areas weaken the relevance of the urban-rural dichotomy and suggest that definitions and labels need to be refined (Harriss and Moore 1984; Widner 1993). In an Africa where cable stations like CNN are watched in every home, where Michael Jackson and Michael Jordan are as popular in the country as they are in big cities, it is archaic to believe that those who live in rural areas are sociologically different from city dwellers. Those who have studied the conditions that led to the democratic process in Africa know that rural movements launched some of the most pressing social demands. The fact that they are more often voiced in urban centers reflects the desire to add a new political dimension to a very old quest for freedom.

A look at the geography of political protest is enough to refute the rural passivity argument. In general, popular protest originated in rural areas, and for a very simple reason: the rural sector suffered more from the economic crisis than the urban sector and thus was the first to revolt. But given the barbarity of authoritarian regimes, this revolt was insidious and subtle and was expressed at the level of everyday actions (Mbembe 1988). Together with urban organizations and networks, rural inhabitants have, as it were, delegated to city dwellers their spirit of opposition. Contrary to popular belief, the eruption of violence and protest in large African cities at the end of the 1980s was above all a rebellion by proxy; the democratic process has actually been orchestrated by peasants, whose purchasing power has been steadily declining for the past ten years. City dwellers were called upon to play a piece composed elsewhere—in the closed circles of family meetings, in the secret network of rural cooperatives, in the informal gatherings of country merchants, and in the weekly church services held in every hick town on the continent. Leading figures in the democratic movement can confirm that the current struggle for social change originated in the rural sector.[3] To find more "scientific" proof of rural involvement in politics, one has only to look at voter turnout in rural areas, which is generally higher than in cities, even when polling places are scarce. Country folk are not illiterate ignoramuses, as some writers like to think, and they are often more involved in the democratic process than city dwellers, who tend to give in more readily to nihilism and discouragement.

The urban-rural dichotomy is thus something of a cliché. Those who perpetuate it and base their analyses on it are engaging in the sociology of appearances. Reality is very different.

Disparate Ethnic Conglomerations and Fragmented States

The resurgence of regionalism and ethnic conflicts in the post–Cold War era has also fueled pessimism concerning the future of democracy in Africa. Horowitz, a specialist in ethnic questions who teaches at Duke University, considers the implementation of democracy to be much more difficult in what he terms "divided societies." His basic argument runs as follows: "Democracy is about inclusion and exclusion, about access to power, about the privileges that go with inclusion and the penalties that accompany exclusion. In severely divided societies, ethnic identity provides clear lines to determine who will be included and who will be excluded. Since the lines appear unalterable, being in and being out may quickly come to look permanent" (1993:18).

Applying this analytic framework to Africa, Horowitz paints a less than cheery picture of the current political situation:

> Togo and the Congo Republic both have northern regimes (based, respectively, on the Kabrai and the Mbochi) that came to power after military coups reversed the ethnic results of elections. Neither regime has had a special desire to accommodate a democratic process it identified with its southern (Ewe or Lari) opponents. Consequently, both took steps to disrupt the process.... Kenya, with its Kalendjin-dominated minority government, finally succumbed to Western pressure and conducted a multiparty election. But the incumbent president, Daniel arap Moi, was able to use a combination of intimidation, violence and ethnic divisions among the opposition to win both the presidency and a parliamentary majority on a plurality of votes, mainly from his own group and several other small ethnic groups. The result is a regime that continues to exclude the two largest groups, Kikuyu and Luo. Likewise, Cameroon's President Paul Biya, presiding over a government supported mainly by Beti and Bulu and opposed by all the rest, benefited from an opposition divided along ethnic lines and an election boycott by the major party.... In a dubiously conducted election in Ghana, the military ruler, Jerry Rawlings, won the presidency, supported by 93 percent of the vote in his own Ewe-dominated area, but polling less than one-third in Ashanti, thus reviving an earlier polarization (1993:21–22).

Horowitz's analysis is weakened by some factual errors. He is wrong to assert that a given head of state is supported by a given ethnic group, to the exclusion of all others, yet this falsehood supports his entire argument. None of the leaders who, in his estimation, automatically won the votes of citizens in their native regions could govern with the exclusive support of their tribes. In fact, one of the most important patterns that emerged in recent African elections is the nonexistence of ethnic voting blocs, the end of monolithic regional support for a given candidate (compare T. Young 1993).

Let us not dwell on Horowitz's abuse of official results of elections that were rigged by authoritarian regimes in order to maintain power and that have been contested and denounced by the international community (Geisler 1993). Let us focus instead on the substance of his discourse. First, there is the arbitrary nature of his ethnic classifications, whose limitations and inconsistencies Horowitz himself has evoked in earlier writings (1985), as have many other anthropologists and historians (Amselle and Mbokolo 1985). Is it necessary to remind those who carelessly use ethnic labels that these classifications, which often go back to the colonial era, served a specific hegemonic purpose? As C. Young has written, "'Colonial science' constructed a wooden and unusable model of 'tribal man' in Africa. There existed, for purposes of drawing administrative subdivisions within colonial territories, a normative map in the alien mind, into which discrete ethnic units could be distributed, with due regard for colonial security calculus. Thorough administrative inquest and competent bureaucratic sifting and winnowing of ethnographic data would permit successful tribal cartography" (1994:75).

That analysis confirms what Vail has written concerning the anatomy of the differential process through which peoples in Southern Africa fell into the ethnic trap:

> The creation of ethnicity as an ideological statement of popular appeal in the context of profound social, economic and political change in southern Africa was the result of the differential conjunction of various historical forces and phenomena.... One may discern three ... variables in the creation and implanting of the ethnic message. First, as was the case in the creation of such ideologies elsewhere, for example in nineteenth century European nationalism, it was essential to have a group of intellectuals involved in formulating it—a group of culture brokers. Second, there was the widespread use of African intermediaries to administer the subordinate peoples, a system usually summed up in the phrase "indirect rule," and this served to define the boundaries and texture of the new ideologies. Third, ordinary people had a real need for so-called "traditional values" at a time of rapid social change, thus opening the way for the wide acceptance of the new ideologies (1989:11).

One must keep such historical phenomena in mind if one wishes to steer clear of what Southall (1970) has termed "the tribal illusion" toward which Horowitz's remarks clearly point. Of course, though it stems from an illusion, the reality of ethnicity today is such that it is impossible to ignore. That said, one must study its origin before according it the importance many Africanist political scientists have given it. It is particularly necessary to ask whether ethnicity is the cause of current political difficulties or whether they stem from a long period of authoritarianism. Otherwise stated, is ethnicity an exogenous and predetermined variable, as Horowitz implicitly suggests, or is it an endogenous variable, whose value is dependent upon other factors that have been ignored?

When Horowitz speaks of the "ethnic results" of elections, he attributes a certain degree of incertitude to a process that, according to the logic of his analysis, ought to have none. If Africans indeed always voted in line with their "ethnic convictions," there would be no need to organize elections, because their results would be preordained—a simple ethnic head count would do. Governance along ethnic lines—which, according to Horowitz, means the inclusion of the ethnic "winners" of elections and the exclusion of all other groups (the "losers")—ought to require an extraordinarily complex institutional mechanism to function. But nowhere does Horowitz speak of either the technostructure or the procedures through which the Kabrai and the Mbochi involve all the members of their ethnic communities—and them alone—in the governance of Togo or Congo!

A few items of information are enough to refute the ethnic argument in Cameroon. During the 1992 presidential election, for example, the principal leader of the opposition, who was ahead in all the polls according to analysts, came from a minority group—English speakers in the northwest. On the eve of the election, 200,000 people, including politicians, intellectuals, and other prominent figures from all regions of the country, went to hear him speak in Yaoundé, the capital of President Biya's native Beti country. (So much for clear-cut ethnic divisions and Horowitz's overly schematic analysis.) Similar events occurred in Kenya, Nigeria, Benin, Malawi, and Zambia—in short, in all places where elections gave voters a chance to express if not their preferences, then at least their dissent.

Much can also be said about the way Kenya has been analyzed through the prism of ethnicity. As Chege has written, "the deluge of so-called scientific literature" (1994:284, n. 15) by experts in development has not yielded significant results. With regard to the impetus behind political reforms, it was not pressure from international monetary funds that caused Moi to call a multiparty election.[4] Numerous studies have shown that financial institutions would have continued as before, for they have never required the accountability of African governments. In fact, one needs the soul of a chemist to attempt to assign, as certain political scientists have done, a precise quotient of responsibility to every group involved in triggering the democratic process. One thing is certain, however: Internal pressure exerted by various groups in civil society was a much more decisive factor in the current reforms than the timid actions of the World Bank and the International Monetary Fund (Barkan 1992, 1993; Chege 1993; Holmquist, Ford, and Weaver 1994; Tibbetts 1994).

Finally, Horowitz's implication that the African opposition consists of tribal representatives who are bitter about their exclusion from power goes beyond mere negligence: It is the type of characterization that is unfair to sub-Saharan Africa. What political scientist would call Bill Clinton a representative of the Arkansas tribe simply because he massively carried his native state? What political scientist would view Jacques Chirac's landslide victories in Corrèze over the years as an example of an ethnic vote in this region? Why is the notion of an electoral base, accepted throughout the world and considered by Western political science as something every serious politician needs, systematically interpreted as proof of backwardness when it comes to Africa?

Though it rests on shaky foundations, the ethnic factor remains a constant in the political situation in Africa. It dominates intellectual discourse because it provides a simple and apparently coherent theoretical model for the analysis of seemingly bizarre, or incomprehensible, phenomena. Political scientists find this both technical and functional analytical framework reassuring, for it allows them to justify the existence of authoritarianism. For instance, Williams notes: "In Africa, where democracy is 'widely approved but everywhere in doubt,' open public participation in politics has tended to be characterized by divisive struggles among ethnic groups over power and resources. Resulting conflicts have led to a general paralysis of productive political activity, a demobilization of participatory institutions, and the seemingly ineluctable turn toward authoritarian mechanisms of rule" (1992:97).

This passage is almost word for word what Sklar wrote a decade ago, (1986:115) presenting the conventional wisdom. Given that few intellectuals wish to promote the idea of authoritarianism, some desperately attempt to devise an "honorable" solution to the problem. They turn to a sort of *consociationalism* with blurred boundaries that might encompass both Nigerian-style federalism and the Senegalese version of "shared" power.[5] Though there is literature on the limitations of Nigerian federalism (Suberu 1993), little exists, unfortunately, on the Senegalese pseudomodel, whose merits are always being sung by the "experts" in constitutional engineering. Albeit poorly understood and little studied, the Senegalese model of government has sufficiently demonstrated its unsuitability as a serious alternative for other African nations (Diop and Diouf 1990).

So we are back to square one; that is, the level of banality and modesty scholars afford themselves when studying the ethnic question in Africa. As I will later demonstrate, the results of their analyses would be more consistent if they agreed to abandon some of their prejudices about the continent.

The Clash of Civilizations and Cultural Inaptitude

Huntington, one of the most prolific and influential Western political scientists of our time, has advanced the hypothesis of a clash of civilizations, in his eyes the best explanatory paradigm of the world today: "It is my hypothesis that the fundamental source of conflict in this new world will not be primarily ideological or primarily economic. The great divisions among humankind and the dominating source of conflict will be cultural" (1993a:22).

Huntington defines a civilization as a "cultural entity" comprising villages, regions, ethnic groups, nationalities, and religious groups that, despite their heterogeneity, constitute a coherent whole. (Let us skip for the moment the syntactic incompatibility of this definition.) Then, using this framework, he identifies the major civilizations in the modern world: "Civilization identity will be increasingly important in the future, and the world will be shaped in large measure by interactions among seven or eight major civilizations. These include Western, Confucian, Japanese, Islamic, Hindu, Slavic-Orthodox, Latin American and possibly African Civilization" (1993a:25). Beyond the arbitrary classification of civilizations, what is most striking in this assertion is the use of the word *possibly* with respect to the existence of an African civilization. It is hard to know what it is supposed to mean here: does Huntington doubt that civilizations exist in Africa today, or does he question the ability of African civilization (in the singular, of course) to "clash" or "compete" with others? In any case, the author's perception of Africa is suspect.

Affirming that Japan alone has been able to modernize without Westernizing, Huntington predicts a great confrontation and advises Western leaders to take preventive measures. Among other things, he counsels the West "to promote greater cooperation and unity within its own civilization, particularly between its European and North American components," "to moderate the reduction of Western military capabilities and maintain military superiority in East and Southwest Asia; to exploit differences and conflicts among Confucian and Islamic states" (1993a:48–49).

I have presented Huntington's thesis because it sheds light on the ideological atmosphere in which certain theories in Africanist political science have been elaborated. His basic premise is that the most authentic quest for freedom belongs to the West, that it holds the copyright now and forever on the expression of democratic principles and their "proper" implementation. Other peoples are completely incapable of conceptualizing democracy, so it is best to leave them to the course of their own histories, all the while protecting the West's precious Greco-Roman heritage from the contamination of heretical civilizations. Huntington presents his thesis even more clearly in his response to critiques of his new theory (1993b).

Huntington's ideas are at the heart of the rhetoric on the cultural inaptitude of Southern peoples (notably Africans) that prevents them from assimilating the democratic model. Their incapacity to incorporate philosophical and political ideals elaborated in the West points to their inability to contribute anything of value to the chorus of nations and to participate in the grand ball of civilizations. This original sin manifests itself politically in various ways: Africans cannot seem to make work the institutions they are always importing (Badie 1990, 1992); African societies and their leaders appear to have adopted an attitude of masochistic complacency toward authoritarianism and patrimonialism (Callaghy 1994); in short, Africa refuses to develop (Kabou 1991).

Although Badie denounces what he sees as the superficial character of democracy in African nations, as well as their importation of governmental models, he does not consider these nations capable of developing alternative models:

> References to democracy, to the rule of law, are as fragile, vulnerable and illusory as the beginnings of an alternative model are difficult to find in the discourse and political practices of African and Asian societies, and this for several reasons. First one must take into account the importance of imported governmental models in the political debate, ... which further dries up the production of new models. Second one must take into account the element of duration.... The third reason for this absence of alternative models is probably the lack, in these developing societies, of well-structured social movements, the nonexistence, within civil society, of at once organized and mobilizing forums of protest.... The fourth factor is perhaps, paradoxically, the overvaluation of politics that characterizes these societies.... The debate tends to turn in circles, around the *modus operandi* of the official political scene; it is much less imaginative with regard to the evolution and transformation of society.... The alternative political function is essentially an oppositional function, with no hope of gaining immediate access to power and that, to borrow Georges Lavau's formula with respect to the tribunitial function, lazily contents itself with the production of a negative discourse (1990).

All the clichés are here: a political imagination held hostage to Western models, a paucity of forums of protest worthy of the name, a dearth of politicians up to the task, a lazy oppositional discourse. In short, democrats in the Southern regions are not worthy of the West's consideration. Are we far from Huntington's thesis? Apparently so, but in reality, no. For we find in Badie the same skepticism toward the ability of African societies to produce a "respectable" (alternative) political discourse.

A number of North American Africanists also subscribe to this logic of disqualifying African democracies on ideological grounds. Thus, Callaghy seems desperate about the inability of African societies (not leaders!) and nations to abandon mediocrity and patrimonialism. This leads him to question the possibility of true political change: "The characteristics of the modal African state are not likely to be altered very much by the varying processes of political liberalization sweeping Africa in the early 1990s.... Under the formal political structure of African regimes, a unifying perceptual and operational cultural idiom has emerged which is deeply embedded in society as well as in the state—that of patrimonialism and patron-client relations" (1994:204,206).

Using the same type of argument, Lancaster is equally quick to paint a dark picture of Africa's future:

> The nature of political institutions in Africa suggests that democracies there are likely to function differently from democracies in the West [nice euphemism!]. These regimes are more open than their authoritarian predecessors, but their accountability to their publics remains weak. It will take time for an undertrained and underfinanced media to play the role it does in much of the West of putting issues on the national agenda, contributing to national debate, and investigating and criticizing government policy failures or corruption. The public may remain politically inert except at elections; even then, many Africans continue to base their votes on cues from village "big men" or ethnic brokers rather than on the government's performance (1993:29).

All those who have carefully followed African politics in the past few years, especially the presidential elections in Nigeria, Cameroon, Benin, and other countries, know that Lancaster's contemptuous description of African voters is not realistic (neither is the presumption of rationalism and political activism she attributes to Western voters), a point to which I shall return later. In fact, this poorly argued Afro-pessimism is a version of Huntington's thesis, which holds that there is no way to civilize these accursed peoples and that it is therefore best to keep them at a safe distance. This concern confirms what Rufin (1982) has written about the West's hands-off attitude toward the chaos in Southern countries and its desire to prevent the invasion of the barbarians, as the Romans had earlier done.

Fortunately, many other scholars have pointed out the shortcomings of Huntington's theory. I will confine myself here to several fundamental contradictions in his reasoning, which is enough to refute his hypothesis. Cultural pluralism, for example, is much more acute in the United States and Canada (which, in Huntington's view, are part of the same homogeneous civilization) than it is in Italy (classified in a different civilization). The geographic zones Huntington hastily and arbitrarily draws are far from monolithic and the five criteria he uses to define a civilization (history, language, culture, tradition, and religion) do not allow one to differentiate in a compelling way between the peoples of the world—none have exclusive rights over their own history, tradition, or culture! One of the paradoxes of what is referred to as "Western cultural imperialism"—which I regard as nothing more than the temptation to subject and mold the other to one's vision of the world—is that it has imposed a certain type of discourse, a certain language and tradition, in short, a single history. Since Columbus's time, the West has endeavored to render civilization uniform, to make it "one" (Said 1993). Even when this attempt failed, there were consequences: The trajectory of numerous peoples was irrevocably altered, the confrontation reshaping the identities of both victims and aggressors (Todorov 1982, 1993). Thus, today it is at once futile and artificial to try to restore the authenticity of civilizations, to try to reestablish the imprints of each culture—as if we were dealing with chemical ingredients.

I could list endless examples of blunders in much of the "scientific" literature devoted to the study of Africa's political transformations. But Huntington's work, replete with errors of fact and judgment, strikes me as enough to discredit research on the topic. Granted, one could simply shrug one's shoulders and conclude that because the social sciences are not among the exact sciences, these errors are par for the course. The problem is that errors made by influential scholars, who are also trendsetters, influence the decisions of politicians and policymakers. In a very concrete way, Africa is the victim of the prejudices and analytical errors of researchers who are accountable to no one. A remark Jacques Chirac made during a trip to Abidjan a few years back is proof of this: "Democracy," he declared, "is a frill for Africa." Now that he is France's president, we will be able to measure the concrete of his vision.

All of this leads to the real question of how to explain the collective blindness of the political science community. How is it that Africa, which does not have a monopoly on complexity, remains so opaque to scholars, so very resistant to their methods of analysis that it makes the theoretical models that have issued from centuries of political thought appear ridiculous? Why do Africanists continue to confuse the subject and object of knowledge? Before suggesting new avenues of research, I shall attempt to respond to these questions.

Theoretical Framework for Analyzing Political Change

In order to advance a theory of democratization that does not fall victim to the aforementioned distortions, it is necessary to proceed in stages. I shall begin by analyzing the reasons for the present confusion in Africanist political science—the genesis, if you will, of misunderstandings. I shall then suggest another way of looking at and studying Africa's new political marketplace.

The Genesis of Misunderstandings

Two types of reasons account for the blindness of some researchers. These reasons are tied either to the development of the social sciences and the attitude of those who wield concepts (I refer to these as external reasons) or to the nature of the new local political marketplace—that is, the new rules of the game and the behavior of the new political actors (I refer to these as internal reasons).

The external reasons can be summed up in a short phrase: the obstinate refusal of global brain trusts (the academy, international development agencies, the banking community) to take sub-Saharan Africa seriously. They are exhibited in two ways:

- Through the West's lack of geopolitical and speculative interest in Africa, a result of the end of the Cold War, and
- Through scholarly contempt for Africa's misuse of certain political concepts and methodologies

The internal reasons have a dual origin:

- On the one hand, the extraordinary agility with which African authoritarian regimes have manipulated techniques of renewal, which has allowed most of them to reinvent themselves and sometimes even to turn to their advantage the desire for change
- On the other hand, what must be called the political *bricolage* of opposition leaders, which is perceptible behind the structural weakness and atomistic tendency of their movements, most of which came to light in a socioeconomic environment conducive neither to risk taking in general nor to political risk taking in particular[6]

Let us examine one by one these four sources of confusion.

The World's Indifference and Intellectual Safaris

It is easy enough to call into question Fukuyama's (1992) ludicrous vision of the end of history. Nevertheless, since the fall of the Berlin Wall, there has been a radical shift in the way the international community—wrongly more than rightly—views and conceptualizes history. The marginalization of Africa is a part of this shift, which was stimulated by increased global competition for volatile, scarce, and expensive capital.[7]

The new world order that came into being after the disintegration of the Soviet Union does not include Africa within its world geography. Unable to discern the smallest sign of hope in Africa's ongoing sociopolitical transformations, the international business community has focused its attention on three areas: the Americas, Europe, and the Pacific. The criteria this community uses to assess its potential interest in disparate parts of the world are limited to such indicators as internal rate of return and net present value, used to measure the immediate value of discounted financial flows expected from investments and the payback period. Given these "objective" criteria, it is neither surprising nor regrettable that easy-profit seekers have avoided the continent.

More troubling is that the indifference of "money makers" appears to have determined the general attitude toward Africa. Despite the success of numerous missions in Africa, the UN is trying to forget the trauma of Somalia and Angola and thus has paid less attention to issues of human rights and democracy. Western governments that used to proclaim their "duty to interfere" in countries where the standards of universal morality were blatantly transgressed have become reserved. The era of the great overseas operations for the protection of human rights appears to have come (temporarily?) to an end.

This new attitude has rubbed off on Western intellectuals. Among Africanist political scientists, it translates into a lack of rigor in their treatment of the continent. The sophistication of the aforementioned theoretical models in fact disguises a certain negligence. When it comes to Africa, one can afford to indulge in approximations, generalizations, even illiteracy. Africa's overall image is so negative that only the most pessimistic types of discourse conform to the logic that governs understanding of the continent. Publications as "prestigious" as the *Financial Times, Der Spiegel,* or *Time* can publish cover stories and surveys built upon falsehoods and factual errors without stirring up a storm of protest, no doubt because "experts" on Africa know that rebuttals will not damage their professional reputations.[8]

The abdication of intellectuals serves the interest of certain players, namely, that of Western leaders who have personally involved themselves in "African affairs."[9] When former French president François Mitterrand was questioned about the efficacy of his support for democratization in Africa, he declared that the increase in the number of African countries having adopted a multiparty system was proof of his success (1993)—as if it were enough for any old Mobutu to proclaim himself a democrat to be recognized as such by France's head of state. Although it is hard to tell whether this type of thinking stems from cynicism or contempt for Africans, it certainly reflects the current trend in the West of intellectual exoticism with regard to Africa. It is no longer necessary even to formulate intelligent answers to legitimate questions.

As a result, and despite the multiplication of sophisticated yet confused theories, the scholarly debate—when it exists—on political transformations in Africa lacks vigor and impartiality. True or false, supported by empirical evidence or not, most analyses are never put through the filter of common sense or rigorous conceptual schemes; one is generally satisfied with what appears "plausible," "original," or "convincing." In recent years the continent has become the El Dorado of wild thought, the best place for daring intellectual safaris, the unregulated space in which to engage in theoretical incest, to violate the fundaments of logic, to transgress disciplinary prohibitions; in short, to give oneself over to all forms of intellectual debauchery—with impunity and in good conscience. Africa is the final frontier for those who like to tinker with ideas; it is the Luna Park for lovers of ideological orgies.

Archaic Instruments of Analysis

It is not at all surprising that Africa has often proved resistant to the assumptions of political scientists and does not fit into (Western) democratic theory. The analytic paradigms that social scientists persist in applying to these complex societies are obviously inapt. All discussions on the meaning and optimal form of democracy hinge upon the idea that "objective," measurable conditions determine its sustainability. Held writes: "Democratic ideas and practices can only in the long run be protected if their hold on our political, social and economic life is deepened" (1987:4). Diamond (1990) reiterates this position when he affirms that in the long run only the emergence of a civic culture can help negotiate one of democracy's intrinsic paradoxes, namely, the conflict between the necessary clash of ideas and the need for consensus.

Within each school of thought, these assumptions translate into a few concepts: the notions of political culture—which includes civic culture and participation—legitimacy, and accountability. Summing up the terms of a prominent debate between eminent U.S. political scientists, Lipset (1990) dismisses Juan Linz (who tends to favor parliamentary government) and Donald Horowitz (who more or less advocates presidentialist forms of government) on the grounds that the only thing that really matters is the political culture of a given people. In fact, most of the current democratic models primarily base their judgment of a political system's democratic validity on this criterion. But the assumptions upon which the idea of political culture is founded are false; for in general—even when they are applied to the well-established democracies of the industrialized world—they stand on shaky ground, as numerous critics have demonstrated (Aron 1972; Callinicos 1991).

Take, for example, the notion of civic culture. Almond and Verba came up with this idea in the early 1960s, and it continues to serve as the centerpiece of current political theories on African societies. There is nothing wrong with the idea per se; the problem lies in the practical application of the supposed elements of civic culture and the criteria used to measure it. Let us begin with Almond and Verba's definition of the term. Their point of departure is the notion of political culture, which they define as follows:

> The term "political culture" refers to the specifically political orientations—attitudes toward the political system and its various parts, and attitudes toward the role of the self in the system. We speak of a political culture just as we can speak of an economic culture or a religious culture. It is

> a set of orientations toward a special set of social objects and processes. But we also choose political culture, rather than some other special concept, because it enables us to utilize the conceptual frameworks and approaches of anthropology, sociology, and psychology (1963:12–13).

Their approach is honest and straightforward, and their willingness to include the research methodologies and perspectives of such disciplines as anthropology, sociology, and psychology speaks to their modesty and the subtlety of their model. They are right to propose a flexible, multidimensional analytic scheme, for the notion of civic culture, derived from that of political culture, must be wielded with great care because it belongs to a vast conceptual field and varies greatly from one society to the next. Thus, when Inglehart defines civic culture as "a coherent syndrome of personal life satisfaction, political satisfaction, interpersonal trust and support for the existing social order" (1988:1203), he points to the implied existence of such notions as a collective attitude, a scale of values, a feeling of well-being on the part of citizens toward citizenship, etc. Such a vast field of study inevitably opens onto various divergences, which make it virtually impossible to perform comparative analyses—unless one falls into the trap of ethnocentrism, which, unfortunately, most scholars who utilize this concept do.

In truth, the definitions social science dictionaries give the term *attitude* transform it into a Bermuda Triangle of sorts from which it is almost impossible to escape. Summarizing decades of multidisciplinary research on the question, Jary and Jary define it as a "learned and enduring tendency to perceive or act toward persons or situations in a particular way.... It is therefore useful to see attitudes as involving three elements: a) a cognitive component—beliefs and ideas; b) an affective component—values and emotions; c) a behavioral component—predisposition to act and actions" (1991:27–28).

Marshall addresses the complexity of the problem:

> Many people do not have well-developed or even superficial opinions on topics that may interest the sociologist. Some would argue that the idea of attitudes is closely tied to the culture of Western industrial society, in which citizens are regularly invited to express their views on public issues, both directly and through the ballot box. What is certain is that attitude scales developed in Western societies do not function in the same way in other cultures. Even the standard simple job satisfaction question attracts a different pattern of response as soon as it is used beyond the confines of Western industrial societies (1994:21).

We can see how difficult it is to evaluate the attitudes of individuals in different parts of the world. Even more difficult is measuring collective attitudes and group behavior by way of individual responses to questions developed within a particular frame of reference. Yet the followers of Almond and Verba do not hesitate to use the civic culture argument everywhere and for everything, even to predict changes in the scale of values from one generation to the next. True, statistical sampling techniques are extremely sophisticated today, and the central limit theorem, with its predetermined margin of error, allows one to sidestep the problem of representativeness and to grasp the essence of a given population. The question nevertheless remains: How can one be sure that surveys conducted by U.S. researchers in the slums of Kinshasa truly reflect the thinking and political opinions of people in the Zairean bush? How can one be certain that the information collected from questionnaires hastily put together and distributed in a few neighborhoods in Dar es Salaam corresponds to the way Tanzanians conceive of and experience politics?

Political scientists who use Almond and Verba's model often fail to take into account the caveats expressed by its authors. For example, in attempting to evaluate political culture in Zambia, Bratton and Liatto-Katundu asked people to fill out a questionnaire based on a few questions: "We address a simple and conventional set of questions which will be familiar to anyone with even a cursory knowledge of an earlier generation of political culture studies.... What do people know about their political system? How do they feel about their government and their fellow citizens? Which political values do they hold dear? And, finally, how do they act politically?" (1994:1). Even if the results are not totally devoid of interest, there clearly is a Western bias in the survey questions. How can one hope to obtain reliable, usable information from Zambian citizens who are asked, only several months after the end of decades of dictatorship, to express their political orientations? How can one expect intelligent answers to such questions as "What is a local government council supposed to do?" How could one be surprised to find that populations long forced to live in a corrupt, inefficient single-party system do not distinguish between the federal government and local authorities? What would the responses be if the survey had taken place in Columbus, Ohio, or Moscow rather than Lusaka? Would researchers rely on the answers to measure the level of political culture in the United States or Russia? It is clear that these types of studies have theoretical, conceptual, and practical limits.[10] The conclusions reached cannot be interpreted in the manner suggested by Almond and Verba's original model.

Although the quantitative problems associated with measuring political knowledge cannot be underestimated (Delli Carpini and Keeter 1993), political scientists who employ such methods to evaluate the civic culture of individuals must also be aware that the collective consciousness of which Durkheim spoke ("the body of beliefs and sentiments common to the average of members of a society" [1968]) is equally difficult to grasp. Dahl, an advocate of the concepts of political culture and citizen competence, has come to recognize their severe limitations: "If democracy is to work, it would seem to require a certain level of political competence on the part of its citizens. In newly democratic or democratizing countries, where people are just beginning to learn the arts of self-government, the question of citizen competence possesses an obvious urgency. Yet even in countries where democratic institutions have existed for several generations or more, *a growing body of evidence reveals grave limits to citizen competence*" (1992:45, emphasis added).

The results of empirical research on the validity of these notions in long-established democracies are disappointing and attack the credibility of the democratic idea. Muller and Seligson (1994) recently developed a model designed to test the nature of and the causal relationship between civic culture and democracy. Their conclusions call into question Almond and Verba's thesis (countries with a high level of civic culture have stable democratic systems) as well as the opposite point of view advanced by Barry (1978) and Schmitter and Karl (1991), which holds that civic culture is not the cause but rather the result of democracy. According to Muller and Seligson, causation is, at least, reciprocal. There is no such thing as a linear correlation between the level of democratic culture and the effectiveness of democracy. One is tempted to agree with this idea in light of the mysterious separation between practical political consciousness and discursive consciousness made by French voters. Analyzing voting patterns in a small French town, Déloye observes that

> voters do not create their behavior, they recreate it at each election, drawing upon knowledge acquired from previous polls. In the voting booth, the voter generally discovers, within the "pool of ordinary knowledge" that constitutes his or her memory, a practical answer that gives meaning to what is happening. Most of the time, s/he instantly associates the present electoral situation with similar experiences s/he has had in the past (whence the difficulty of modifying, even marginally, this internalized behavior). This reflexive form of competence anchors voter behavior in the personal history of the voter.... The power of this voting habit, justified by practical voting consciousness, paradoxically explains why the voter has such difficulty formulating the meaning of and reasons for his actual behavior (1993:88).

To some extent, these comments are similar to Rohrschneider's remarks concerning the consolidation of values within the German elite. Studying the manner in which democratic institutions in former West Germany modified the behavior of politicians in former East Germany (a process known as "value convergence"), he observes that the lack of democratic culture does not negatively affect the outcome of the political game, since the institutions progressively shape the political behavior: "I find that the socialist and parliamentary institutions in the East and the West, respectively, have substantially influenced elites' conceptions of democracies in Germany, leading to a value divergence across the East-West boundary. Yet the findings also suggest that a partial value convergence in terms of liberal democratic rights among postwar elites has taken place. The results support an institutional learning theory, but they also suggest that support for liberal democratic values has been diffused in East Germany" (1994:927). In an epigraph to his article, Rohrschneider quotes a member of parliament from East Berlin, who serenely declared: "I think entirely in dialectical terms." This loyalty to Marxism parallels voting habits in a small French town: both phenomena belong to the same type of determinism, which is institutional rather than cultural in the narrow and almost ethnological sense in which political scientists often understand it. Paradoxically, this leaves more hope for the idea of democracy than one may have initially expected.

Proposing an elaborate mathematical model devised to question the dogma of civic culture, Muller and Seligson shed light on some of the practical difficulties in measuring civic culture across the world. It invites one to reexamine Inglehart's model, generally considered the cornerstone of theories based on the idea of civic culture, which consists of four variables: (1) a country's level of economic development in 1950, as measured by its gross national product (GNP) per capita; (2) the percentage of the labor force employed in the tertiary sector, which is used to determine the size of the middle class; (3) a composite measure of civic culture over 1981–1986 that reflects the general public's average level of life satisfaction, interpersonal trust, and lack of support for revolutionary change; and (4) a country's years of continuous democracy from 1900 to 1986. Democracy is measured on the seven-point scale Gastil developed for Freedom House, which has published a yearly report since 1972 (see Gastil 1991).

An analysis of Inglehart's model reveals the arbitrariness of its logic and the reason it cannot be transferred to the African context. Even if we put to one side the accuracy of the indicators used to measure the level of economic development (economists increasingly view GNP as a poor indicator of prosperity), the fact remains that the idea of a middle class takes on a very different dimension in sub-Saharan Africa, as do the problematic notions of *level of life satisfaction, interpersonal trust,* and *support for revolutionary change.* Whether one adopts Inglehart's model or Muller and Seligson's, the measurement of democracy poses an even greater problem: How can one employ a simplistic seven-point scale to interpret what is happening in Rwanda, Zaire, Congo, Madagascar, Senegal, Libya, or Sierra Leone? And how can one compare the situations in these countries to what is going on in the United States, Scandinavia, or the Islamic republics in the former Soviet Union? One cannot. Despite their high level of sophistication and the good faith of their authors, these models are decidedly inadequate to the task.

The results of recent research likewise invalidate the idea of civic culture. Verba et al. conducted an extensive survey in the United States that led them to conclude that citizens who are involved in traditional forms of political activism (participation) are in no way representative of the social groups to which they belong. This conclusion confirms the thesis earlier advanced by Bennett and Bennett (1986). Given that the question of representation lies at the very heart of democratic thought, such discoveries ought to serve as a wake-up call to researchers and policymakers: "Those in public life are more likely to be aware of, and to pay attention to, the needs and preferences of those who are active. Thus, it would seem to matter for the democratic principle of equality that studies of citizen participation in America concur in showing political activists to be unrepresentative in their demographic characteristics of the public at large" (Verba et al. 1993:303).

Of course, one may question whether observations of this sort apply to Africa—once again, much research remains to be done. But it is already clear that the theory whereby one surveys a group of activists involved in various forms of political participation in Dakar, Lusaka, or Nairobi and deems the results to be representative of the political hopes and needs of the Senegalese, Zambians, or Kenyans warrants discussion. Adopting the opposite approach—that is, seeking to discover why some citizens do not participate in political life—Brady et al. (1995) developed an original model with surprising results. For example, they found that certain resources such as time and money count at least as much as civic competence; and that some citizens are inclined to express their political views conventionally, whereas others tend to use different avenues of expression, which as yet have been studied little, if at all. One must keep this crucial finding in mind if one truly wishes to explore and understand the new African political marketplace. Unfortunately, few Africanist scholars have done so.

The other criterion of analysis found occasionally in Africanist political theory (generally in the works of rationalists) is that of legitimacy. In theory, the idea of legitimacy is less contentious than the concept of civic culture advanced by culturalists, for it appears to encompass less controversial notions. However, if one takes a closer look, as Weatherford has done, one cannot fail to see that its various dimensions are no guarantee of a smooth, controlled analysis. How, for example, is one to verify whether a given political system actually meets the following criteria:

> Accountability (Are rulers accountable to the governed via a process that allows wide, effective participation?); Efficiency (Is the government set up to accomplish society's ends without undue waste of time and resources?); Procedural fairness (Is the system structured to ensure that issues are resolved in a regular, predictable way and that access to decisional arenas is open and equal?); Distributive fairness (Are the advantages and costs allocated by the system distributed equally or else deviations from prima facie equality explicitly justified on grounds that define "fair shares" in terms of some long-run, overarching equality principle?) (1992:150)

These questions are, of course, troubling but so very important if one is to provide the word *legitimacy* with real content. They might be asked by an Algerian in Algiers or by an Angolan in Luanda, but also by an American in Washington, a Frenchman in Paris, or a Japanese in Tokyo! The sad truth is that one would likely receive a variety of discordant responses to these questions regardless of the country in which they were posed. And what one perceives at the level of the political and institutional system (the macro-level) is but a single aspect of legitimacy. One must also study the meaning of legitimacy at the level of individual beliefs and hopes (the micro-level), which means investigating such notions as interest and involvement in politics ("the psychological feeling that political participation is worth the opportunity cost of trading off time and commitment from other occupations," as Weatherford puts it); faith in collective action, that is, in the trustworthiness of other people; and a certain degree of optimism with respect to one's country and to the power of voters. All of these not only warrant analysis but would unquestionably open up important debates in any country.

We have come to the end of our theoretical excursus. Having begun with the idea that a liberal democratic model exists to which African countries, despite the political reforms of the early 1990s, have not managed to conform, we have arrived at the idea that the evaluative criteria of said model are too arbitrary to be taken seriously and that no country in the world could pass the democratic test anyway—assuming it were possible to design such a test. Many years ago this observation led Dahl to describe democracy as a goal after which polyarchic Western governments strive but never reach (1971). It is a shame that Africanist political scientists have not taken to heart the modesty implied in this lesson. As for African heads of state, they do not hesitate to exploit these contradictions in order to "legitimate" their authoritarian regimes and revamp their approach to politics.

The Art of Political Aggiornamento: A Revamped Discourse

The opacity of the new African political landscape cannot be attributed to the egocentrism and ignorance of Africanist political scientists alone. The remarkable creativity of African leaders has also contributed significantly to the present confusion. Because of the rapidity with which they have brought their discourse and repressive techniques up to date, African dictators have managed at once to create uncertainty about their abilities and will and to sell the international community on the ludicrous idea that the future of Africa depends on them and them alone. As a result, thought is by and large confined within the boundaries they have erected and only their point of view is included on the agenda of university scholars, political brain trusts, and international banking institutions.

Through an incredible reversal of fortune, all of Africa's dictators—from Senegal's Abdou Diouf and Djibouti's Hassan Gouled to Morocco's Hassan II and Zaire's Mobutu—who were losing strength in the early 1990s succeeded not only in maintaining power but occasionally in strengthening their control over their countries and in changing the issues of debate, this at a time when the dictators of the former Eastern bloc were toppling like bowling pins. If one is interested in advancing thought on democracy in Africa, it is necessary to examine this near miracle (the techniques of political survival used by African dictators) in order to understand why it occurred.

Initially shocked and stunned by the 1990–1991 popular uprisings, African leaders quickly regained their composure and began to decipher the vocabulary of the new era.[11] They came to understand that the imprisonment of their opponents was costly and difficult to manage: The democratic myth appeared to have ignited a firestorm of political activism, and the number of people wishing to become involved in government increased exponentially. Whereas the opposition had previously been confined to a handful of leaders not only known and "on file" but mostly in exile, it now extended to countless masses. These illegitimate governments had to address the problem of controlling an ever increasing number of adversaries. Already overcrowded, prisons could no longer hold them all.

Since direct violence was no longer effective, heads of state quickly classified it as an obsolete tool, an outmoded weapon—at least against certain types of leaders.[12] It was therefore necessary to devise new techniques to rally people to their cause, to rewire the circuits of official propaganda, and to modernize practices of exclusion. That is why African leaders have developed a discourse centered on democracy. In the name of pluralism, they do their best to fight words that strike them as unorthodox. Their retorts warrant attention.

The discourse of African heads of state centers on four themes: (1) the political immaturity of the population; (2) the lack of financial means to organize efficiently the democratic process; (3) the denunciation of outside interference and violations of their national sovereignty; and (4) the demand for cultural relativism, which gives them license, on "moral" grounds, to design their own democracy. In their eyes, democratization is a mere cosmetic; thus, they busy themselves with the elaboration of a "new" ideology to explain their refusal to adopt the principle of alternation of power. Cameroon is a striking example of this strategy. The primary goals of official discourse are to make a mockery of popular demands, to engage in sophistry, and to create deliberate confusion. Let us take a look at some of these new techniques and at the new crib sheet for authoritarians. Concentrated on Cameroon, the discussion that follows also sheds light on what is happening in Morocco, Côte d'Ivoire, Kenya, Zimbabwe, and other countries.

- *Cultural relativism against democracy:* It all begins with the repeated use of cultural relativism clichés. The celebration of the myth of uniqueness is likewise one of the government's new themes. In a speech given in Yaoundé in 1991, Paul Biya proclaimed, "Cameroon is Cameroon!" so as to justify his refusal of the National Conference—a popular meeting during which all the politically active groups in the country redesign the rules of the political game and elaborate a new electoral agenda. In so doing, he was following in the footsteps of some of his minions, such as Emah Basile, the deputy and mayor of Yaoundé, who rejected the idea of a multiparty system by declaring to the National Assembly in 1990: "We don't want imported models!" Beyond the puerile quality of such a slogan, especially in a country where those in power refer and defer daily to French constitutional law, it is necessary to call attention to the resurgence of a certain form of national pride. It is a rather laughable nationalism, however, because its essential function is to rationalize the maintenance of a repressive system by giving it a "philosophical," "legal" foundation and an "intellectual" framework.

By refusing to import political models developed in Benin, Nigeria, or Congo (for example, the Supreme National Conference), the authorities not only were expressing contempt for "little countries" but were simultaneously affirming, "We'll democratize at our own pace." Understood in this idea is the following: "We refuse to use outside ideas because they do not belong to the reality of our culture or our history." The reasoning is specious, as it is in all sophisms. First of all, the cultural precepts that are referred to are rarely identifiable. Lévi-Strauss and Eribon criticized this type of monoculturalism, which forgets that "*toutes les cultures résultent de brassages, d'emprunts, de mélanges, qui n'ont cessé de se produire, bien que sur des rythmes différents, depuis l'origine des temps* [all cultures are a result of brewing, of borrowing, of mixing; a process that has not ceased, though always with differing rhythms, since the beginning of time]" (1990:212).[13] Multicultural by virtue of its formation, Cameroonian society has, of course, produced its own synthesis that citizens may conceivably wish to retain today. But to disgrace and discredit a political system from the Sahel while glorifying a hybrid form of presidential government is completely incoherent.

The cult of Cameroon's uniqueness likewise appears in the comparisons leaders often make between their own country's performance and that of other countries where the economic and political situation is deemed to be worse. State-run television regularly devotes programs to the "catastrophes" that occurred in Congo or Zaire, insinuating that the disaster was brought on by the organization of national conferences in these states. It is comforting for leaders to invoke such notions as "intellectual sovereignty"; they can slyly refer to the "Westernization of the political order," which Badie and others have denounced, and to distort the debate on democratization.

Burkina Faso's president Blaise Compaoré dips into the same well of cultural relativism, declaring: "I do not believe that there exists a set of immutable principles for the political organization of a state. Each state must prove extremely imaginative and inspired if it is to find the mechanisms capable of combining political forces that do not always share the same options. Every society inevitably has a specific form of political organization. Just as every people evolves in function of its own cultural experiences" (1995:55).

The president of Equatorial Guinea, T. Obiang Nguéma, justifies his adherence to cultural relativism via the rhetoric of political illiteracy:

> Like all African nations, Equatorial Guinea is in the process of democratizing. This is why we have adopted a governmental policy that we have baptized trial democracy. For we cannot be considered as totally democratic. It is a new process. To speak of democracy, one needs a well-informed, well-educated people able to face the problems that emerge with democracy. The country must also have sufficient financial resources if democracy is to develop normally.... Africans see democracy as a way to make money, to obtain important positions, to live like kings, forgetting that their responsibility is to craft the nation. A great majority are not yet aware of the true meaning of democracy. Ignorance and poverty are, of course, factors that slow its development" (1994:102).

• *The "do-nothing" strategy:* In the 1960s and 1970s, when African opposition leaders living in exile in the West denounced human rights violations in their countries and called for the establishment of a multiparty system and for free and fair elections, governments invariably replied by way of solemn communiqués. Anxious to preserve the respectability they had won by lobbying the most influential international media, autocrats vehemently rebutted all accusations. The demands of opponents were reduced to "posturing on the part of men hungry for power" or "attacks on national security" (compare Eyinga 1978), and insults were a large part of official replies. The ideologues of the single party always justified their responses on the grounds that because the people were not yet ready for pluralism, the maintenance of national unity, "patiently won" at the price of a long civil war, required sacrifices in the realm of human rights. For decades, the discourse of authoritarians centered on this theme.

Since the mid-1980s, African governments have evolved considerably. Amid the panoply of arms used against opponents, invectives remain a favorite weapon, but the content and timing of governmental reactions are now more original, more in keeping with the spirit of the times. Subscribing to the axiom that "there exists no historical law that provides that a people shall revolt at a certain threshold of despotism, famine or abuse" (Vargas Llosa 1993:2), African authorities presently opt for a do-nothing strategy. At first view, this does not look like a strategy at all, since it does indeed consist in doing nothing for as long as possible. In the face of their failure to improve the economy, of growing demands of all kinds, of scandals uncovered by the press, and of criticisms from the international community, governments often counter with silence. It is as if African heads of state think that by adopting a contemptuous attitude, they can wear down their opponents, keep them outside the arena of debate. Doing nothing has become a consummate political virtue. And sometimes it works! Sheer exhaustion has caused some members of the opposition to team up with those in power, for they feel their effort to change the course of history ended in failure (for example, in Morocco, Tunisia, Zaire, Senegal, Nigeria, Cameroon, and Gabon); it has driven others to radicalize their discourse and thereby fall into the trap of blindness or populism; it has led still others to abandon politics (for example, in Zaire and Kenya)—which is the chief objective of governments seeking to reduce, in any way possible, the ranks of the opposition.

• *Disqualification and defamation as a weapon:* A new function ascribed to official discourse is the use of discredit and defamation as a strong weapon against recalcitrant members of the opposition. To each of the opposition's demands, the government responds with censorship (silence) or systematic vilification (words). This was the case in May 1990, when Cameroon's chief opposition leader, John Fru Ndi, led a march in Bamenda for the establishment of the Social Democratic Front party (SDF). The authorities prohibited the protest march and deployed a large number of troops in the northwest region of the country. Thousands of protesters showed up, defying the Cameroonian army, which opened fire and killed six people. Unable to control the outpouring of emotion generated by the affair, the government launched a disinformation campaign centered on discrediting those who had organized the march. Over several days, journalists on Cameroon's only state-run television station explained that the deceased had been "trampled to death" by other protesters.[14] Poorly disguised archival footage was used to back up this claim. The protesters were presented as "wild gangs" from Nigeria who had sung the Nigerian national anthem during the march. John Fru Ndi was accused by the state press of being a common swindler who had been responsible for the bankruptcy of the Cameroon Bank, from which he had purportedly borrowed CFA 400 million that he never paid back.[15]

The same tactic was used between July and September 1992, before the presidential election slated for October 11. The regime got the Paris-based African press to run articles singing the praises of Paul Biya's government and demolishing his opponents. Biya's "success" was celebrated, his economic and political results deemed enviable. The other candidates were all impostors. John Fru Ndi, the opposition front-runner, was portrayed as the former cook (!) of Prime Minister Simon Achidi Achu. Yondo Black, who played an important role in establishing a multiparty system, was accused of being a crooked lawyer. The intellectuals in the front lines of the battle for freedom of speech were presented as "tribalists," and "illiterate" ones to boot. Yet again, discredit and defamation served to belittle those guilty of the crime of imagining that things could be run differently. Only the glossy paper and dazzling photos of *Jeune Afrique* and *Africa International* outshined the *Cameroon Tribune*.

Similarly, Zaire's dictator Mobutu uses insinuation to discredit his adversaries. Never at a loss for ludicrous ideas, he has declared that the "politics of food" is the only way to explain the behavior of those opposed to his regime: "Know that they come see me, eat at my table. Sometimes planes land in Gbado at two o'clock in the morning, and you wouldn't believe who wants to have a chat. And I'm there, I receive them, and the planes take off again at 5 a.m., and no one's any the wiser. Listen, I'm not going to say anything more" (1994:20). He also engages in sophistry: "It's quite simple: in the minds of some of my fellow countrymen, the transition means nothing more than the departure of President Mobutu, his eviction, outside the context of any popular vote, and their installation—without elections. I said no! The people are sovereign, they have their say in this. All the more so since they're the ones who elected me, and many times over" (1994:16). And when asked his opinion on the reasons for popular protest in Zaire, he responds without a chuckle: "Oooh!… It's because of my personality, you see. I'm not always pleasant to behold, my head has an unpleasant shape, my name too no doubt. I make people feel uncomfortable, there you have it" (1994:21). Not a word is uttered about his catastrophic performance as Zaire's leader for the past thirty years. To pacify the international community and maintain power, he need only discredit his opponents.

- *Resorting to the paradigm of ethnicity:* To "explain" the difficulties of democratization in Africa, official discourse constantly resorts to the ethnic or tribal argument. Nearly two decades ago, Kotto Essome observed: "Because it explains everything, the 'tribal' excuse defies all explanation. Universally invoked as the fateful, ancestral cause of Africa's 'ethnic' divisions, it excels in diverting attention from their genesis in colonialism and from the ravages on the fringes of a market economy that catalyzes and reinforces their institutionalization"(1985:33). Although the "tribal" is lacking in scientific substance, the ideological mystification of "tribalism" has allowed African governments to deflect public opinion from the only question that really matters: their abysmal thirty-year record of rule. By reducing even the most corporatist opposition demands, criticisms, and social tensions to "manipulative" efforts on the part of one or more ethnic groups to the detriment of others, African heads of state often succeed in eliminating debate on the economic failure and social bankruptcy of their countries. They systematically sidestep the issues raised by the opposition by bringing them back to the question of slicing up the mythical "national cake" among the different tribes.

Thus, when Cameroonian attorney Yondo Black was arrested in February 1990 because he sought to create a political party, the government accused him of having tried to use his title of traditional tribal chieftain to organize the takeover of the government by the Duala. Next the government elicited a "show of support on the part of traditional Littoral tribal chieftains for President Biya." Wearing exotic tribal garb and ornaments of royalty, some went on television stating that the Duala community had not mandated Yondo Black to defend its interests. Although that had obviously never been the intention of this former president of the bar association, the government had achieved its objective: it had created a diversion so that attention would not be focused on the real question raised by Yondo Black—respect for political pluralism written into the constitution—and had lent credence to the idea that he was motivated not by nationalism but by tribalism.

The ethnic argument has nourished the practices and discourse of authoritarianism in the past few years. Thus, it is easy to see why the official ideologues became flustered when, after thirty-three years of exile in France, the writer Mongo Beti decided to return home in February 1991 (see Kom 1991a). Born in Mbalmayo, a true son of the south province (Biya's native region), Mongo Beti has steadfastly opposed the regime. In his case, it was impossible to trot out the old "tribe-with-hegemonic-ambitions" argument; something else was required. Taken aback, out of catchy ideas, the government first organized a campaign on national television devised to show that Beti was, of all things, French! His identity papers were presented on television along with copies of visa request forms he had filled out in Paris in order to make the trip home. Subsequently, J. Owona, general secretary of the presidency and second in command, published a vitriolic article in a "private" newspaper published by the presidency in which he besmirched the writer's family and accused Beti of having been co-opted by other tribes (Owona 1991).

• *The cult of fatalism:* The efficacy of modes of political communication that use paralogisms and distortion depends on their capacity to maintain the illusion of power. To imprint these new "truths" into collective memory, the regime attempts to exploit the factor of time. It seeks to impress these theses on the general psychological environment—in a Braudelian sense.[16] It endeavors to restructure the episteme by creating the conditions for fatalism on a massive scale. Its goal is to discourage the greatest number of citizens, to take away their interest in politics—in brief, to reduce political participation to the lowest possible level.

Through police brutality and various types of subterfuge, political opinion remains focused on considerations that do not invite debate. Such measures as censorship, the prohibition of privately run media, the imprisonment of recalcitrant journalists, the silencing of dissenting voices, the exponential increase in official propaganda, and the reinforcement of police and administrative powers have not so much recreated the climate of terror found in these nations during the 1960s and 1970s as they have created a collective weariness and discouragement.

More sophisticated, if hardly original, techniques are used to reach the same goal: sap the foundation of citizens' hope and faith in the possibility of a different world. Thus, the enlistment of intellectuals in the apparatus of repression is not designed to breathe new life into the existing system but rather to convince dreamers and utopians that "every man has a price" (compare Mbock 1985), that it is better to put up with a corrupt (and sated) leader than to risk the alternation of power, which would come down to a political takeover by young, hungry wolves—even more inclined to rob the public coffers than those in place.[17]

Whenever the government wishes to justify the imprisonment of a writer, the torture that takes place at police headquarters, the rigging of the register of voters, the stuffing of ballot boxes, or the nonpayment of salaries, it finds at its disposal a pleiad of "professors-with-a-long-list-of-diplomas" (that's the way they are usually introduced on public media) ready to explain such decisions. Cameroonians watched on television an "eminent" professor of public law criticizing the National Conference on the grounds that "it is not provided for by the dictionary" and that "a Belgian would not understand it." They were not surprised when he was later appointed minister of culture. They likewise witnessed the promotion of a "great philosopher," who had long called for the "dictatorship of renewal" (official ideology), to a high-ranking position within the administration of the University of Yaoundé. They have seen "world-renowned intellectuals" make meager attempts at theorizing tribalism and then assume the directorship of big-budget public agencies.

The same strategy of "conversion" has been used successfully against numerous political "opponents": those who work for the government and whose only role is to create diversions; those who created parties in the hope of receiving state financing; and those who tired of waiting for the alternation of power and thus resigned themselves to joining ranks with the "presidential majority" in exchange for a seat on a board. Such maneuvers, which involve the combined interests of urban elites, coteries, mysterious lobbies, and various pressure groups, are not related to a given policy or political idea, but that does not prevent the government from presenting them as proof of the existence of a dialogue among the nation's different political families. It also shores up the idea in the collective unconscious that alternation of power serves no purpose, that it might even be dangerous insofar as it would upset the delicate balance ("dialogue," in official parlance) of political forces.

Without question, these new political techniques (the cosmetics of authoritarianism) have helped cloud the perception of Western and African political scientists. They underscore the need to refine analysis of African sociopolitical transformations. As the Beninese philosopher Hountondji has pointed out, "The major problem in the sphere of political analysis is to know not so much how a regime defines itself as what objective function this self-proclaimed definition has in the political game which the regime is playing" (1983:93).

Official African discourse stems above all from the idea, endorsed by numerous intellectuals, of the negatively marked specificity of the African political arena, for the political philosophy behind most theories of modernization supplies cultural relativism with a theoretical framework of which African heads of state take advantage (Coleman and Halisi 1983). When Huntington affirms that "the most important political distinction among countries concerns not their form of government, but their degree of government" (1968:1), he elegantly justifies the suspicion of the universality of forms of political organization and, in so doing, de facto concedes the validity of any form of relativism that claims to be able to govern "better"—that is, according to measurement criteria that may be defined only locally. Huntington's initial criticism is no doubt well founded, but it leads one to a slippery slope that African dictators have not hesitated to start down, reinforcing their barbarisms with all sorts of philosophical justifications.

The Political "Bricolage" of the Opposition

In the face of the creative maneuvering by African heads of state, the opposition cuts a sorry figure—but this does not reflect the dynamism and seriousness of rural and urban populations, who do not hesitate to make sacrifices so as to manifest their desire for freedom. Wole Soyinka has often spoken of an Africa betrayed from within. This observation, which was subsequently developed by Ayittey (1992), certainly applies to the political arena, where the inconsistency and capriciousness of actors in certain countries is such that long hoped for change appears unlikely. There are several problems regarding opposition leaders. First, very few of them were prepared to fulfill their roles. Although the Côte d'Ivoire's Laurent Gbagbo and Gabon's Paul Mba Abessole have a great deal of experience fighting political battles, the same cannot be said of the vast majority of current opposition leaders, often former big shots in the regime who transform into its most bitter rivals.[18] Cameroon's Jean-Jacques Ekindi is an interesting case in point. A former political baron of the single party who organized in March–April 1990 a national march against the establishment of a multiparty system, a staunch critic of the coordination of opposition parties in 1991—two months after the first opposition party was legalized—he resigned from the ruling party in May 1991 and became the general secretary of said coordination in August. Similar examples can be cited for Gabon, Togo, Congo, the Central African Republic, etc.

Quite often, then, the career paths of opposition leaders are inconsistent, which raises the question of these leaders' true motivations, their loyalty to the causes to which they have committed themselves (if loyalty can be said to exist in politics), and their leeway to maneuver vis-à-vis the regimes they claim to oppose. But given that politics is not an art of the straight line, as Winston Churchill's tortuous ideological trajectory amply demonstrates, the seriousness of African politicians must not be judged on their successive party affiliations alone. This brings us back to our initial reservation concerning this category of African opposition leaders: It is their flexibility of spirit that makes their behavior so unpredictable—and always "justifiably" so.[19]

Almost everywhere opposition parties seem paralyzed. Ruling heads of state have custom-built adversaries; that is, the latter are often ready to celebrate the virtues of the old order, often incapable of transforming collective despair into an avenue for change. Despite the institution of a multiparty administrative system, public discourse remains one-dimensional insofar as the new leaders have not suggested alternative political programs. The numerous recognized opposition parties revolve around a few individuals, exhibit a rigid, centralized structure, and function in the same way and with the same ideas as the old single party. This organizational deficiency leads one to think that Africa's multiparty system is but a conglomeration of multiple "single" parties.

I believe these are the principal reasons for the current confusion in Africanist political science. Next I shall attempt to propose an alternative vision of the political arena.

Outline of a Theory of Democratization in Africa

Having addressed the genesis of the misunderstandings that cast doubt on the relevance of Africanist political theories, I will now move on to an analysis of the space of politics. I will explain the new rules of the political game, interpret the current transformations and changes in attitude, and examine Africa's contribution to democratic theory. Adopting Braud's definition of the political arena as the "site of (peaceful?) competition for the right to monopolize coercion, to lay down the law and to guarantee its effectiveness in society as a whole" (1992:6), I shall analyze in more theoretical terms what is at stake in the current political battles and how the rules of the game and the behavior of the actors have changed.

The Reconfiguration of the Political Arena and the Capacity to Disguise

Many who have studied the African political game have spoken of the hunger for power that drives political actors but have not investigated their true motivations (Bayart 1989). These writers forget that power is never an objective in and of itself; rather, it helps one attain other goals, which are by and large clearly expressed. By analyzing competition for power in sub-Saharan Africa, one can better grasp the multiple dimensions of the present democratization process.

In the period immediately following independence, power in Africa was conceived as a sort of privilege, indeed a monopoly, held by a group of individuals and occasionally divvied up among members of a clique, along the lines of Krueger's (1974) rent-seeking principle. At the time, this "substantialist" conception of power, to use Braud's terminology (1992:10), was the most widespread in Africa. Numerous writers have referred to its most perverse forms as "neopatrimonialism" (Callaghy 1994; Médart 1994).

This paradigm is no longer operative today. Even the most extreme forms of African patrimonialism have undergone revision. Far from being a system of mere privilege trafficking and influence peddling, patrimonialism is attuned to the social exigencies of the times and seeks to craft a type of power that is less direct and primitive, more equilibrated, and, in a certain sense, interactive. The naked power that characterized the first three decades of African independence has given way to a much more subtle form of political action that I shall term power in disguise. It consists in the ability to appear to be something one is not (as witnessed in the techniques for the renewal of the symbolic order) and sometimes does not even require the threat of violence to succeed. A minimal level of obedience to government authority is guaranteed not only by the conviction of citizens that the state has methods of public and private retaliation but also by their very disenchantment, a result of the capability of authoritarianism to disguise itself.[20] In societies with a highly developed sense of spirituality, the craftily manipulated politics of confusion allows leaders to capitalize on the psychology of fear, to play with people's emotions, and to exploit the entire range of emotions.

The specificity of African power also lies in the very nature of the institutional arena in which political competition is played out. The usual dichotomy between rigid political systems characteristic of dictatorships (where competition is restricted because access to power is blocked) and flexible systems (where the various actors divide among themselves, in a more or less inegalitarian manner, positions of power on the local and national levels) cannot account for the subtleties of the African model. Both systems are combined in a semirigid model in which access to the political game is blocked less by way of restrictive constitutional provisions than through the practical, everyday implementation of laws and rules. Cases like that of Cameroon, where the constitution of May 20, 1972, stipulates that "the President of the Republic defines and implements national policy," or Côte d'Ivoire, where a code of election law was adopted in 1995 for the specific purpose of keeping the candidate the administration feared most out of the race (French 1995a, 1995b; *New York Times* 1995), are exceptions, not the rule. In general, the textual framework of competition has been modernized to the point that access to the political arena is blocked not through institutional constraints but through abuses of the new legal liberties. Thus, when Zaire's president Mobutu Sese Seko officially legalized 322 "opposition parties," he knew very well that the effect on the political outcome would be the same as legalizing none; the excessive number of parties allowed him to trivialize the function of opposition to his government and opened up various possibilities for political manipulation—the heads of most of the parties were loyal to him, and these precious allies were numerous enough to defeat any proposal by the parties to take action against him. Most African dictators quickly understood and mastered this classic technique of barring access to the political arena via excessive politicization.

The evolution of the balance of power in the African political marketplace can be illustrated as a function of the number of parties, as shown in the Figure 2.2, showing the atomization dynamics of the political marketplace. This figure highlights the predatory strategy of African governments. In countries where the ruling (and former single) party reluctantly endorses the idea of political competition, it is possible to multiply deliberately the number of opposition parties to weaken the opposition as a whole. Authoritarian governments are powerful when the political game is dominated by a single party, as was the case in most of the continent in the 1960s and 1970s, or in countries where there is no political party at all (Nigeria and Uganda in the early 1990s). However,

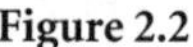

Figure 2.2

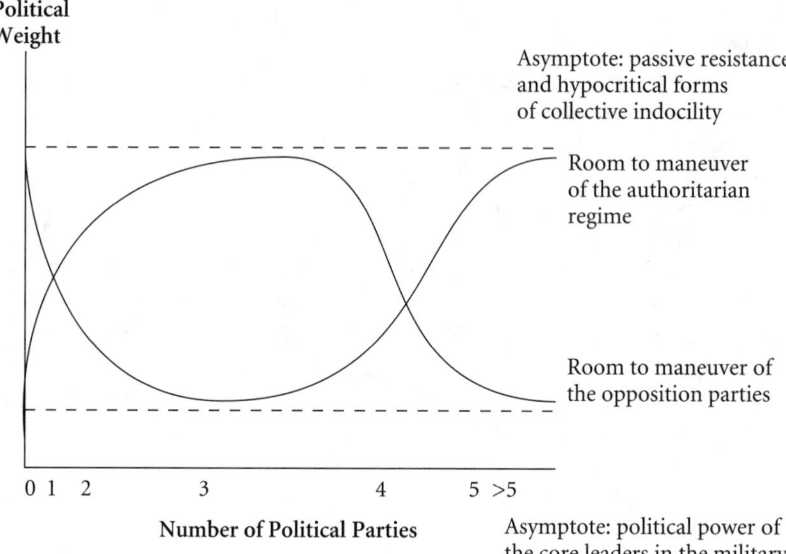

there is always an upper and a lower limit to any political power in Africa, whether it comes from the government or its opponents. These structural limits, which are represented by the two asymptotes in Figure 2.2, have been very important in the democratization process: Even under brutal dictatorships by single-party regimes, the government's room to maneuver was constrained by various forms of passive resistance and informal techniques of collective indocility—illustrated by the higher asymptote. Facing new forms of strong, popular opposition in the early 1990s, African governments were obliged to open up the political market and tolerate some competition. Immediately following such a concession, their political power dissipated, as did their ability to repress opposition (represented by the downward sloping curve). Even at the peak of a democratic explosion, there is a limit to the weakness of authoritarian regimes: Some military leaders in the army can be neither removed immediately nor circumvented. They represent, therefore, the lower limit of the decreasing political weight of authoritarian regimes (the lower asymptote).

The opposition parties' room to maneuver tends to increase exponentially immediately after the legalization of the first two opposition parties (the upward sloping curve). Thus, the optimal moment for radical political change lies somewhere between three and four parties, when the gap between the two main political actors is the greatest—the point at which the power of the authoritarian government has weakened drastically, and the strength of opposition leaders has reached its highest level. If major constitutional changes do not occur at this time, it is very likely that the country will move to another phase of political history; this is the second stage of the democratization process, typically characterized by major setbacks in political reforms. Beyond four or five parties in the political market, the authoritarian regimes are able to regain a monopoly: They support the establishment of an infinite number of new "opposition parties" that are totally under their control and that are used to challenge or ridicule their strongest competitors. Discord is almost inevitable among so many opposition leaders, some of whom invariably end up claiming "ethnic" or "regional" legitimacy, which enables them to join a coalition government in the repressive system they pretended to oppose. Such strange moves have devastating psychological effects inside and outside the country, for they send negative signals to the other players who are involved in or who are watching the game: Those in popular resistance movements are discouraged by what they see as their leaders' lack of commitment or even betrayal (especially by those who later make deals with the government they opposed), while international opinion is quick to conclude that opposition leaders lack clear vision, strategy, and consistency. Such was the case when opposition leaders became ministers in the government they had opposed after the 1992 presidential elections in Cameroon and Kenya, the 1993 presidential race in Senegal, and the 1995 legislative and presidential elections in Benin and Côte d'Ivoire, respectively.

Thus, by flooding the political market with as many political parties as possible, the government is eventually able to trivialize (or even marginalize) its opponents. Of course, it is usually well known that most of the newcomers are in fact political allies of the sitting government, but it does not matter, since their official status as opponents entitles them to official respectability, public funding, campaign time in the public media, etc. The actions of these newcomers finally erode the political appeal of the other opposition leaders, who are quickly labeled "radical," "irresponsible," or "violent" people. This is one of the main paradoxes of multiparty politics in Africa: the higher the number of opposition parties, the weaker the opposition is as a whole, and the stronger the authoritarian regime becomes. It all boils down to monolithic pluralism, for the political weight of the two main political actors may grow or diminish, but it returns to the starting point. A political baron of Cameroon's former single party used a nice metaphor to describe the current situation of atomization of the political market and ideological unanimity. Some political actors are sopranos, he said, others, baritones, but they're all singing the same song (Ntsama 1993).

The Cohabitation of Two Worlds

The original character of political struggles in sub-Saharan Africa is also attributable to the multidimensional nature of the political arena and the weak differentiation between the organic and the functional. The political arena is multidimensional insofar as two distinct levels of political activity exist: one visible, the other invisible (Monga 1995a).

- Researchers tend to focus on the visible level of the political arena, made up of three main types of actors: institutions provided for by the constitution (the executive and legislative branches, the judiciary, the highest governmental agencies, the military); political organizations (parties and affiliated associations); and various organizations of civil society. I call this the technostructure of government.
- Few people even suspect the existence of the invisible level, which is likewise divided into three primary categories: international pressure groups (European politicians who receive financial backing on the sly from Africa, Western diplomats working in or on Africa); transnational financial networks (including international agencies such as the International Monetary Fund [IMF] and the World Bank, as well as businessmen, large corporations, and banks with commercial interests in sub-Saharan Africa); and sects, religious groups, and other private transnational organizations. I call this the superstructure of the political marketplace. Figure 2.3 illustrates the two levels as a longitudinal section of the African political marketplace.

The democratization process was intended to reaffirm the principle of an effective balance of power via the division of responsibilities among the different branches and agencies of government. But even in countries that adopted new constitutions allowing such balance to occur, the exercise of power is still stuck between the known and the unknown level. This has resulted in the blurring of the institutional boundaries that the revision and clarification of the rules of politics sought to introduce. Thus, alongside the legislative, departmental, and judicial branches of government are informal networks of power, which are extremely active and powerful, and through which most important political and economic decisions are made. That is why the hopes public policymakers placed in democratization have not materialized—the decisions reached in the informal political circuit tend to cancel out official government programs. The elaboration of economic policy comes up against the conflicting agendas of the various actors. Researchers who do not grasp the structural subtleties of the sociopolitical environment simply conclude that Africa is resistant to economic reforms and that the adjustments that need to be made if these moribund economies are to be saved cannot take place within the context of democratization.

Figure 2.3

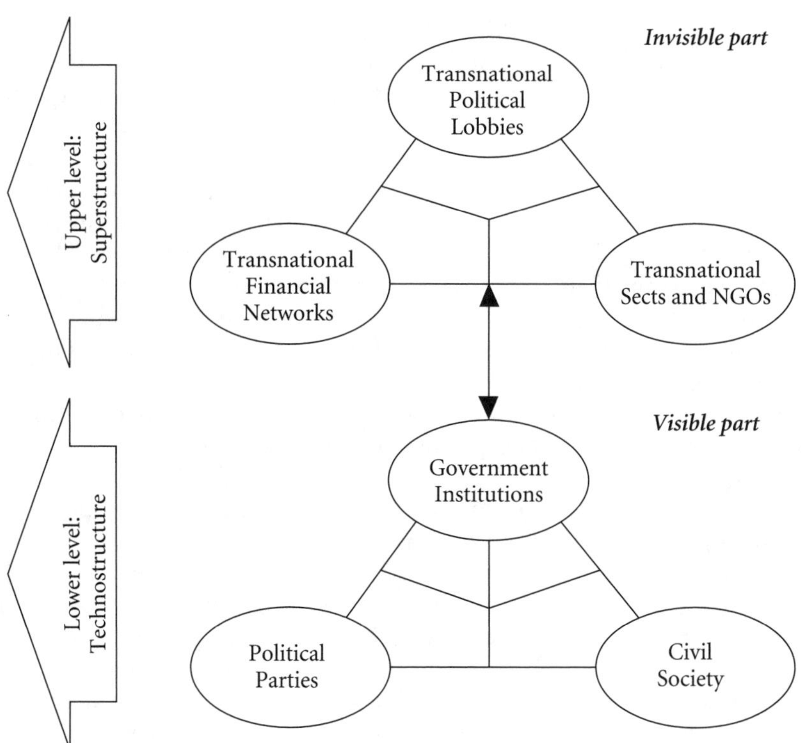

In countries where the process of public policy development is mysterious, where the semantics of politics needs to be redefined, it is imperative to investigate the goals of political actors and the rules of political life in order is to understand the dynamics of the current situation. To begin, let us examine the uses and perceptions of power in Africa.

Uses, Efficacy, and Perceptions of Power

The disenchantment and utter confusion resulting from the "failures" of Africa's first democratic governments intrigued and unsettled most analysts, who were eager to see confirmed their culturalist theories on the structural incapacity of African peoples to negotiate democracy. Hence, the civil war that broke out in Congo in 1993 and 1994, the fiery or Ubuesque conflicts pitting the prime minister against the presidents of the republic in Mali (1993), Niger (1995), and Madagascar (1995), the merciless battle between Benin's head of state and his main political rival, the president of the National Assembly (1992–1995)—all of these events, which are typical (or so it was thought) of authoritarian regimes alone, have cast considerable doubt on the possibility of democratic consolidation in Africa. It is necessary to examine the political environment and imagination of these regimes in order to understand such events and to get past the indignant attitude of researchers toward these democratic "setbacks."

To grasp the meaning of what is at stake, one must begin by classifying political actors according to their motivations. Certain leaders of political organizations, having found nothing better to do in society, seek power out of spite. This partially explains why, for example, there are more established parties in Benin than there are seats in the National Assembly. Others become involved in politics out of revenge, having lost the important positions they once held in the political system. Despite democratization, the African political class is the same as it has always been. Still others enter politics not to change things but to defend the interests they represent—interests that generally concern the few, cross ethnic lines, and exhibit no particular ideological bent. Around 98 percent of Africa's political actors fall into these three categories. In their view, the alternation of power is more intimately linked to the alternation of men than to the alternation of approaches to government. According to the law of large numbers, a fundamental rule of probability theory, these leaders are much more likely to gain access to power than others. It is not surprising, then, that their actions obey a separate logic, their interests lie in the maintenance of the status quo rather than in change, and their agendas reflect the concerns of a minority of social groups instead of the hopes and dreams of the majority of the population.

We will have to wait until the fourth category of politicians, at present a tiny, fragile group, grows large enough to effect deep changes in the way politics operates in Africa. The forefather of this group is no doubt the Senegalese historian Cheikh Anta Diop, the leader of an opposition party (the Rassemblement National Démocratique [RND]) founded during the Léopold Sédar Senghor years, who has become so disillusioned about his ability to influence events that he has chosen to withdraw his party from elections. The RND's involvement is limited to championing a few issues.

Signs of the emergence of this new race of politicians attuned to the needs of the population are perceptible here and there, but for the time being, democratization continues to make do with the politicians at hand. Their mediocrity in no way affects or reflects the people's desire for freedom or the quest for democracy on the continent. If the depth of democratic feeling were judged solely on the basis of a nation's leaders, then neither Japan nor Italy nor Canada nor even the United States would pass the test. Why do political scientists tend to demand of Africa that which they do not expect from other regions of the world?

Another problem arises from what I shall term Braud's paradox, whereby a government has much more difficulty effecting change when it takes power in a preexisting environment of legitimacy:

> If socio-economic structures are by and large seen as satisfactory, if common values have been strongly internalized by the different segments of the population, if, finally, the political regime appears properly adapted to the expectations of social groups, governments and those seeking to replace them have little latitude to act. As for advocates of radical change, they have no chance of running institutions.... The alternation of power is as frequent and smooth here as the parties or opponents are similar to one another, sharing in fact more or less common social conceptions. On the other hand, as soon as this condition is lacking (or appears to be lacking), democratic alternation of power becomes a major political problem (1992:19).

This paradox takes a different form in black Africa, where the ingredients for desired change are in no way lacking—the painful failures of the past forty years have prepared even the most timid spirits for a revolution in the institutional framework and the exercise of power. But two problems exist that weaken the capacity of new leaders to bring this to fruition: the proximity of the ideological positions of politicians, old and new, as the categories proposed earlier suggest, and the money factor, so very important in these lean times. In countries in dire economic straits, some of which are forced to depend on outside aid to pay the salaries of civil servants and to cover the government's operating expenses, there is little room to maneuver in the area of public policy. Once in office, the leaders who have been duly elected (or whose legitimacy is uncontested by their opponents) find themselves held hostage to economic realities. A case in point is Niger's president Mahamane Ousmane. The centerpiece of his 1992 campaign was a virulent attack on the IMF's and the World Bank's programs of structural adjustment. No sooner had he won the election against the former single-party candidate than he had to convince the international financial community of his seriousness. In the end, Ousmane had no choice but to swallow the bitter pill of structural adjustment, for which the voters never forgave him. Only months after assuming office, his government lost a vote of confidence in the National Assembly and a chaotic coalition government with a hostile prime minister ensued.

Contrary to Braud's prediction, it is not so much the population's acceptance of existing values and socioeconomic structures that weakens the ability of new governments to enact change. If his paradox remains apposite—that is, if the new leaders' freedom of action is inversely proportional to their legitimacy—it is because they almost always inherit a disastrous economy but almost never try either to explain the reason for the rigorousness and brutality of their economic policies or to conceive alternative programs of development. Caught between a demagogic, superficial critique of the IMF's programs of adjustment and an incapacity to envision new horizons and possibilities, they find themselves trapped in a legitimacy without content. Albeit democratically elected, these new statesmen are scorned by the international banking community and are eventually dropped by the very people who brought them to power. This is the syndrome of powerlessness to which the governments of Niger, Mali, Congo, the Central African Republic, Zambia, Madagascar, and São Tomé and Principe have fallen victim.

Pakistan's prime minister Benazir Bhutto said recently, in an effort to explain the disaffection toward newly elected governments, that the problem is that people believe democracy lowers inflation and reduces unemployment. Her statement mirrors what Benin's president Nicéphore Soglo said following the 1995 legislative elections:

> After a good campaign, many candidates among the members [of my] government were surprised to see parties show up at the last minute in villages, bringing either something to drink or an envelope, along with ballots in their name. This is why they did so well in certain areas. Many were surprised by this. But I explained that after seventeen years of economic decline—let us not forget that purchasing power fell 2% a year during the 1980s—it wasn't surprising to see people leap at the chance to take that money (1995:60).

Such explanations are facile and do not withstand scrutiny. In reality, the problem is less a matter of the civic incompetence of the people than of the political incompetence of the leaders who claim to represent them. These are two very different notions that one should not use interchangeably.

On the other end of the spectrum, authoritarian regimes that have managed to stay in power through a subtle trade-off between brute force and disguised power—governments of such nations as Morocco, Mauritania, Senegal, Côte d'Ivoire, Cameroon, Chad, Gabon, Togo, Burkina Faso, Kenya, Zimbabwe, and Tanzania—receive subsidies from and the blessing of the global banking community. Alas, they too have had little if any success in implementing public policy (Mosley 1991; World Bank 1994). This leads me to advance a model of political efficacy (see Figure 2.4) that runs counter to Braud's observations and that measures a government's ability to enact political and economic reforms (necessary to increase citizen involvement in the res publica) in terms of its level of legitimacy.

Thus, the use of political power depends less on who the leaders are and what they know than on whether the people see them as legitimate. Hence the necessity of reexploring this mundane concept, which few Africanist scholars bother to do.

Figure 2.4

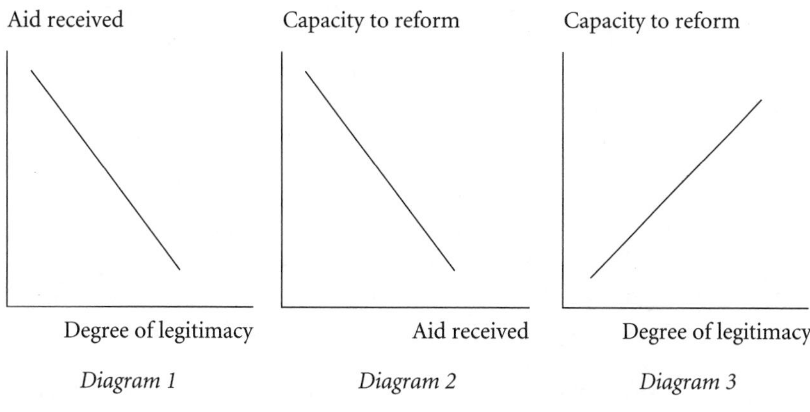

The international financial community earmarks priority funds for authoritarian regimes; in so doing, it devalues the notion of legitimacy as conceived by the population of a given nation.

Aid given to political regimes without institutional mechanisms to ensure the accountability of politicians aggravates the dysfunctions of the political system and discourages the implementation of necessary reforms. Nevertheless, the amount of economic aid is inversely proportional to the ability of the government to enact reforms.

The experiences of such democratic states as Botswana and Mauritius demonstrate that the more the population perceives the regime as legitimate, the more likely it is to support the implementation of public policy aimed at redressing the economy.

New Strategies of Mythologic Legitimation

Aware of the intensity of popular resistance (active and passive) to their regimes, African governments endeavor to develop ideological mechanisms of socialization and regulation that are in fact techniques of legitimation. To this end, they have attempted to devise political mythologies.

The first problem they confront is finding a frame of reference that cuts across class and ethnic lines, necessary for the elaboration of a system of representation centered on values acceptable to the entire population. But in countries where historical traumas (slavery, colonization, failures of the independent state) have left deep scars, ideological antagonisms have escalated. The insidious undermining process begun by the colonists and pursued by the local consuls and proconsuls working for the colonial powers profoundly altered the perspectives adopted by different indigenous social groups. Having experienced the same history, the same dramas, the same "culture," and the same destiny, populations became convinced of the existence of an intimate, age-old identity of dubious origins. This terrible assumption gave rise to a considerable amount of suspicion—indeed hatred—and entire ethnic groups unknowingly became hostage to cruel, cynical warlords. The political incompetence of leaders (not the so-called civic competence of populations), tolerated elsewhere, has sometimes led to savage violence, as witnessed by the events in Liberia, Rwanda, Burundi, Somalia, Angola, and Mozambique. Care must be taken lest the same scenario repeat itself in other countries (compare Chapter 7).

The multiplicity of collective memories necessarily implies different interpretations of the tragic and different social constructions, which is why certain heads of states do their best to incorporate these diverse perceptions of reality into hegemonic strategies (cultural or ideological) for the construction of socializing structures intended to serve their goals. Myths play an important role in this process. For decades, the most popular myth in African politics was that of solidarity, celebrated by politicians via slogans of a nationalist flavor or in favor of national unity. Regional integration was the leitmotiv of public discourse, even though the slogans actually served the politics of exclusion (Kamto 1987). Things have changed: The *myth of protection* has replaced the old standby and has comfortably installed itself in political discourse. Those entering the race for power now affirm that their goal is to protect people not only from the totalitarianism of the sitting government but also (and especially) from the supposed aggression of "rival" groups (ethnic, socioprofessional, etc.). The goal of national unity has given way to strategies designed to fragment society: The objective of politicians is no longer to appeal to the population as a whole but to shore up enough ideological or geographical support to make their views heard in the national political marketplace. The political action of many new players is confined to carving out an "ethnic" or "regional" base that allows them to bring something to the table when negotiations begin among respective "representative" groups. Given that everyone must claim to represent some group or other, the rhetoric of politicians often centers on the theme of protecting this group, whose overall size matters less than the size of its mouth.[21] The myth of protection serves the purposes of a rather primitive political mercantilism.

For a while, the *myth of competence* occupied the scene. At the time of the first popular uprisings (1989–1992), the new politicians were expected to be competent "technocrats," expert in the fine points of management and well versed in the arcana of international finance. The reasoning behind this expectation was clear and simple: The failures of the first three decades of independence clearly pointed to Africa's urgent need for nonpartisan cadres able to get the continent back on track—the "politics of politicking" came later. The dire economic situation of African countries dictated that the major political players (dictators and their principal political rivals) take a back seat to former officers of the World Bank, the IMF, or some other international banking institution charged with putting the house in order. This is how the myth of competence came to be born. Alassane Ouattara, a former IMF executive, became prime minister of Côte d'Ivoire; former World Bank administrators André Milongo and Nicéphore Soglo were named to the same office in Congo and Benin, respectively; and coming from major international institutions, Zoumana Sacko became prime minister of Mali and Ahmadou Cheifou, prime minister of Niger. Heads of state feverishly sifted through the list of expatriates until they found one unknown (and politically insipid) enough to be named prime minister.

Was this a matter of naïveté? Whether or not, the myth soon faded away. With few exceptions, the mediocrity of the technocrats—combined with the ferocity of the opposition leaders and the fact that the people, impatient for change, were not fooled—was enough to invalidate any subsequent candidacy from abroad. In western Africa, these politicians are referred to as "vacationers," expatriates who take a vacation from their jobs in the West to assume the temporary position of prime minister or even to run for president in the tropics.

Finally, the *myth of legitimation,* which aims at reaching "an effective consensus on institutions so as to reinforce the obedient attitudes that facilitate their functioning" (Braud 1992:37), has slowly begun to emerge but has yet to come to the fore in most African countries. Although the institutional sanctification that generally solidifies democracy is far from sight, most political and community leaders in Africa now prefer right to might. For example, the Islamic fundamentalists who have taken up arms against the Algerian authorities invoke the nullification of the 1991 elections as the primary reason for their anger; the armed factions involved in the bloody battles in Congo in 1992–1993 also demanded respect for the law. In the 1995 fight between the supporters of the prime minister and the proponents of the president of the republic in Niger and Madagascar, both sides called for respect of the constitution. Albeit superficial upon occasion, these references to the law are a positive sign, for in the past combatants never bothered to recognize the constitution or to come up with any legal pretext for their acts of violence. "Moral" discourse alone, accompanied by vengeful slogans, had been enough to justify their actions. The increasingly frequent appeal to the law suggests the return of an ethical exigency that must not be overlooked.

How long will the current political myths last? It is difficult to say. The conditions for the endurance of myths—the mobilization of leaders around their diffusion so that they might be accepted by the population—do not appear to have been met. This is all the more true in that a large fraction of politicians are content to respond superficially to the people's demand for physical safety and self-esteem, of which Africans have been deprived for four centuries. The anxiety associated with, on the one hand, the outside domination of the colonial era and, on the other, the denial of civil rights prevalent in the postcolonial era is still very much present (Diop 1979). Most politicians answer this anxiety with frivolous symbols. The semiological codes upon which they rely to transmit their worldview and leadership qualities do not meet the criteria of endurance as defined by anthropologists: They do not draw upon local moral values, collective memory, or even the various resources of African languages. Thus, during presidential campaigns, people were shocked to see some sitting heads of state adopt as symbols of their goals animals they had hastily selected on the advice of European advertising agencies little familiar with the subtleties of the local imagination. On 1992 Cameroonian presidential campaign posters, a photo of President Paul Biya was superimposed onto the image of a growling lion, with the caption: "Man-Lion." Zaire's Mobutu has long compared himself to a leopard and always wears a fake leopard-skin hat. In both cases, reactions were mixed—people were not sure whether these attempts were designed to scare them or attract their votes. During the 1992 campaign, Kenya's Daniel arap Moi chose the rooster as a symbol, which elicited sarcastic remarks as to his strength and courage. Côte d'Ivoire's Henri Konan Bédié adopted the elephant after doing violence to the constitution and the election code in order to disqualify his principal rivals. His adversaries were quick to point out that his methods were indeed elephantine.[22]

Elements of a Theory of Democratization

This nonexhaustive inventory of the particularisms of African political life suggests that researchers should show a little more modesty in their judgments. The metamorphosis of the collective consciousness these past few years is such that one is obliged to return to Held's basic question: "Is democracy an essentially Western project or is it something of wider, universal significance?" (1994:4). Responding to such a question reopens the old philosophical debate on universalism versus cultural relativism, on narrow rationalism versus unlimited culturalism. Elsewhere, I have attempted to put forth an argument and analytic framework reconciling these two approaches (Monga 1995b). At the moment, I wish to conclude by emphasizing the main lessons and theoretical exigencies that Africa brings to and imposes upon political science and by suggesting a simple conceptual model of democratization that incorporates these principles.

Africanist political scientists have too often attempted to use reductive analytic paradigms to study political problems in Africa. In their models, they frequently confuse causes and effects, parameters that matter and those that reflect isolated epiphenomena, and what economists term endogenous and exogenous variables. My analysis calls attention to a few essential points that will serve as the basis of my model:

• First, the democratization process in Africa is dissimilar to that which has been observed elsewhere. In Africa, it is a matter of a difficult and ongoing confrontation between unequal forces (those of repression and those of freedom), between, on the one hand, opposition leaders who are often politically incompetent and almost always discounted by the international community and, on the other, heavily armed authoritarian regimes that have outside support and the blessing of international political and financial organizations. This latter, apparently insignificant detail is in fact important; we must remember that the West, the former Soviet Union, and the entire world community actively contributed to the collapse of Communist regimes in Eastern Europe and to the fall of military dictatorships in Latin America.[23]

• The central, if often subterranean, role civil society plays in the current transformations does not so much affirm itself as it must be inferred. Given the weakness of opposition parties (a reflection of leaders' severely limited freedom of action), the breadth of the social movements that have arisen in sub-Saharan Africa these past years can be adequately explained only by internal dynamics whose scope must be measured, mechanisms understood, and operational codes deciphered. If the action of civil society is responsible for the groundswell of social movements on the continent today, then an analysis of democratization must be centered on it.

• The typology of the causes of the so-called failure of the democratic process in Africa generally consists in an inventory of the manifestations and effects of this failure (rather than the causes of existing problems) or in a study of routine institutional problems, which are found to some extent in all democracies, including those in the industrialized world. Paradigms that rely on the notion of *political culture* and suggestions by Pambou Tchivounda (1982) and Michalon (1994, 1995) for *ethnic federalism* need to be reevaluated and submitted to a simple test: are they valid in all regions of the world? The answer is fairly clear: in general they are not. For instance, if measured through *civic competence,* the level of political culture in the United States would be almost the same as it is in Mozambique; and ethnic tensions are certainly a major political issue in Canada, as they are in Malawi or Burkina Faso![24] In my judgment, these paradigms do not help one conceptualize logically the democratic phenomenon, which has other determinants upon which one needs to focus. One of the most important is that the major political players reach a consensus, not on the division of power among competing elites, but on the rules of political competition.

• The linear and teleological approach to democratic consolidation is by and large erroneous. The idea that it is possible to pinpoint the precise moment when this consolidation occurs—that it is a function of the number of free elections organized in a country or any other fixed quantitative criterion, which can only be arbitrarily established—is ludicrous. Nothing is static, nothing gained once and for all. Democracy as a quest for greater public welfare is an ongoing process, a daily battle between opposing forces—the forces of change coming from civil society, on the one hand, and authoritarian regimes, on the other, who likewise attempt to grab hold of fragments of civil society.

• In the short term, democratization is realizable in a given political marketplace only if the majority of existing political forces in a country feel it is in their interest to participate in developing the rules of the political game. In the long term, democratization is sustainable only on certain conditions: the implementation of the agreed-upon rules; the maintenance of a formal political system—in the mechanical sense of the term, implying human and financial means; and the existence of informal rules (1) that either enable the rules to be continually brought up to date as the interests of the principal players evolve or allow for the emergence of networks of social communication to facilitate the circulation of information among major political players and (2) that provide for the nonviolent, unobtrusive adjustment of political behavior, which gradually transforms normative democracy into (the illusion of) a long democratic tradition.[25] Finally, the democratic spirit becomes engraved in the collective imagination as over the years citizens enlarge the space of what the great British jurist J. F. Moulton termed "the domain of obedience to the unenforceable" (1925). Human actions continue to fall into the three categories Moulton defined: on the one end, those prescribed by law, which all are expected to obey; on the other, those that depend solely on the will of the individual; and in between, those that arise more or less voluntarily and that are neither imposed by law nor born of pure individual will. It is to this third category of actions, where human behavior results from a blend of individual consciousness and respect for the law, and which is "nearly as strong as positive law," that Moulton refers. Here "obedience is the obedience of a man to that which he cannot be forced to obey. He is the enforcer of the law upon himself." There is, I submit, a strong, positive correlation between the existence of this third domain of human actions and the sustainability of democracy and democratic deepening.

• A country's level of political development, if such a thing may be said to exist, must be measured above all on the basis of the degree to which the different political players have reached a consensus on the rules of the game. More than any other variable, this consensus determines (1) the validity of the concept of democracy as it is conceived in a given nation, (2) the manner in which it is implemented, and (3) whether it will be successfully maintained. It therefore plays an important role in the consolidation of democracy, the quality of which will later depend upon the strength of Moulton's third domain of human action.

• When forces for change manage to decipher the different forms of behavior within civil society and channel them into greater participation in political life—which may be "invisible" to traditional political scientists—they will succeed in imposing a broad consensus on the rules of the political game, which will subsequently translate into a true liberalization of politics. If, however, the forces of repression (at the present time, authoritarian regimes still in power) have enough financial and human means to limit the intrusion of civic organizations into political life, it is unlikely that a consensus will be reached on the political agenda and on the rules of competition. The democratic process, in that instance, would have little chance of consolidation.

These assumptions and observations may be graphically illustrated in Figure 2.5. The reasoning behind this simplified model of democratization partially corroborates Przeworski's point of view:

> Democracies last when they evoke self-interested spontaneous compliance from all the major political forces.... To evoke such compliance, democracy must simultaneously offer to all such forces a fair chance to compete within the institutional framework and to generate substantive outcomes; it must be fair and effective. Yet under some historical conditions, these requirements cannot be simultaneously fulfilled by any system of democratic institutions. Foremost among such conditions are periods of profound economic transformation (1991:x).

My analysis of the African body politic leads me to temper Przeworski's idealism—in my view, democracy is never "fair." As soon as people start competing for power, the concept of fairness must be wielded with great caution, even when the various stakeholders agree upon the results of negotiations.

Conclusion

It is high time political scientists and, more generally, Africanists in the social sciences reevaluated the theoretical frameworks through which they analyze political phenomena in Africa and adopted a more imaginative approach to the subject. To return to Sklar's remark cited at the outset of this chapter, I would say that Africanist political science lacks legitimacy at the moment and thus offers little of value to the social sciences. Political scientists must free themselves of the models to which they are presently

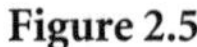

Figure 2.5

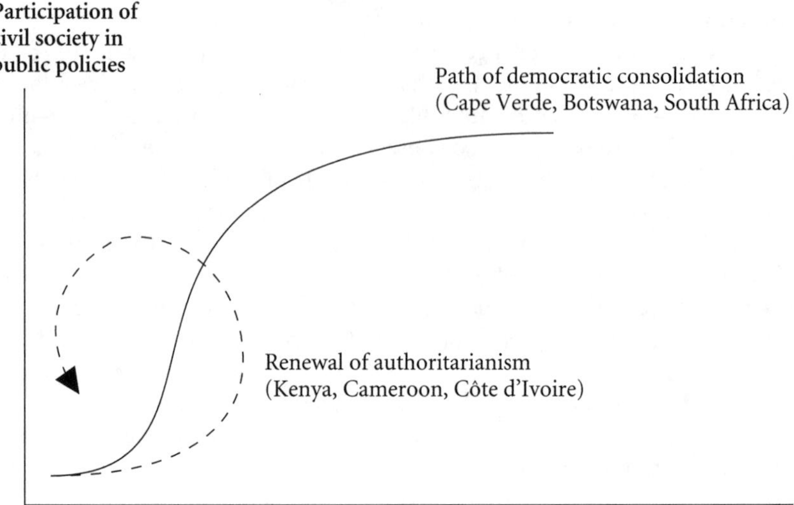

chained and follow the advice of de Certeau (1984), who advocates a close reading of the way in which people invent their daily lives.

The bloating of the social imagination, brilliantly analyzed by Ka Mana (1991) and exhibited by the eruption of actors with strange political habits on the political scene, must not stop one from seeing the forest for the trees. Beyond the outrageous behavior and missteps of politicians, which are in no way confined to Africa (compare Castoriadis 1987), the continent is doing its best to get by, to survive neglect—that is, to struggle against historical determinism. It sometimes gropes and staggers along, zigzags more than it advances in a straight line, but its desire to be free of the scorn of outsiders and of its own self-doubts is, in my view, obvious. That is why I am attempting to understand the intimate determinants of the population's political behavior and to decipher the hidden rationality that appears to govern daily life.

Notes

1. Hermet (1983) and Badie (1988) belong to the first school of thought; Touraine (1992) and Lefort (1981, 1986) to the second.

2. The suspicion with regard to elected representatives and hence to the active exercise of citizenship goes back to Rousseau's *The Social Contract,* written in 1762: "Soveriegnty cannot be represented, for the same reason that it cannot be alienated ... [for] the people's deputies are not, and could not be, its representatives; they are merely its agents; and they cannot decide anything finally. Any law which the people has not ratified in person is void; it is not law at all. The English people believes itself to be free; it is gravely mistaken; it is free only during the election of Members of Parliament; as soon as the Members are elected, the people is enslaved; it is nothing" (p. 141).

3. Interviews with the following opposition leaders: Laurent Gbaggo, Côte d'Ivoire (April 1990, April 1993); John Fru Ndi, Cameroon (May, October 1992); Paul Mba Abessole, Gabon (February 1992), Mountage Tall, Mali (June 1991); Aristide Sokambi, Central African Republic (June 1991).

4. According to the most serious economic journals, the global financial community was in fact staunchly opposed to political transformations in Africa, for it considered that the uncertainty of such developments would be bad for business. Compare Geisler (1993:631).

5. The notion of *consociationalism* warrants a few comments. Lijphart (1977) coined the word from Johannes Althusius's concept of *conociatio* in his *Politica Methodice Digesta* (1603) to suggest a new way of conceptualizing democracy in what he calls plural societies. Lijphart presents the models as follows:

> In a consociational democracy, the centrifugal tendencies inherent in a plural society are counteracted by the cooperative attitudes and behavior of the leaders of the different segments of the population. Elite cooperation is the primary distinguishing feature of consociational democracy....
>
> [It] can be defined in terms of four characteristics. The first and the most important element is government by a grand coalition of the political leaders of all significant segments of the plural society.... The other three basic elements ... are (1) the mutual veto or "concurrent majority" rule, which serves as an additional protection of vital minority interests, (2) proportionality as the principal standard of political representation, civil service appointments, and allocation of public funds, and (3) a high degree of autonomy for each segment to run its own internal affairs" (1977:1,25).

First, the idea of a plural society sounds like a pleonasm. At this time of globalization and triumphant multiculturalism (whether illusory or real), I cannot think of any country that is not a plural society. Second, I doubt the effectiveness of those political coalitions that are designed to share the "national pie" equitably among various segments of society, for this is exactly what most African leaders have attempted to do since independence—we now see the results of such strategies. As far as proportionality of representation is concerned, besides its utopian aspect (how do we define a segment?), one must recall that African leaders' attempts to implement such a concept led to the adoption of public policies based on the strange idea of "balanced regionalism," that is, the classification of people using teleological ethnic labels conceived for the very purpose of the operation. In countries such as Cameroon or Rwanda, the main outcome was the legalization of injustice and arbitrary policies. Finally, the vague formulation of Lijphart's fourth principle (a high degree of autonomy for each segment of the national population) reveals the practical difficulties of its implementation: Even if "successful," this would lead to a Nigerian-style centrifugal federalism; the worst case would be endless claims of micronationalism by various political entrepreneurs, as witnessed in the former Yugoslavia.

6. My definition of political risk goes beyond the classical analysis of country risk used by investors. It includes the social risk taken by each member of the community to express his ideas publicly against the prevailing institutional practices, and current social and cultural habits. I believe there is a direct correlation between political risk and the democratic project's chances of success.

7. At the conference on "Word Behind Bars and the Paradox of Exile," organized by the African Studies Program of Northwestern University in November 1994, I listened to Dennis Brutus's stirring reflections on disenchantment. The famous South African poet was wondering whether so many lives had been sacrificed over the years simply to conquer voting rights in order to insert the country into the world market economy—at the price of devaluing human beings and destroying the environment. One should not dismiss his remorse on the grounds that it reflects the disillusionment of a nostalgic Marxist. According to *Washington Post* journalist Bob Woodward (1994), the U.S. president asks himself the same questions, since his room to maneuver in the economic policy is severely limited by the attitude of a small group of bond traders on Wall Street. James Carville, one of President Bill Clinton's election advisers, confirms the limits of political power in the world's greatest democracy: "I used to think that if there was reincarnation, I wanted to come back as the president or the pope. But now I want to be in the bond market: you can intimidate anybody" (quoted by Woodall 1995:3). A rather sad assessment of the financial markets was made by French president Jacques Chirac, who once described speculators as the "AIDS of the world economy" (Woodall 1995:3).

8. At a conference sponsored by the African Studies Association (Orlando, Florida, November 1995), Howard French, the *New York Times*' correspondent in West Africa, explained that the editors of major U.S. newspapers view Africa as a training ground for young foreign correspondents because it is the only place in the world where a mistake made by a journalist has no negative consequences (it affects neither the newspaper's reputation nor diplomacy and finance).

9. The expression is taken from Péan (1983), who studied the no-man's-land of patrimonialism that characterizes Franco-African relations. On the same subject, see also Glaser and Smith (1992), Médart (1994), and Martin (1995).

10. The research methodology used to carry out the survey was sound, respecting most scientific standards. The problem lay in its applicability and effectiveness. The 100-item questionnaire was, for example, translated into four Zambian languages (Bemba, Nyanja, Tonga, Kaonde), but it is well known that only a tiny minority of Africans can read the language they speak fluently. What is more, the way certain notions that are foreign to the collective imagination are understood can significantly alter responses. In the section of their study entitled "Conventions and Caveats," Bratton and Liatto-Katundu note, for example, that

> respondents appear to have misunderstood some items because they were vague or difficult (the ten-point numerical scale used for questions on political trust proved too difficult for a

few respondents who were old and illiterate, engendering a few meaningless responses); … sometimes, they tried intentionally to mislead the interviewer (for example some people didn't want to reveal that they had a radio in the house for fear that it would be stolen.… We also failed to capture situations in which a household owned a radio, but it was broken or had no batteries) (1994: Appendix, and n. 11 and 12).

11. For a listing of important events, see Bratton and Van de Walle (1992:32).

12. My purpose here is not to suggest that physical violence against political opponents is no longer practiced in Africa. The recent attempts by the military to assassinate opposition leaders in Togo and Cameroon and the murders of Nigerian political opponent Ken Saro-Wiwa and Burundi's elected president demonstrate the continued use of this radical tactic.

13. Laurent Gbagbo, the Ivorian opposition leader, criticized such approaches by saying: "We do not want an Ivorian type of democracy. We want democracy, period." Interview.

14. Following this affair, CRTV lost most of its credibility, and the journalists who participated in the government's disinformation campaign were held up to public scorn, most notably Z. Ngiman, who had read the government's communiqué on the air. Under public pressure, he was forced to elucidate the affair. He cosigned an open letter to the minister of information denouncing governmental pressure and later published a book on the incident in which he explained how the government had forced television journalists to malign John Fru Ndi's SDF. See Ngiman 1993.

15. See Ekani (1990:2) The defamation campaign did not have the desired effect on the public. Moreover, in a suit filed by the SDF, a courageous judge in Bamenda recently ruled that the government pay FCFA 10 million in damages weekly to the chairman of the SDF.

16. Deciphering the manner in which things are inscribed within time, Fernand Braudel isolated three elements of duration and demonstrated how on the surface events express conjunctural fluctuations, which are dependent, in turn, upon slow structural shifts.

17. Many executives in Yaoundé, as well as many peasants in the back country, use the following reasoning: "It's better if Biya stays in power because he's already gobbled up so much that he might actually get down to work. If we replace him with a younger man, we'll have to wait until he, too, has done his share of gobbling up." The rationale has held true in other African countries.

18. It is likewise necessary to distinguish here between leaders with pre-1990 experience fighting political battles inside their countries and exiled leaders who engaged in them from the outside alone.

19. In this regard, the career path and discourse of A. F. Kodock, secretary general of the Cameroonian UPC "opposition" party, are instructive. After criticizing and ardently fighting the Biya regime for several months, he was appointed to the cabinet, which increased tensions within his political family. Asked by the press to explain the dramatic shift in his position, Kodock mentioned divisions within his party and blundered that he was ready "to hang on even to a serpent in order not to drown." Beyond the Freudian slip of comparing the head of state, his new boss, to a serpent, his comment reveals the tremendous and, unfortunately, typical cynicism of "new" African politicians.

20. State violence now takes various forms in sub-Saharan Africa. In addition to the traditional policing agencies (the military and state and local police), the government uses private militias, Praetorian Guards of sorts who answer only to the head of state. Generally better trained and better armed, the "soldiers" of these paramilitary organizations are recruited along ethnic lines and have an antagonistic relationship with the national armed forces which, in theory, are already at the service of the government. This "private" dimension of state violence, which existed in various Latin American countries during the 1970s, is a relatively recent phenomenon in Africa.

21. For this new type of politician, it is no longer a matter of trying to represent the largest number of voters but of appearing to be the intrepid defender of a given social group—majority rule losing its raison d'être. The only thing that counts is speaking in the name of a particular constituency and presenting oneself as both its advocate and agent. In essence, one must loudly and clearly proclaim that one is speaking for a disenfranchised, long-suffering, excluded group.

22. Occasionally, African autocrats' attempts at mythological legitimation are so awkward that they backfire. See, for example, Toulabor (1981).

23. An instructive example of this political double standard is the awarding of the Nobel Peace Prize to Lech Walesa in 1983. This highly significant political and symbolic gesture, orchestrated by a group of Western democrats and humanists, increased world recognition of this union leader and apprentice electrician who had founded the Solidarity Movement in 1979. The free world was also sending a clear message to Poland's General Wojciech Jaruzelski and his Soviet sponsors. Aside from a few intellectuals such as Nigerian Wole Soyinka, awarded the Nobel Prize for Literature in 1986, freedom fighters in Africa (politicians like Walesa) have never benefited from such direct support. Well before the establishment of the Solidarity Movement, people were fighting for change in Africa; they were openly silenced, forced to exile, prison, or death. And all the while Western democrats remained silent. As Walesa was being awarded with the Nobel Prize, Laurent Gbagbo, leader of the clandestine Ivorian opposition, who had taken temporary refuge in France, was "under surveillance" by the French socialist government, which described Félix Houphouët-Boigny, the Ivoirian Jaruzelski, in panegyric terms ("the sage of Africa," "the founder of the modern Côte d'Ivoire," etc.) that might have come from the mouths of communist autocrats. Western governments have praised all of Africa's dictators, from Morocco's Hassan II, to Mali's Moussa Traoré, to Somalia's Mohamed Siad Barre.

24. The boisterous remarks—reinforcing tribalism—that Quebec's separatist leader, Jacques Parizeau, made on the evening of the October 30, 1995, referendum on independence amply demonstrated to any remaining doubters the limits of the myth of national unity achieved through multiculturalism. Similarly, the reaction of U.S. citizens along racial lines to the verdict in the O. J. Simpson trial underscored deep ethnic division in the United States. This has yet to incite any "expert" to call into question the effectiveness of U.S. democracy or even to suggest that Lijphart's theories on plural societies be applied to the United States.

25. The idea that the experience of democracy is an illusion may seem cynical. I concur with Dahl and others that democracy is necessarily a utopian horizon as soon as it is given more than a purely "political" content (the right to vote). Admittedly, some people live their utopias better than others.

3

Changing Identities: Memory, Culture, and Revolt

Je suis fier d'être un bâtard culturel.
Si chacun reconnaissait sa bâtardise,
il y aurait moins d'intolérance dans le monde.

*

I'm proud of being a cultural bastard.
If each of us claimed our own bastardy,
there would be less intolerance in the world.

—Rachid Bahri, Algeria

Many of the social scientific works on Africa surveyed in Chapter 2 used culturalistic paradigms to explain the slow rate at which political reforms have been enacted on the continent. I highlighted the contradictions in these works and observed that they rely heavily on the rhetorical figures of a mysterious black Africa, as well as on the stereotypes about Africa's so-called specific historicity, to explain today's political ineptitude. To paraphrase Said (1993), what is most striking in these writings is the implied notion of bringing morals and civilization to reluctant barbarian peoples and the disturbing, selective attitude of not using the same rigid ethical standards to explore the determinants of political failures elsewhere on the planet. The key assumption in this "rationale," which seems compelling even to some African intellectuals (M'nteba 1992, Owusu 1992), is that African peoples are not "serious" in their quest for freedom, because they are not used to self-government and because they understand only brutality and violence. Moreover, that is why they are so quick to engage in civil wars or ethnic tensions. Such contempt toward the process of social change in Africa can only lead to an intellectual vacuum in many important areas of public policy and to some mistakes in the design and implementation of the nation-building project.

In this chapter, through an analysis of cultural politics, I will examine, on the one hand, how African governments exploit this dearth of knowledge and, on the other, how artists react to and attempt to counteract this effort. On the basis of cultural relativism, governments have tried to impose an official historiography of national culture as a means of political legitimization. Artists and intellectuals have resisted the official discourse in various ways, attempting in their work to circumvent the mainstream historiography of culture. This chapter is about the silent conflict between these two forms of logic. It is about the clash between a single official narrative built around the idea of culture and an infinite number of informal counternarratives.

In the first section, I argue that the conceptual frameworks used by African governments to back up their relativistic views of national culture are inconsistent, to say the least. Adapting West's method of periodization of the history of cultural politics in the world (1990), I challenge the validity of the concepts and notions behind hegemonic public discourse on national identities in sub-Saharan Africa. In the second section I discuss the authenticity of collective memory and traditions that are supposed to sustain and justify public policies in the domain of culture; I show that the celebration of the past is mainly designed to articulate the hegemonic discourse of domination and sometimes leads government propagandists to fall into the fundamentalist trap. However, there is always a strong response from below: Even in the face of violence, African societies resist anything perceived as a symbol of a dominating state and see through even the most subtle techniques for the appropriation and rearticulation of official discourse on culture.

Ethical Stakes Poorly Evaluated

As I argued in Chapter 2, democracy is often perceived as having a cultural foundation that enables its social structures to deal successfully and quickly with the challenges of pluralism, which is why the paradigm of culture is invariably present in public discourse in Africa. However, the emphasis placed on the importance of cultural factors in political and social development has increasingly been reduced to the level of empty, demagogic promises made by African politicians for the sole purpose of spicing up their speeches and appearing up to date. When officials speak in public, they feel obligated to brag about the philosophical richness of tradition and to underscore the critical necessity of "valorizing African culture." The spell cast by their words is so strong that one catches oneself taking them seriously, even though one knows that nothing will remain of them tomorrow.

This chapter was inspired by what strikes me as the ineffectiveness of cultural politics as it has been practiced in African nations over the past thirty or so years of independence. Indeed, it is questionable whether one can speak of a true *politics* here, for the inconsistencies of officials in both discourse and action are so numerous that the very existence of their strategy may be mere hypothesis.

A crossroads of peoples and civilizations, Africa is first of all a profusion of different types of social structures, and as a result, it abounds in cultural potential. Unfortunately, only its superficial aspects tend to be retained—those that the tourism industry celebrates by way of slogans on promotional brochures. Behind all the pretty words, there is nevertheless the force of the myths, beliefs, customs, and visions that form mankind's collective memory and determine its future. Thus understood, culture does not correspond to the exotic superficialities exalted from time to time on state-run television (potbellied "traditional" dancers, charlatans dressed up as sorcerers, etc.). Traumatized by distressing problems, African peoples have tended to repress the remaining vestiges of an authentic culture. Of course, far from the indiscreet cameras of tourists, far from the voyeuristic gaze of short-term visitors, people continue to invent in their daily lives an approach to the world (and thus to other cultures) that helps them give meaning to the era in which they live.

Thrown off balance by a political, economic, and social crisis without clear beginning or end, African peoples have witnessed, and have been powerless to stop, the collapse of the value systems that long governed their social organizations. There has been a demise of so-called traditional cultures, many of which now appear obsolete. Insofar as they do not allow peoples to conceptualize and give meaning to modernity, they do not stand up well to today's problems and seem even less well adapted to future challenges.

Oswald Spengler once wrote:

> [A culture] dies when [its] soul has actualized the full sum of its possibilities.... Every Culture stands in a deeply symbolical, almost in a mystical, relation to the Extended, the space, in which and through which it strives to actualize itself. The aim once attained—the idea, the entire content of inner possibilities, fulfilled and made externally actual—the Culture suddenly hardens, it mortifies, its blood congeals, its force breaks down, and it becomes *Civilization* (1926:106).

This sympathetic but somewhat naive reading of the "normal" course of a culture obviously cannot be applied to Africa, whose inhabitants have been forced to suffer other forms of violence. The German philosopher did not conceive of the possibility of a cultural confrontation that would upset the evolutionary cycle he described. African cultures were not given the time to go through all the phases of prosperity; rather, they collided with the harshness of history, resulting in problems of identity for many of their peoples. Caught within the upheavals of politics and history, Africans have been obliged to fit themselves into social molds that were conceived by others and to improvise the development of new codes and cultural markers.

Though one need not link the consequences of this confrontation to the notion of decline, one must nevertheless recognize that the primary difficulty in speaking of African culture today consists in clearly establishing what is authentic in this expression. How can one evaluate a culture in which the principal actor does everything possible, for whimsical or serious reasons, to muddy the waters and dissolve himself in his various representations? How can one define what remains of the indigenous in their way of being? These are questions that have yet to be answered by those who have undertaken to define Africa's identity. In what follows, I shall first consider the hypothesis as to the existence of political cultures in Africa, examining the conceptual components of this notion. I shall then analyze the authenticity of various schools of thought, whose theorists consider themselves as representatives of today's culture.

The first issue to be addressed is straightforward: does African culture exist? This question, which sounds like a joke, haunts the mind of anyone who examines cultural politics in Africa. In order to answer it, one must first define the notion of culture—already a challenge, since Kroeber and Kluckhohn (1952) identified 160 definitions in the literature—and then determine what is truly indigenous in the current worldview of the peoples on this continent. The impossibility of such an endeavor goes without saying. The question must nevertheless be raised and debated. A discussion of underlying principles allows one to evaluate the redundancies within official discourse on culture and to measure the gap that exists between the real urgency of preserving, valorizing, and reinvigorating collective spiritual heritage and the politics of folklorizing all sorts of practices incorrectly considered as representative of African civilizations.

Semantic Doubts

The idea that there is a culture identical for all human beings has preoccupied philosophers since Socrates. Based on the notion that people possess a set of fixed characteristics stemming from reason, this theory led to a rethinking of everything that appeared to be specifically tied to biology or geography. For several centuries, philosophers defined culture as all that in human society that is socially transmitted. The spirituality of the individual, for example, was part of the common foundation of universal culture even if the manner in which it manifested itself varied in different places and eras. The antithesis of this point of view was developed notably by nineteenth-century anthropologists, such as Edward Tylor and Lewis Henry Morgan, who defined culture as a conscious creation of human rationality.

Later, Sartre also rejected the overly broad generalization, arguing that the nonexistence of God, creator of all human beings, implied de facto the nonexistence of an indivisible human nature and culture:

> Not only is man what he conceives himself to be, but he is also only what he wills himself to be after this thrust toward existence. Man is nothing else but what he makes of himself.... Man is at the start a plan which is aware of itself, rather than a patch of moss, a piece of garbage, or a cauliflower; nothing exists prior to this plan; there is nothing in heaven; man will be what he will have planned to be (1947:18–19).

Social anthropological conceptions of culture are based to a great extent on Tylor's assumption that culture and civilization are synonymous. However, archaeological approaches tend to distinguish material culture, or artifacts, and practices and beliefs, the nonmaterial or adaptive culture. Indeed, as Marshall pointed out,

> Modern ideas of culture arose through the work of field anthropologists such as Franz Boas, around the turn of the century, and tend towards relativism. The intention is to describe, compare, and contrast cultures, rather than ranking them, although Boas and some later North American anthropologists have also been interested in the processes by which cultural traits may be borrowed or otherwise transmitted between societies (1994:105).

The debate surrounding the question is considerably more advanced today, as both sides appear to accept the idea that everything that constitutes the biological essence of human beings is mediated through several cultural strata. Thus, human nature is always actualized in the culture to which one chooses to belong. One's vision of the world, one's approach to all types of problems, one's actions and reactions concerning the difficulties of daily life, one's feelings about things, all stem primarily from various cultural phenomena. While it is certainly a legitimate concern for African intellectuals to object to Eurocentric hegemony posing as universalism, as Chinweizu and Madubuike (1980) eloquently did, it is also illusory to claim to evaluate the culture of human beings exclusively in terms of skin color, as certain theorists of negritude or even Pan-Africanism have attempted to do. Appiah (1992) made this point brilliantly.

The Imprints of History

It is necessary to specify the field of inquiry: what is the meaning of *culture* for Africans who are said to be acculturated? It is difficult for Africans to avoid this problematic issue. On the one hand, the elements of their culture have not been defined systematically; on the other, the forces and violence of history have created blurred and debatable boundaries. And even if one accepts Tylor's classical definition of culture as "a learned complex of knowledge, belief, art, morals, law, custom and any other capabilities and habits acquired by a man as a member of society" (1871:2), there are ambiguities that Etounga-Manguelle, among others, has addressed:

> African society today has piled very different strata of time on top of one another. Onto a very old layer concerned with the relationship between the sexes, kinship, and religion has been superimposed an intermediate layer concerned with the teachings of the law, with Islam, writing, and the domination of men. To this layer a third, modern one is joined that concerns French, English, Portuguese, or Spanish colonization and raises the question of money, urban life, and education (1990:31).

This complication of the essential problem—that of definition itself—leads one to express a semantic doubt about everything that has been officially presented as constituting African culture. For no sooner has the factor of time been added to the equation than one is forced to admit that its mental makeup, its political and social structures, its legal system, its cultural practices, and even its language have been affected by historical processes that resulted in a power structure in its disfavor (slavery, wars, conquests, colonization). Everything that is customarily brought under the heading of "national cultural heritage" has by and large been borrowed from those who falsified the history of the continent through the brutality of their methods. Everything, even what is known as the cultural universe of Africans' ancestors, was profoundly shaken by the double tragedy of slavery and colonization.

Without lapsing into what Bayart (1989) calls "the paradigm of the yoke," a sort of persecution complex to which a large fraction of the African intelligentsia has fallen victim, one cannot fail to agree with the Zairean Ngandu Nkashama when he laments that

> by treacherously inserting us into an historical process begun in a different political and economic context, by stealing from us other myths (social, cosmic) and other poetic metaphors, by surreptitiously spiriting away a different knowledge—and not only simple "technology," which does not come to us (in terms, at any rate, of a capital asset) as a legacy from our ancestral group (what is it henceforth?)—we can only be received by our partners in the human race as pilgrims, if not as usurpers (1985:33).

In sum, there is little among those "cultural riches" that Africans currently tend to (over)value that actually belongs to them. And the emblem of their authenticity is too often altered by the violence of the mark of others. Bamileke or Yoruba art objects are assessed on the scale of values established by Africa's (former) masters—what Ngandu Nkashama calls "the standard of canonical measurements and transistorized metrics." Ancient Zulu dances are evaluated by specialists of Maurice Béjart or Merce Cunningham. The polyphonic songs of the Pygmies from the forests in eastern Cameroon and southern Congo are analyzed by musicologists trained in the school of Mozart and Stravinsky. New national literatures tend to imitate the French "new novel" because the imagination of writers is held prisoner to techniques in vogue in the West and because the critics whose role it is to appreciate and make known this literature do not have any other intellectual reference points.

The Ambiguity of Being African

The object of the gaze of others rather than the subject of its own future, African culture is subjected to new forms of subjectification. A grammar of human history, this culture has been strongly conditioned by the fact that it has borrowed methodological processes from others in order to validate its own knowledge and update the rites of initiation. As a result of very strong historical ties, Africans are enmeshed in what Foucault (1969, 1976) has termed *episteme,* and their roots will continue to draw sustenance from it. Is it possible to sever this technological and psychological legacy from their "biological" heritage? Is it reasonable and desirable to envision this intellectual disconnection at a time when the imperative of economic development (and hence of integration in a world more than ever dominated by the influence and power of the West) requires that they fit their minds into conceptual molds invented by others?

The essential question is how to come to terms with the ambiguous adventure that Africans' existence in the contemporary world represents. They are trained and educated in an environment to whose construction, development, and renewal they have contributed very little. How are they to believe in the utopia of an "authentic" African culture, that is, one from which the influence of history has been purged? Is not the real challenge to manage the ambiguity of being African today in such a way as to leave their mark and their creativity on everything that comes to them from outside and that global political and economic realities require they assimilate—if they do not wish to be pushed to the margin of history? If Lévi-Strauss (1958) is correct in asserting that language is the very foundation of culture, is not the first step toward liberation the invention of new languages? Would it alone help Africans subvert from within the invasion of "universal" culture in which they have so little say?

Redundancies in the Discourse and Management of Virtualities

Let us get back to politics. Without clearing the semantic doubts raised earlier, official ideologues have undertaken, with an almost admirable obstinacy, to exalt within each African country a virtually mythic "national culture." Orphans of the mystique of lost traditions, they have turned conceit and symbolism into instruments of political propaganda. When they pronounce the words "African culture," the expression takes on a sort of syntactic incompatibility. But no matter: All they care about is the celebration of a ceremonial folklorism capable of satisfying the desires of tourists.

Slings and Arrows of Utopia and the Exhaustion of Myths

Nostalgic for a "traditional culture" complete with every virtue, officials dream of the dawn of an era soon to come in which Africans would turn to their ancestors in order to explore other avenues of access to modernity. It would not take much for them to imagine the young replacing their jeans with *bila* (the traditional loin cloth) or chucking their electric toothbrushes, so little in keeping with our customs and environment, in favor of a good old bamboo shoot. It is a handful of fundamentalists who suffer daily from the slings and arrows of their utopia. As Appiah reminds us, a process of cultural aggiornamento has been going on for a very long time:

> We must not fall for the sentimental notion that the "people" have held onto an indigenous national tradition, that only the educated bourgeoisie are "children of two worlds." At the level of popular culture, too, the currency is not a holdover from an unbroken stream of tradition; indeed, it is, like most popular culture in the age of mass production, hardly national at all. Popular culture in Africa encompasses the (Americans) Michael Jackson and Jim Reeves; when it picks up cultural production whose sources are geographically African, what it picks up is not usually in any plausible sense traditional. Highlife music is both recognizably West African and distinctly not precolonial; and the sounds of Fela Kuti would have astonished the musicians of the last generation of court musicians in Yorubaland. As they have developed new forms of music, drawing on instrumental repertoires and musical ideas with a dazzling eclecticism, Africa's musicians have also done astonishing things with a language that used to be English. But it is as English that that language is accessible to millions around the continent (and around the world) (1992: 58–59).

In fact, the dreams of the fundamentalists have been kept alive by the inflamed rhetoric of politicians and the attendant establishment of gimmick institutions. Designed to organize and disseminate "national cultures," these institutions have actually done nothing more than manage virtualities insofar as the men in charge of running them have had neither the material and conceptual means nor the actual will to exploit existing possibilities.

Cameroon provides a good example of this ambition and its limitations. As early as 1962, President Ahmadou Ahidjo signed a decree creating the Federal Linguistic and Cultural Center. Based in Yaoundé, the capital city, this research center's mission was "the compilation, preservation, and diffusion of Cameroon's national cultures."[1] Well before the establishment of the Office of Cultural Affairs within the Ministry of Education, Youth and Leisure, it was the state's primary cultural institution. Researchers conducted a few studies throughout the country and the center prepared Cameroon's contribution to the much vaunted Festival of Negro Art held in Dakar in 1966. But its activities were soon hampered by the inefficiency of its bureaucracy and the inadequacy of its means, notably with regard to the valorization of Cameroon's linguistic heritage.

Rather than calmly examining the reasons for its failure, the authorities opted to rush ahead, instituting the Service for Cultural Development within the Ministry of Education in 1965. This new entity was subsequently transformed into the Office of Cultural Affairs, described as "the governmental arm of cultural action" (Bahoken and Atangana 1975). Under its aegis, various events were organized that were cultural in name but largely political in aim. Cameroonian productions and artists (theater companies, village dance groups, rural musicians) were exported north. The basic marketing strategy was as follows: The artists were to preserve the image of their country—that is, of their government—while abroad and "sell" to the rest of the world the image of a mythical Africa, with its exotic, lost civilizations, the evocation of which was intended to arouse feelings of guilt among European audiences. Sponsored by such organizations as UNESCO, these tours were favorably received and allowed those in power to maintain relatively high ratings in international opinion, which was, of course, the goal. Small matter that Cameroonians were little involved in what they saw as political posturing.

In 1967, influenced by the "revolutionary" dogma of the time, Cameroon's head of state signed another decree whose terms appeared to have been taken directly from the Marxist vulgate, calling for, among other things, the "national consolidation of activities for the young and for the education of the people."[2] Its terminology was forceful, the content of the new agencies it created less substantial. A number of youth centers were indeed established throughout the country, most notably the Federation of the Arts and Humanities, managed by both the Ministry of Education and the Ministry of Youth, whose mission was to coordinate the activities of theater companies and dance groups. But in reality, these were yet again gimmick agencies lacking clearly established goals and run according to the whims and personalities of the government officials appointed to head them.

During the first convention of the Cameroonian National Union (single party), held in Garoua in 1969, the Cameroonian president gave a speech in which he "acknowledged the importance of emotions" and "the affective and spiritual reality of tribal collectivities" and praised "the cultural content and richness of the Cameroonian people's traditional values." These slogans, designed to reflect the mood of the day, were embraced and applauded by the official media. They were accompanied by the creation of regional entities (cultural and youth centers) intended to rally the young around the *idea* of culture. As before, there was no follow-through, not only because the government had a poorly defined national strategy but also because it had finally unveiled its true conception of the role of cultural leaders and the debate of ideas.

The exhaustion of the myth of prosperity fostered after independence contributed to the government's increasing rigidity and further strengthened its reflex to shut down thought. The attainment of political sovereignty (the replacement of European government officials with nationals) had not improved the living conditions of Cameroonians, and the population exhibited a clear loss of confidence in the idea of the state and hence a lack of interest in the official cultural discourse. Through the use of slogans and the creation of so-called national institutions designed to celebrate the past, the government was trying to reshape people's understanding of politics. Thus, cultural politics was conducted as a set of narratives purveyed by authorities, civil servants, intellectuals, and various groups of civil society. Yet it turned out that people at the grassroots level were at the same time developing some counternarratives; that is, a broad range of means (and a fretwork of assumptions supporting those means) by which they would contest the dominant reality of cultural politics.

At the beginning of the 1970s, the young began to show signs of protest, such as the memorable student strikes at the University of Yaoundé. Suspecting that several intellectuals had encouraged if not fomented the movement, the Cameroonian president decided that the best way to block the road to "subversion" was to enlist in the single party all those capable of stirring up ideas. This was not done to stimulate action in the party (which, though not a state party under the constitution, was assigned the task of setting public policy), but rather to compromise as many intellectuals as possible and to keep a watchful eye on heretical thinkers.

Thus, while his Senegalese counterpart, Léopold Sédar Senghor, tolerated within his country the presence of intellectuals and cultural leaders (Cheikh Anta Diop, Pathé Diagne, Jean-Pierre Ndiaye, etc.) whose activities might provoke criticism among the young, President Ahidjo outlined his ideas to his country's cultural leaders, clearly articulating the role he assigned to culture: "Every effective cultural action is at root an enterprise, if not a political one, then at least a civic one" (1973). Given that the government was growing more and more repressive, few men dared to distance themselves from the party line. Two important meetings of the Higher Education Council and the National Council on Cultural Affairs confirmed the adherence of scholars to the party line. The two events brought together scholars from around the country who were presented as leaders in their fields. Bahoken and Atangana have captured the essence of the texts adopted after days of debate:

> The Commission [the first, devoted to policy development] settled upon the basic idea that the university, which was called upon to involve itself in the realities facing the nation through the medium of politics (whose principles were defined by the party), should be integrated into the party structure. The university would no longer constitute, as it had in the past, a separate world or, to borrow the President's phrase, a place for "thinking heads totally removed from the realities facing the nation." ... The duty of researchers, professors and students alike was to become activists in the Cameroonian National Union and to contribute in a concrete way to the formation of the national consciousness (1975: 37–38).

Acknowledging that it ultimately fell to the experts to devise the ways and means of transforming the university into a veritable political instrument, the commission advised that "the engagement of the university take place at the level of structure, course content, and people, so that it might in the end produce citizens who speak the language of their country and reason as Cameroonians concerned with the stature of their nation" (1975: 37–38). The resolutions adopted ran along the same lines: "Whereas cultural renewal, if it is truly to become a political instrument in the service of the nation, must be placed within the sphere of the Cameroonian National Union Party ... [we] recommend that the Cameroonian cultural and artistic movement engage itself politically in accordance with the ideals defined by the party" (MINFOC 1974).

It is easy to understand the ineffectiveness and pointlessness of subsequently established institutions: from that date forward, the political slant imposed upon the results of studies conducted in various "laboratories" at the University of Yaoundé ensured that little was accomplished, except, perhaps, some sort of naive management of party slogans. The conference on Cameroonian cultural identity held in 1985—at which there were a few excellent participants—and the States General on culture (1991) were both organized by the government for the sole purpose of creating a political diversion. Neither was able to generate enough enthusiasm to instill a new sense of confidence in cultural leaders or to trigger a real debate on the question of national identity.

The Time for Counternarratives and Refutations

Ensconced in their certainties, preoccupied exclusively with the political aspects of their actions, forgetful of passing time, those in charge of what passed for cultural politics in Africa missed the arrival of modernity and all that it called into question. As a result, they failed to notice the irruption of new ways of seeing and thinking in the daily lives of those peoples they thought would forever remain in the dark.[3]

Of course, on the pretext of celebrating the authenticity and the splendor of collective memory, a number of prominent figures have continued to promote archaic mentalities and anachronistic social conventions. Responsible for a palpable obscurantism, these antiquated souls have been challenged and defeated by the advocates of a new order who do not feel any allegiance to the habits and customs of their ancestors. Below the surface have developed new ways of being that have bold visions of the future and a thoroughly "subversive" conception of art. They have helped us forget the shame of things past.

Beyond Remembrance of Things Past

For many years, it was extremely difficult, if not impossible, to dispute the effectiveness of what Africans presented to the world as the essence of their cultures. Western intellectuals and Africans invariably felt the need to respect certain customs and traditions, occasionally criticizing their origin but never daring to pass judgment on them. It was only in 1990 that a Cameroonian writer, Etounga-Manguelle, had the courage to start a ripple in the pond of certainties. Offering a brutal analysis of the (non)functioning of Africa's systems and a no-excuses approach to hard truths, his book endeavored to decolonialize African citizens from their feelings so that they might question their value system.

Seeking out those conditions in which a type of hope differing from the current definition—a string of self-congratulatory slogans—might be born, Etounga-Manguelle reformulated some of the questions surrounding the difficulty of being African today: What African has not privately deplored the cultural and psychological stumbling blocks that have made their peoples "social misfits," marginalized players in the construction of history? Who is unaware of the burdensome aspects of the African family? Who does not recognize the futility of certain "folkloric" rites and ceremonies? What African has not suffered or seen someone suffer as a result of witchcraft, that plague Amnesty International has forgotten in its inventory of attacks on human rights?

Etounga-Manguelle belongs to the same school of thought as Yambo Ouologuem, who in *Le Devoir de violence* (*The Duty of Violence,* translated into English as *Bound to Violence*) examined the receptiveness of precolonial African societies to slavery and colonization. Emphasizing their propensity for disorder, inversely proportionate to their ability to take on the responsibilities involved in shaping their destiny, he rooted out the seeds of failure. These seeds are not found in Africans' chromosomes or in their political and economic structures, but rather in the outdated precepts that govern their behavior. The unresolved question at the end of this century is whether the intellectual and psychological approach these peoples have to problems is compatible with the demands and realities of our time.

An example of the necessity of this type of questioning is African peoples' collective approach to the future. They have little inclination to plan for the future and thus have insufficient control over the notion of uncertainty. This attitude is found in their intensely spiritual relationship with the divinity, in their desire to cohabit with nature (seen as a divine space) rather than dominate it as do other peoples, and in their concept of time management. In the eighteenth century, Scottish explorer Mungo Park lamented the fact that "the African shows little interest in the future. If there is something important that he has to do, it does not matter to him whether he does it today, tomorrow, or two months from now" (quoted by Comte 1988). Though this observation may strike us today as something of an ethnological cliché, we would be wrong to dismiss it altogether. Servan-Schreiber has returned to it and critiqued it:

> Time in Africa has both a cultural and symbolic value that plays an important role in the manner in which time is experienced. As such, it is both a source of richness and a handicap. It is a source of richness insofar as it is satisfying for individuals to live in time at their own pace, something they do not wish to give up. But it is also a handicap insofar as we are in competition with other countries that do not employ the same work methods and in which competition at the level of productivity, for example, is tied to a more rational use of time (1985).

Etounga-Manguelle corroborates Servan-Schreiber's assessment when he relates the indignant response that the man on the street in Lagos gives in order to justify his free conception of time: "The watch did not invent man!" Likewise, Djiboutians describe "hurried time as an 'outside' joke" (Monga 1990c). Despite insinuations by some of Gobineau's followers (Lugan 1989), this fatalism obviously is not biological. For if Mali, which opened the world's first university during the Middle Ages (in Tombouctou), no longer has a single institution of higher learning, it is the result of a political failure itself caused by a naive and whimsical conception of culture.

Indicted, therefore, is so-called traditional culture, which is at once archaic and pretentious, and which "defies time because it considers itself to be at the beginning of time." Of arguable authenticity (compare

Mudimbe 1988), it produces conceptual handicaps that make it difficult to decipher the future. It authorizes not only authoritarian practices to prevail in everyday life but also the dictatorship of the community over the individual, the excessive cult of conviviality (which is evidenced by a taste for celebrations), the conflicted relationship with wealth in general and money in particular, and the bloated role of the irrational (witchcraft, religious fundamentalism, and paganism) in peoples' daily lives. It transforms Africa's countries into totalitarian, cannibalistic societies. Its incapacity to meet the challenges of our time—which has made most Africans "stowaways" in this century—speaks to the urgency of a veritable aggiornamento. Africa must bring itself up to date if it wants to embrace this century, something that can be accomplished without losing the humanism associated with its ancestral traditions. The challenge, therefore, is to reconcile the sociability that is the essence of Africanness with the autonomy of the people, necessary if Africans are to affirm themselves as autonomous political, economic, and social agents. In other words, the real challenge for the advocates of democracy and self-empowerment is to transform the current celebration of cultural immobilism (which is done by African governments mainly for political purposes) into a dynamic discussion over the function of culture and the need for alternative visions. Indeed, in all African countries, the struggle has already begun between, on the one hand, governments and their fundamentalist flatterers and, on the other, prodemocracy apostles, who are trying to develop counternarratives through arts.

Memory Forgotten

There appears to be a multidirectional evolution taking place. Among those to whom I refer as "fundamentalists" of a mythic culture, there is a tendency toward radicalization. On the part of the young, especially those who live in urban areas, there is a strong desire to free themselves of the postulates established by their ancestors, to adapt the cultural environment of the family to their own temperament, and to leave behind the imprint of their ideals. Battle lines have been drawn between those who want to restore a waning traditional "moral order" and those who view themselves as the apostles of a postmodern, fragmented cultural identity in tune with the turbulent state of the world.

The Fundamentalist Temptation

The official ideologues of African culture, whose utopian conception of social relations and brutal theory on Africa's integration in the world have been critiqued earlier, still seek to "reconstruct" in each citizen a mental landscape that belongs to an irretrievable past. On the pretext of celebrating what they see as the "eternal values of our cultures" (compare MINFOC 1985), they have developed a discourse aimed at an excessive socialization of individuals and at an absolute respect for the established order. Committed to the idea of a single truth, they advocate a form of positivism claiming to encompass the entire complex of reality. Philosophers dedicated to totalizing systems and a return to myth, they measure the truth of an idea in terms of what they deem to be constants of history. I call this perversion of memory the *fundamentalist temptation.*

At the present time, this temptation is expressed in all parts of the country through the medium of so-called cultural associations and socioethnic organizations. The extent of their activities cannot be precisely determined. Defining themselves as mere extensions of earlier movements active during the colonial period (the Ngondo, the traditional Duala Assembly in Cameroon, or the Bwiti in Gabon are good illustrations of the resurgence of such movements), they have a simple goal: to provide the existing precepts of each community with a moral content and to protect community interests.

The ambiguity of their agenda lies in their second objective. How can one establish a moral boundary between the celebration of the tribe and the incitement toward tribalism? How can one differentiate the instance in which people from the same ethnoregional group come together to shore up their common spiritual foundation so as to integrate themselves within the national community from the one in which they calmly devise strategies to increase their own power and material wealth to the obvious detriment of other groups in the country? How can one accept the idea that every African state should be conceived as nothing more than a conglomeration of different "ethnic" groups?

Of course, the pretext here is to reconstruct frayed identities, to realize possibilities, and to organize collective resistance against the transformation of unified subjects into multiple ones; in short, to take old philosophical values (fraternity, solidarity, mutual assistance), battered, in their view, by modernity, and turn them into reality. The actual goal of the members of these associations—political domination—is never stated. But an examination of the facts and an analysis of the action taken by (or in the name of) these cultural associations clearly prove their interest in increasing the political power of the "ethnic" or social groups that they are supposed to represent.

Some countries have witnessed recently an attempt to polarize national politics through a war of political tracts designed to create ethnic tension. In Cameroon, the Essingan ethnopolitical group has been pitted most notably against the Laakam. The former is supported by the political barons from the central and southern regions of the country and has the backing of the official press—the government daily, the *Cameroon Tribune,* publishes its communiqués. The latter comprises officials from the western part of the country and has taken positions that clearly indicate its willingness to defend only "the interests of the Bamileke community."

In addition to rebutting these pressure groups' claims concerning their affiliation with earlier movements, it is necessary to put into perspective the confrontation between these two lobbies. The tabloids make much ado about mere epiphenomena, and the strategy of those in power is to do their best to exploit them. By showcasing the opposition between the Essingan and the Laakam, the government creates a diversion, succeeds in changing the terms of the current political debate, lends credence to the idea of an upcoming civil war, and arouses the fears of Cameroonians—even as it allays those of the international community by affirming that the nation's recent troubles concern only a few extremists in the rival Beti and Bamileke communities. The strategy is subtle but hardly original: the French and English colonists employed the very same tactics in the 1950s during decolonialization. They too claimed that the fight being led by the Union des Populations du Cameroun (the nationalist party) was not aimed at achieving independence but rather at establishing a hierarchy among tribes.

Culture and Violence

In the face of these associations, with their dubious definitions of micro-citizenry and their vitriolic theories of inequality, in the face of these illusory attempts to sunder the cultural arena through its division into monolithic ethnic blocs, the young have endeavored to develop different points of view and different behaviors. If one concurs with Foucault (1966) that an underlying structural configuration shapes the culture of a given era, and that a specific mode of knowledge undergirds a civilization (Sheridan 1985), molds the collective unconscious, and renders possible the formation of new discourses and behaviors, then it might be said that in our case this social base has been increasingly marked by violence. Given that each culture develops within the framework of an "historical a priori" (episteme), urban civilization in sub-Saharan Africa today bears the stigmata of the political and social upheavals that have occurred time and again since independence. The necessities of daily life have caused a large number of people, notably the young, to devise various methods of revolt against the current social system. Having understood that it is futile to follow precepts that are continually violated by those who endorse them, young people from Dakar to Djibouti have rejected Descartes's first moral maxim: "to obey the laws and customs of my country" (1962:24). The lifestyles they have invented in order to survive involve different factors. Theirs is a true urban culture that rests upon the truth of violence. Its effectiveness, in their eyes, is beyond the shadow of a doubt. Violence has tended to reduce the part episteme plays in their approach to life's problems and difficulties. Respect for political, parental, or traditional power—discredited by its tendency to exacerbate injustices and its inability to bring about public prosperity—has increasingly declined and young people have manifested their disgust through a greater need for violence.

To the aggressive instinct that Freud described as a fundamental characteristic of the human species, one must add the revolt against social norms, which everyone knows were established for the purpose of being, well, ridiculed. The perversion of collective memory has given rise to the violation of laws and to the creation of a different form of popular culture, less passive, more arrogant. Thus, in the slums of Cameroon's large urban centers, and in depressed areas generally, young people have developed a Rambo culture, because a certain type of film is their only escape from local bars. In their eyes, Sylvester Stallone, Chuck Norris, and Arnold Schwarzenegger are visionaries of freedom and have displaced Césaire, Anta Diop, or Mongo Beti.

Whether uneducated or educated but unemployed these young people have nothing around them except the abdication of intellectuals and the rhetoric of politicians. There are no role models to emulate, no emblematic figures to stimulate their minds. And as the government appears unwilling to accord any significance to college degrees; as the myth of education crumbles in the face of a system that produces more and more unemployed, disenfranchised, and marginalized people; as the number of unemployed continues to rise, but no public policy is developed to address the problem of inclusion and to prevent delinquency, Rambo becomes an escape valve. The young form gangs and organize their survival around terror. Of course their actions demonstrate a perverted vision of excellence, but the formation of gangs along other than tribal lines announces the emergence of a form of popular culture that disrupts current models.

A Subversive Conception of Art

Within this tumultuous conceptual framework, one in which a chaotic political culture has given rise to all sorts of perversions, African art has painfully attempted to find its way. Insofar as the ethical substratum of a work of art promotes the possibility of a different way of life, artists have become increasingly bold. Without engaging in Manichaeanism, artists from all fields may be said to fall into two basic groups: those who have the support of the government and those who do not. On the one side are those intellectuals and artists who subscribe to the official view of art as first and foremost a reproduction of tradition and hence a means of defending the established order, even if—indeed, especially if—the established order involves political power. The goal of their work is to imitate what came before or to celebrate things as they are. For in their eyes, everything is always for the best in the best of all possible worlds. One might counter their arguments with the criticisms Hegel leveled at the advocates of a Platonist theory of art: "This superfluous labour [of imitation] may even be regarded as a presumptuous game which falls far short of nature. For art is restricted in its means of portrayal, and can only produce one-sided deceptions, for example a pure appearance of reality for *one* sense only, and, in fact, if it abides by the formal aim of *mere* imitation, it provides not the reality of life but only a pretence of life" (1975, 1:42).

In reality, only a few African artists and intellectuals content themselves with this mimetic theory of art (compare Kom 1991b). Most fall into the second category and do not consider the goal of art to be the celebration of long lost myths, a perspective that empties art of any content or meaning of its own insofar as its object is imposed from without. Championing a popular culture attuned to the times, to the imperatives and concerns of modern life, they conceive of art as the expression of an idea, as the spiritual transfiguration of new truths. This is how one must understand the words of the musician Toto Guillaume:

> Getting an album out every six months is like punching in at the factory. Before I can present something to the public, I have to feel something go off inside me, some inner development.... When you're just starting out, you have a tendency to do what other people are doing. But over time you start feeling the need to make your own statement.... I like tradition, I just have very modern ideas. I think we need to get our music out of the ghetto and start putting it on the market. The artistic war today is fought with missiles. We're not fighting with bows and arrows or spears anymore" (Monga 1988:236).

Refusing to fit themselves into preestablished molds, African artists eagerly embrace their role and seek to convey the specificity of their doubts and emotions. Whether writers, philosophers, musicians, singers, comedians, actors, or painters, they draw inspiration from the need to change the order (or, more precisely, the disorder) of things. Strengthened by the force of their convictions, they endeavor to leave the imprint of their values and beliefs on society. They believe that art should be a reflection of both social realities and human dreams. That is why the main themes that drive their work are the striving for a better world, criticism of the prevailing sociopolitical order, and resistance to any kind of totalitarianism. In other words, they tend to attribute a utopian function to art—in the sense suggested by Bloch (1988). This explains why, for example, the singers Lapiro de Mbanga and Ben Decca felt they should lead the public demonstrations in support of protecting human rights that took place in Douala in January 1991.

On January 1 of that year, a Cameroonian army patrol broke into my house at six o'clock in the morning and dragged me to a filthy cell in a police station in Douala. I had been arrested like this before, so I did not even bother to ask the police for an explanation. As always in this part of the world, the police had no other warrant than their revolvers and machine guns. Several days later, I learned from an article in the official press that I had been arrested for "contempt of the President of the Republic and official bodies" as a result of a piece I had written in a local newspaper criticizing democratization, "Cameroonian style." According to the official press, I deserved a five-year prison sentence without possibility of parole and a fine of FCFA 5 million ($20,000).

On January 18, after a bizarre three-day trial, the Cameroonian judicial system gave me a six-month suspended sentence and fined me FCFA 300,000. Given the seriousness of the charges against me, the relative clemency of the court can be attributed to the massive show of popular support for my cause. In Douala and other cities throughout the country, tens of thousands of people had decided to confront the forces of order so as to express their solidarity with my cause—something never before seen in Cameroon. My work as an economist and my "status" as a writer might account for the support of intellectuals, but I remain convinced that above all it was the work of a group of well-known artists in the streets and working-class neighborhoods that raised the consciousness of the masses.

My trial would no doubt have been just another political trial had Lapiro de Mbanga, André-Marie Tala, and Ben Decca not decided to dedicate themselves so completely to my cause. Among other things, they created an advocacy group, made daily trips to working-class neighborhoods wearing T-shirts printed with slogans demanding freedom of expression, and distributed pamphlets asking people to show their support for me. All of this was unheard of in a regime where the word *democracy* was a rhetorical artifice and where people never dared express their true thoughts in public.

Stunned by the sudden awakening of a civil society everyone thought had been immobilized by thirty years of political monolithism, unpunished police brutality, and repression raised to an art of government, the power base around Paul Biya was thoroughly humiliated and lost its assurance. The official political ideologues had to come up with an explanation for the slap in the face to the president of the republic and also had to find a way to restore the authority of the state and its institutions. Held accountable for the disorder and anarchy, Lapiro de Mbanga and the other artists involved in the affair were subjected to slanderous accusations in the official press and had their songs banned on national radio and television. As if that were not enough, the National Center of Studies and Research (CENER, the political police) asked John Salle, another popular singer, to compose, posthaste, a song along the lines of the official slogans. Financing came from the military budget, and in late January the song was hastily recorded. It was later turned into a video shown daily on state-run television. This surprising reaction by Cameroonian authorities was proof of a new phenomenon: the consciousness that both politicians and civil society had of the power of music. This was further evidenced by the fact that several months after the trial the government engaged in a strong seduction-intimidation campaign aimed at the artists who had come to my defense. Considered by the authorities as the leader of the popular uprising, Lapiro de Mbanga was severely pressured by police officials, who eventually succeeded in getting him to "reverse" his position: The singer publicly denounced the goals of the Cameroonian opposition, though he had been its most prominent member. His statement, of course, did not fail to raise all sorts of questions as to the reasons for his sudden change of heart.

The Lapiro de Mbanga case reveals a great deal about the changes now occurring in black Africa. Throughout the continent, music is now considered a legitimate and effective way to get one's message across, that is, a counternarrative to the official cultural politics. An important threshold has been crossed with respect to the perception politicians, intellectuals, and businessmen have of African music. An increasing number of artists have begun to engage themselves publicly—in order to defend their rights, but also to address concerns of a political nature.

*
* *

In truth, what strikes us today as the "discovery" of the power of music was more the doing of the politicians than of the artists themselves. Artists have always thought of their art as a medium of expression for the ethical goal toward which we all strive. This conviction—timid, of course, and virtually clandestine—was hidden from view by the paternalism and superficiality of the musicologists who evaluated African music. Indeed, sociologists and musicologists have long analyzed African lyrics through the prism of the methodologies in vogue in their fields.

Based on traditional methods of observation, this musical historiography has allowed for the detection of forms of language that are understandable only within Western analytical paradigms. Hence, the recognized importance of the griots, keepers of the ancestral moral order and heralds of collective memory, has unfortunately lent credence to the false idea that musical satire can occur only in linear form. The conclusion that has thus been drawn is that contemporary African music is incapable of transmitting a message of protest, but that is not the case. The disappearance of the griots has been counterbalanced by the emergence of singers who wish to exploit fully their freedom of expression and explore taboo themes. The language and the register in which they work differs from those of their ancestors, and new tools of measurement are required if one is to detect and appreciate what they are saying.

If one agrees with Attali (1977) that a society ought to be judged more on the basis of its sounds, its music, and its taste in entertainment than on its statistics, then it is necessary to alter one's approach to African social realities: Africa must not only be "seen" but "heard." Its countries cannot be understood by simply analyzing their sociopolitical and economic structures. By deciphering the lyrics and the sounds of different types of music in Senegal or Djibouti, one is better able to perceive the concerns and hopes of these peoples.

To understand properly the production of music in black Africa, two levels of reading must be distinguished. On the one hand, the use and the extent of freedom of expression need to be evaluated through both the lyrics and what lies beyond them, for language is multidimensional and can sometimes be accessed only with the aid of a few well-defined keys. On the other hand, what appears as an expansion and appropriation of freedom needs to be explored on a strictly musical level (instrumentation), for freedom of expression is not confined to lyrics. It likewise involves the choice of instruments and the philosophy behind the way they are played, the combination of sounds, the construction of harmonies, and the development of arrangements that give a musical work its stamp of originality.

Let us begin, then, with the lyrics. Roughly speaking, the evolution of African song may be divided into three periods. Originally, it served chiefly as a means of keeping popular memory alive and celebrating societal values. During the colonial era, it functioned as a rite of exorcism—exorcism of the concerns and difficulties of daily life and of the violence of a colonial government seen as illegitimate and treacherous.

Love songs, songs of war or protest, odes to the dead, prayers, incantations, and lullabies first and foremost celebrated the possibility of happiness and the necessity of hope. This dimension has been missed by a number of commentators because the first artists to record albums sang the ideology of love. Because these artists had to seek financial backing from French and Belgian producers, who were few in number and little inclined to invest in material with a message, the first songs to be recorded were bland and vapid. This, of course, gave credence to the idea that African songs were just another form of entertainment.

The context in which contemporary African music was born did not lend itself to great ethical declarations, at least not in a form easily deciphered by using ordinary criteria of analysis. Thus, when Congolese Joseph Kabassele, alias Grand Kalle, formed the African Jazz Band in Léopoldville (now Kinshasa) in 1955, he had no idea that the ensemble would become the first important band in black Africa. Bringing together his fellow Congolese Tabu Ley Rochereau and Luambo Makiadi (Franco), as well as Jean Serge Essous and Cameroonian Manu Dibango, Kabassele, now considered a pioneer, no doubt invented modern African music. From the beginning, his idea was to offer the African public songs celebrating the sensual delights of existence. According to Manu Dibango, "You had to be nuts to go into the music business in those days. Not only was the road a precarious one, but you ran the risk of being called a deserter in the fight for national independence" (Monga 1983:67).

It was only in 1960, after the great debates on colonialism, that Grand Kalle recorded his hit song, "Indépendance tchatcha," which for years would serve as the banner of African music. Following on his heels, the Congolese Franklin Boukaka attempted to start a "revolutionary" trend and stir up social and political protest. In his most famous song in Lingala, "Le bûcheron," he said:

Ba voti tango ekomaka
Nakombi moto ya bango
Nakomituna mondele akende
Dipanda to dzua ya nini (Bemba 1984)

Which can roughly be translated as follows:

Only when the time comes for electoral campaigns
I become their body.
I am starting to wonder whether the colonial masters actually left this country.
To whom is devoted the so-called independence we fought for?

In spite of Boukaka's enormous popularity throughout central Africa, he did not meet with much success. The reasons for his failure are threefold: First, artists were less sensitive to this type of combat, preferring to express their subversive vision of the world through instrumentation. Second, the 1960s saw the rise of authoritarian regimes, which plunged African countries into a long period of darkness. Third, the production, distribution, and promotional arms of the music industry long closed their doors to artists considered dangerous because of the nature of their work and the possible impact of their discourse of protest on a population prepared to receive it, given the tragic conditions of daily life.

A confused and tumultuous second phase of music expressed the disenchantment that followed, in the wake of independence. Lyricists ceased to be prophetic and became preoccupied with everyday problems. Reality was echoed in these songs rather than challenged, and no effort was made to change society. The great ethical goals of the colonial period were progressively abandoned and the entire complex of traditional values began to unravel.

There were, however, two notable exceptions: Francis Bebey, from Cameroon, and Pierre Akendengue, from Gabon. Ceaselessly referring to what they considered Africa's cultural heritage, they succeeded in establishing a small but significant trend. They channeled their freedom of expression through African parables and allegories, which they used to transmit their critical vision of the world. In "King of Pygmies," one of his best-known songs, Bebey employed humor and feigned ingenuousness to ridicule the pretentiousness of certain African heads of state:

> In our camp
> there's a little man
> who claims to be the king.
> Everyone laughs when he says
> that his father was a king.
> Because everyone knows that in our tribe
> there has never been a king.
> We don't think that a crown
> serves much purpose on hunting trips. (1983)

Akendengue's lyrics were in the same vein:

> I never get any rest
> I never get any sleep
> My nights are filled with nightmares—the tears of children
> Who are hungry and who want every day
> A little more …
> The sun bites into my body
> I sing
> The tse-tse flies suck on my blood
> I sing. (1973)

If one excludes the work of such "oddballs" as Bebey and Akendengue (who, not surprisingly, had to live in France for a number of years), there was no song on the market that could be termed subversive before Nigerian Fela Ransome Kuti burst upon the scene. His arrival in the early 1970s inaugurated the third phase of contemporary African music. There was a large public response to his message and a trend began to take shape.

Some of the movement's artists—Ivoirians Alpha Bondy and Serge Kasy among the most prominent—have since turned to reggae, in their view a better vehicle of expression for oppressed peoples' yearnings for freedom. Returning to highly complex forms, other artists have introduced a discourse of revolt into the most sophisticated musical structures (Euba 1989; Kwabena Nketia 1990). Still others, such as Zaireans Ray Lema and Lokua Kanza, Senegalese Baaba Maal, Malian Salif Keita, and Cameroonians Koko Ateba and Nkembe Pesauk, have taken inspiration from the textual framework and techniques of popular singers in the West. The electrifying force of their songs remains a source of concern for political authorities.

The unfolding of freedom of expression in black Africa is best observed on the level of the music per se. If one takes seriously both the axiom that all music speaks—even in the absence of lyrics—and the need to decipher the unspoken dimension of this art form, one can attribute some of the social upheavals of our time to the impact of different types of African music.

This postulate is not fortuitous. The new generation of African artists has clearly chosen to favor the music itself over the lyrics. The Senegalese *sabar* of Youssou Ndour and Ismael Lo, the Cameroonian *makossa* of Toto Guillaume, and the Zairean *rumba* of Koffi Olomidé illustrate this phenomenon. Nzete has shown how the stars of Zairean music define their priorities, always to the detriment of the lyrics: "When there are more syllables than will fit in a given rhythmic sequence, the author-composer always cuts one out. When the length of a word doesn't disrupt the rhythm, we leave all the syllables in" (1991:99). This technique allows the artists to accommodate the lyrics to the pulse of the music and to preserve the melody by modifying the pitch curve of words—no easy task given that in most African languages pitch is all that distinguishes certain words from others. The preference given to the rhythm has also led to the suppression of elements of syntax. Thus, when the tempo is fast, most subordinate clauses and almost all adverbial complements are dropped.

Taking tremendous liberties with the techniques governing lyrical composition, African artists underscore their desire to free themselves of the criteria established by musicologists. Artists give importance to musical composition, often to the detriment of the lyrics. Consequently, if one wishes to get at the essence of these works, one must study the various sound configurations, examine the instrumental discourse as a whole, and unearth the ethos buried within the harmonies and arrangements.

Such an endeavor requires the adoption of a multifaceted, expansive approach that integrates both what is termed traditional African music and what is referred to as modern or popular African music. The debate between the "old" and the "new" is far from over, but because producers, distributors, and promoters are interested in only what they think (rightly or wrongly) is in demand, only "modern" African music has gained the attention of the music industry's principal players. This has caused Angolan guitarist Mario Rui Silva to remark: "We must not allow the success of this music to eclipse Africa's other music. We have a tendency to forget it, but another one exists. From the Pygmies through the Bochimans to the Bamilekes, the Fulani, the Hausas, and the Zulus, all the populations of Africa have their own ancestral music. In purely structural terms, this music has no reason to be jealous of any other" (Monga 1983:68).

Francis Bebey has said much the same thing:

> We only call it "traditional" music because we don't recognize it for what it is. It continues to advance towards the future whose course it is destined to upset through the renewal of sincerity. It speaks of man, eternal and diverse, steadily moving through the maze of poverty and misery; it speaks of injustice, racism and segregation; it proclaims to the world of the disenchanted the joy of living as long as there is dance, the joy of hearty laughter. It reinvents life around legends as old as our first ancestor. It plays its flutes, koras, mvets, and sanzas with the delicacy of harmony; it beats its tom-toms with the brutality of passion; it calls to the gods and opens men's eyes to the invisible. It wishes to be known, studied and respected for what it is, and not admired for what we wish it were (1981:38).

However, the idea of an either-or opposition between these two forms of music—if it is indeed possible to reduce all the different types of music that are found in Africa to these two broad categories—is not justified. Each has its own function and role. Rarely recorded, listened to less and less, traditional music has certainly suffered from its association with the past and the fundamentalist discourse of some of its practitioners. It is rare and elicits twinges of nostalgia reflective of contradictory, anguished feelings toward modernity, dizzying and difficult to control. But the place of traditional music remains an important one inasmuch as tomorrow's popular music will draw inspiration from it.

Popular music is indeed very popular and has taken over the airwaves. In touch with the problems of daily life, in tune with today's atmosphere of disorder, it is often syncretic but nevertheless contributes to the development of a new social order. Though it is fumbling and repetitive, though it sometimes appears neurotic or lost in the fun house of such fleeting trends as disco, reggae, funk, rap or *zouk,* popular music has never stopped playing an essential role—that of recording the frenzied chronicle of our collective meanderings, ambitions, and dreams.

It is therefore illusory to perform a Manichaean reading of the different types of African music and to establish a moral hierarchy among them. Through their work, individual creators express their desire to explore the unknown order of things, to elaborate new and exciting sound combinations, and to contribute to what will later be the memory of their people. This is how one must understand Manu Dibango's words when he declares:

> When you're a musician, you don't get up one morning and say to yourself, "I'm making African music"; you say, "I'm making music." Period.... All along people have accused me of "stealing." But how can you create anything if you don't use what's out there? All creators are a little like vampires. Painting, literature, the information industry, they all function like the music industry. Some musicians are afraid of tapping into this universal dimension. But without this perspective, what's the point of being born? What good is curiosity, energy and movement if you live behind bars, feet and hands tied, in a little corner of the world for seventy years? (1991:4)

The lucidity and realism of this approach have allowed Dibango to reach a worldwide audience and to position himself as a singer who remains in touch with the times but also with his African identity. This positive approach to art is deeply significant. Rejecting the nondestiny that conservatives offer us, it expresses the will to extract a little emotion from the universe that constantly beats us down and underscores the ability of humans to contribute to the construction of a different world.

In all fields, these types of artists have always been the most numerous. Although the work of the first African writers was somewhat conformist, the generation that gave African literature its letters of nobility was also the one that introduced dynamism into the subject matter along with social and political protest. Moreover, from Mongo Beti to Simon Njami or Ben Okri, writing has often been a space of revolt against the established social or aesthetic norms, despite the inevitable constraints imposed upon the imagination by the use of foreign languages (Muhando Mlama 1990; Midohouan 1991).

I must also mention the remarkable deconstructive/reconstructive efforts of several African thinkers. Through the power and originality of their work, they have opened up new perspectives on African culture and have contributed to the development of a new set of working principles for its study. They have triggered that indispensable cultural update, alone able to inject a sufficient dose of authenticity into culture so that it might invest without fear in the future (compare Ndiaye 1976; Fonkoué 1985; Mudimbe 1988).

Per Capita Anxiety Rate and Gross Domestic Happiness

Musicians, singers, and dancers are at the forefront of the effort to transform reality. The sounds, noises, and forms of African music increasingly set the tempo of social change. Africans have always known that most musicians were sorcerers, entrancing the populations of whole cities and altering the beliefs of entire peoples through the magic of their instruments, bodies, and voices (Bender 1991). They have also become preachers and futurologists. Their art is not merely an avenue that focuses the world's attention on Africa's plight; it is also a way of telling what the future holds in store. In the words of Francis Bebey:

> On a purely political and economic level, our countries appear to be going nowhere. But if you listen to the music of the young, it becomes clear that sweeping changes lie just around the bend. The new sounds I am hearing in African music announce social upheavals. Let me give you an example. The voice of Bailly Spinto, from the Ivory Coast: it predicts cataclysmic events, announces a great rebellion still in the process of formation—it doesn't matter what words he happens to be singing.[4]

In other words, if political scientists and sociologists wish to understand the way African societies function, they need to go beyond statistics and macroeconomics in order to decipher the sounds and the music of Africa. The rates of inflation and unemployment may allow for the calculation of a fictive gross domestic product, but only music can help us measure the per capita anxiety rate and gross domestic happiness—fundamental underpinnings of culture.

Miséréor's Fast *and* Guernica

Although the plastic arts in Africa are not among the techniques of cultural expression that one associates with a long and rich tradition, they must be considered, for a number of exciting and influential developments have occurred in painting and sculpture during the three decades of independence. If such artists as Zairian Liyolo or Cameroonian Gédéon Mpando, sculptors of the principal monuments that "adorn" our capitals (they uglify them in fact), have made a travesty of the plastic arts, it is because the authorities have chosen to make them important figures despite their lack of talent, creativity, and charisma. Fortunately, sculptors such as Damian Manuhwa (Zimbabwe) and painters such as Iba Ndiaye (Senegal), Zogo, Manuela Dikoume, Othéo, Pascal Kenfack, and especially René Tchébétchou (Cameroon) are now demonstrating that one can successfully promote a different conception of art.

The refusal to conform and the desire to rebel is prevalent in the works of all these artists, particularly in Tchébétchou's. When the eye rests upon one of his paintings, it ceases to operate as an optical instrument in search of pleasurable emotion. Rather, it is assaulted and transformed by the diversity of styles, by the willed shift in pictorial techniques—in short, by the multiple dimensions it perceives in the work of an artist who appears to have freed himself of the psychological constraints imposed by tradition.

It is true that some of his paintings seem to have been inspired by the impressionism of a Monet, a Pissarro, or a Degas. There are the gradation and the nuances of color, the fragmented brush strokes used to render the brilliance of a sky or the shadows of a face. There is also the light, predominant and exultant. Precise contours and details are abandoned. Other paintings pose the essential question of cubism: how to represent a three-dimensional object on a two-dimensional surface. Different facets of the same object are assembled in a single painting; the naked object is exposed, opened from within, presented not as it is seen but as it is thought by the artist. And though Tchébétchou has incorporated the influence of Miró and Picasso into his work, he has not lost sight of his African identity. Bearing witness to this are his great kaleidoscopic frescoes, among which is one of his finest paintings, *Miséréor's Fast,* a panorama of daily African life. The manner in which it is conceived, the order in which the scenes are presented, and the attitudes of the characters bring to mind Miró's *Soirée snob chez la Princesse* (*Snobbish Evening with the Princess*), or Picasso's phenomenal *Guernica*: The characters, limp and spiritless, mirror their destiny; the situations are tragic, heart wrenching. The Western references suggested by this painting do not take away from the authenticity of a culture deliberately oriented toward the universal. Black African culture, let us not forget, has likewise made a large contribution to humanity's common heritage. Neither should we forget that African society as depicted in Tchébétchou's paintings today is in the same sorry shape that European society in Spain was at the time Picasso painted *Guernica.* Finally, neither the turmoil of an artist nor the personal anguish that stimulates creativity is the exclusive province of a single race. In a word, suffering is color-blind.

*
* *

In view of all that has been said, a few remarks are in order concerning the future of cultural politics in Africa. Both technological evolution and social revolutions will no doubt make it necessary for Africa's peoples to adapt themselves continually to new dynamics. Countries that are little prepared for the so-called global battle of culture (encompassing, of course, geopolitical and economic struggles) run the risk of being swallowed up in a standardized culture: if music from elsewhere is all that is heard, and the most readily available literature—that is, from Europe and the United States—is all that is read, then Africa's young people, like the rest of the world's youth, will be "Americanized." In many African countries, those in power oppose the very idea of democracy on the grounds that it is a threat to "authentic" African culture and a challenge to secular values of respect to the chief (the authoritarian head of state).

Obviously, one should be wary of overestimating the effects of the so-called Western influence on Africans' values, for artists and some intellectuals will always develop counternarratives to any form of universal narrative—as they did with official cultural politics and its hegemonic narrative. For centuries now, experts have described Africa as totally "deculturized." Of course, they are the same experts who lament that the continent has yet to "free itself" of the cultural habits that impede its development.

Juxtapositions of different cultures are part of the normal course of history, and encounters with other civilizations help peoples make adjustments necessary for the survival and renewal of future generations. Moreover, it would be ill advised to judge the substance of a culture based on a given era lifted from the continuum of history. Culture, by its very essence, is dynamic, constantly in flux. And like all other peoples, Africans must contend with an ever changing identity. In the current quest for democracy, it is not a liability.

Notes

1. See the Presidential Decree No. 62/DF/108, March 31, 1962.
2. Decree No. 67/DF/503, November 21, 1967.
3. Balandier (1985) and Vattimo (1987), among others, have suggested interesting frameworks to analyze the effects of new ways of seeing and thinking in people's daily lives.
4. Bebey, interview.

4

The Emergence of New Patterns of Free Expression

Je suis un homme de forêt et de haute savane. Je suis donc quelque peu étranger à la ligne droite. Dans la forêt, on ne peut pas se déplacer en ligne droite. Je soupçonne la ligne droite d'avoir un côté censure par rapport à l'existence.

*

I am a man of the forest and the savanna.
So straight lines are somewhat foreign to me.
In the forest, it is impossible to move in a straight line.
I suspect that, with respect to existence,
straight lines have a censuring aspect.

Sony Labou Tansi, Congo

In nearly four decades of independence, numerous unsuccessful attempts have been made to graft Western political systems onto African nations. Yet alongside these failures, new ways of structuring and negotiating reality have emerged, and hitherto unknown expressions of identity are taking shape. This important phenomenon has largely gone unnoticed by Africans, who have not made the necessary shift to another social frame of reference, one that would allow them to perceive the originality of this new mind-set.

If, on the scale of brutality, African autocrats have been unable to "elevate" themselves to the level of their cohorts in pre-Gorbachev Eastern Europe or in Latin America during the Pinochet era, it is not only because they are "apprentice dictators," to borrow Mongo Beti's pithy phrase, but also, and especially, because African peoples, despite rampant injustice, intellectual bankruptcy, economic illiteracy, and cultural erosion, have invented numerous forms of passive resistance.[1] In the process, and through their daily behavior, African peoples have likewise expressed the desire to affirm their specificity and to create a different way of life. They have invented veritable modes of democratic production, developed new forms of critical thinking, and ceaselessly endeavored to change the logic governing their relation to all types of power (especially political and traditional authorities). Surreptitiously, in the small events, gestures, words, and actions of daily life, there has evolved a true ethos of resistance, a subtle sort of civil disobedience that cannot be described in the language to which we are accustomed.

This life(saving) strategy of resistance, whose form and content I will later define, is turning social relations upside down in certain countries. Slowly but surely, a model of subservience to power is giving way to a confrontational one, which has, of course, profoundly altered social relations. Sites of protest are being formed, new languages formulated, original discourses affirmed; they have their secret codes and keys, their meanderings and mysteries.

Misled by what Balandier (1971) has called "the illusion of the durability of societies," few Western analysts have discerned this movement. Even the most critically minded African sociologists and political scientists do not appear to have noticed the development of these new strategies of popular insubordination—with the exception of Mbembe (1988). One would think that Africa's failed efforts to adopt Western models of government would suggest to these scientists the possibility that democratic notions are being articulated differently on the continent and that they have given rise to new types of behavior. Instead, researchers have been content to watch the failure of numerous efforts to establish different forms of government: presidential, semipresidential, parliamentary, and so forth. In the guise of explanation, they have trotted out the usual dichotomies—tradition versus modernity, center versus periphery, equilibrium versus disequilibrium—rather than observing and analyzing the reality of daily life. Nonetheless, it has become increasingly clear that the failure to construct democratic institutions in all of sub-Saharan Africa has contributed to the emergence of other modes of attaining liberty.

As a result, and in the light of a sociological grammar subtended by a macroscopic vision of things, it seems useful to try to reformulate the political syntax of those countries. This point of view is as yet poorly defined, and it requires the adoption of a tentative, multifaceted approach. I am keenly aware that any effort to define and evaluate new and revealing elements of social reality runs the risk of ambiguity. The temptation is great to compile a heterogeneous inventory of "sociologized" epiphenomena simply because they produce syncretic combinations. I am nevertheless convinced that by using de Certeau's approach (1984), it is possible to trace the outline of a space of expression hidden behind the unsaid and to decipher its language. For if African peoples are adroit with words, they are also quite skilled in the use of silence and other means of expression to convey their defiance of political authorities, who are themselves subject to what Fabien Eboussi Boulaga has called "functional illiteracy" and who appear incapable of comprehending the possibility of dissent.[2]

The first section of this chapter presents some general guidelines to approaching the banal in everyday African life. The second section explores the meaning of disorder by looking at the way political changes are conceived in the imagination of African leaders. The third section focuses on informal and unusual forms of reappropriation of freedom, through sexuality, body expression, or music. The fourth section concludes with the need to integrate the psychoaffective dimension into social and political analysis.

A Different Understanding of the Banal

A striking aspect of African peoples' struggle for political recognition is that they have developed an impressive set of informal frameworks to conceptualize their propensity to create counternarratives against the prevailing official discourse. Their quest for dignity—as Cornel West defines this notion; that is, self-confidence, self-respect, and self-esteem (1990:27)—has occurred on unusual social and cultural terrains. Authoritarian uses of culture to prevent people from discovering the charms of liberty have required persistent popular techniques to hold pessimism and self-contempt at bay. Thus, selective appropriation and reinterpretation of official ideologies including linguistic innovation in rhetorical practices and stylizations of body forms (hair styles, ways of walking, standing, talking, singing, working, etc.), have been some of the strategies employed, transforming public discourse into new, silent yet powerful vectors for collective insubordination.

I shall begin with a few preliminary remarks about the informal systems of resistance that African peoples have developed and their ability to carve out spaces of individual and collective freedom. I shall then emphasize the power of language, question the validity of the assumptions of African hedonism, and examine certain a priori notions that are often used by social scientists to analyze the so-called African mentality.

Study What Lies Beyond Language

The problem began the moment sociologists and anthropologists forgot one of the fundamental principles of the social sciences: the existence of a dimension beyond words. Though this important sphere of communication should not have been neglected, most Africanists who studied urban language, for example, confined themselves to an analysis of the language per se and failed to examine the ineffable dimension of the words. But ever since linguists discovered functions of language beyond its "referential" or "propositional" aspects (Crystal 1987:10–13), and since Klossowski (1969) lent philosophical dignity to the simulacrum, we have known that words have only figurative meanings. Mired in their desire to be at the forefront, most researchers have been blinded by their conviction that each word is univocal. Unable to see anything beyond the obvious, they can interpret neither what is suggested by verbal dynamics nor what lies beyond the words themselves.

Of course, the axiom that Africans, like all human beings, are defined above all by their language allows one to stop at appearances and to view as useless—or insane—the conception of another frame of reference for thought. But this axiom cannot stand up to the very definition of language, that is, the conceptualization of a vehicle allowing access to reality, in all its complexity and most ephemeral nuances. If one accepts, therefore, that the essence of a message is not reducible to the word, then it is necessary to elucidate to the extent possible the element of mystery that is consubstantial with all language; and this so as to be able to grasp its precise truth (Martin 1988; Chomsky 1987; Hagège 1985; Fontanier 1968). Such an effort must be made by anyone wishing to penetrate the complex souls of African peoples, whose psychological habits must be read at several levels.

One way of pursuing meaning behind popular forms of discourse is to pay close attention to new languages. Following numerous philosophers as widely separated by doctrine as Plato, Aristotle, Kant, Hume, Wittgenstein, or Quine, all of whom were able to pursue metaphysics in the general structure of language, Davidson concludes: "In sharing a language, in whatever sense this is required for communication, we share a picture of the world that must, in its large features, be true. It follows that in making manifest the large features of our language, we make manifest the large features of reality" (1977:244). When studying African political realities today, it is therefore necessary to accept the existence of a dimension beyond language, even more pronounced in Africa than elsewhere.

Take the example of the Zairean civil servant, caught red-handed in an act of corruption, who calmly responds that he is only applying "Article 15," an imaginary article of the constitution stipulating: "Do whatever it takes to get by!" (Péan 1988). It is necessary to go beyond mockery and analyze the multiple dimensions of language at work here. Or take the example of the Douala taxi driver who replies, after you have offered to pay him FCFA 125 (the ordinary fare) to take you to a location that strikes him as far away: "I didn't hear a word you said. Speak up!" He is telling you to up the price, to offer him something extra, give him a "reason" for going out of his way. The fact that he claims not to have heard really means that you are supposed to agree with him that the posted fare is out of line with the actual distance involved. And his "Speak up!" translates his willingness to let you take the initiative in negotiating the new fare. One can easily imagine how devastating these techniques would be when used by actors in local political markets, and how misleading language can be to those researchers who limit their surveys to superficial analyses of words they hear in the streets of Dakar or Harare.

African Hedonism, an Imported "Value"

Next, one must rid oneself of widely circulated clichés. As Owomoyela puts it, "Even within the discipline of African studies scholars continue to propagate and popularize concepts of Africa and Africanity that are hardly distinguishable from those of Joseph de Gobineau or Captain Nolan" (1994:78). For example, building upon the ludicrous idea that the search for pleasure is a notion perpetually in vogue in certain cultures, some researchers have concluded that eudaemonism is a typical trait of Africans (White 1988; Robertson and Klein 1983; Naipaul 1980, 1984). Roughly speaking, one could say that in the past few years, this pseudoaesthetics has been the characteristic feature of the literary and philosophical school developed by most commentators. Worse yet, other researchers have used it to elevate hedonism to the level of a basic precept of a supposed African political philosophy. Expanding Senghor's famous maxim, "I dance, therefore I am," they have made the desire for pleasure part of the definition of the African political personality. This is how one must read their commentaries on the so-called African imagination—which is sometimes nothing more than their own exotic vision of the continent.

Making flattering remarks about African mentality and turning this imagination into a potential model for understanding the world changes nothing at bottom (Barley 1983, for instance). Filmmakers (for example, Sydney Pollack, the director of *Out of Africa*) who celebrate the sensuousness of an Africa at once romantic, cozy, and radiating an atmosphere of naive joviality think they are putting up a good show when they argue that Africa represents for them a lost paradise, a land of smiling men, mythical women, and fauna found nowhere else in the world. The reasoning is simplistic, and the racism all the more subtle in that it is inverted, presented in the form of a false compliment. Several excellent studies have shown that the hedonist label some would like to stick on black peoples is either a characteristic imposed upon Africa through rhetoric or an imported "value," created in order to validate the idea of the exotic "other"—"closer to nature" (removed from intelligence and control), as West puts it, and "more prone to be guided by base pleasures and biological impulses" (1993:88).[3]

Refuting Certain A Priori Conceptual Notions

If Western social scientists seeking to analyze African reality had understood, as did Kant, that the power of knowledge is limited to the form it takes and that the only accessible objects of knowledge are phenomena shaped by the structure of the observer's mind, then the ethnocentrism of their studies would have had a certain charm. The possibility of conceptualizing other forms of "Africanness" was even more difficult for them given their underestimation of Africans' refusal to be mere instruments of reason. Immersed in spirituality, imbued with an active and inventive vitality, Africans have had a tendency to free themselves of the tutelage of the god of reason, which has not only been forced upon them for the past four hundred years, but which feels like a girdle that fits too tight. The logic of this presupposition has led Africans to reaffirm and rehabilitate the concept of contradiction. A substratum of dialectics, the foundation of thought, contradiction is above all the condition sine qua non for the development of a personal sense of freedom. This, in turn, allows one to conceive of other freedoms and to survive (1) the hardships and cruelties of everyday life, (2) the totalitarianism of political power, (3) the theological deliriums of fundamentalists attached to a traditional culture little adapted to the times, and (4) the yoke of the family—obsolete but still very much present. In this regard, one cannot overestimate the necessity of updating some rituals, which would allow the continent to soften the sociopolitical and financial burden of the ceremonial structure around which African life is organized: marriage, baptism, mourning, funeral rites (Monga 1994b).

How can we reaffirm and rehabilitate contradiction to the prevailing philosophic discourse on Africa? By stripping immutable rituals of their apparent attributes. By blowing up the conceptual principles that have shaped thought on the behavior of Africans. By ceaselessly inventing new frames of reference so that the deep significance and meaning of events might be properly evaluated. In other words—and beyond the inevitability of entropy—it is a matter of dominating and negotiating the crisis of the African Man, the *Muntu* (Eboussi Boulaga 1976), so as to perceive the sparks of positivity within the most anodyne daily actions, so as to capture the spirit lurking in the shadows of the most ordinary words, so as to discern the beginnings of a new way of seeing and living. In sum, it is a matter of finding the flowers the manure has produced.

Without falling into the exuberant but dubious determinism of some neo-Africanists, I will discuss several aspects of the new forms of dissent—which constitute, above all, a subversive and silent approach to the world. First, I wish to reconsider, in a positive light, the intensity of the confrontational relationship between African civil society and the various powers it must face daily. Ever since Hegel demonstrated that consciousness does not involve a passive apprehension of reality but rather a struggle between two opposed figures, two beings seeking to annihilate the other in order to gain respect, the idea of a master-slave dialectic has been accepted. In the African version of this dialectic the lower rungs of society, considered to be dominated and miserable, are sometimes cast in the role of active social agents, capable of playing an important part in the debate, taking the reins, detailing their complaints, and turning in their favor the various discourses and resolutions. In short, they would be a force to contend with—a far cry from the widely held view of the passivity of Africa's peoples.

Next, I wish to suggest that these microattitudes should be judged positively. African peoples' mental outlooks—if I may use this phrase without overgeneralizing—indicate that they have been able to conceptualize, if not freedom, then at least insubordination and indocility, notable and noble signs of the desire for democracy. The reality of daily life indicates the existence of micropowers arranged in a complex strategy and disseminated throughout the entire social body. The sense of anxiety one might feel toward the future of societies that are imploding, losing their traditions, and witnessing the disruption of a long-established hierarchy must not allow one to lose sight of the permanence of equilibrium, subtended by new combinations of the elements. That is why the images filmmaker Wim Wenders shows of a city like Berlin or Los Angeles allow us to perceive an interesting economy in the permanent social intimacy of these cities, where the squeamish see only chaos and the destruction of the old order. Similarly, Jean Rouch's remarkable films, notably those dealing with everyday life in Abidjan, have brought to light the ways in which people actually conduct their lives and have uncovered the harmony of existence that injustice and cruelty hide from view. Could not sociologists, anthropologists, historians, and philosophers also begin to see the realities filmmakers have perceived?

Having examined the spiritual framework that governs the collective will to resist and to live otherwise, I wish to stress the necessity of relativizing certain historical notions such as decline or decadence. Though we have yet to develop a way to measure gross domestic happiness, as Imbert (1984) has advised, we can nevertheless remain skeptical about speculations on the idea of decadence. Aron (1973) was rightly wary of the term, which he judged more appropriate for social studies than for dry statistical analysis, and preferred to use "lowering" (*abaissement*). One inevitably strays unless one gets past the political meaning of decadence—the cultural influence and the historical vitality of African civilizations can be grasped in other ways. The best proof of this is that the "collapse" so often evoked in no way corresponds to Plato's famous equation, which political scientists still insist on using in order to explain decline.[4]

In Africa's large metropolitan areas, the methods of insubordination are so sophisticated that in certain areas one occasionally stumbles upon veritable laboratories of philosophy. Since the publication of Yambo Ouologuem's famous novel *Le Devoir de violence* (*The Duty of Violence,* translated into English as *Bound to Violence*), we have known about African peoples' thirst for disorder, which is intimately linked to their desire to surpass and organize this disorder. We also know that nihilism is a viewpoint prevalent in the tropics. Nietzsche, Schopenhauer, and Cioran have their counterparts and followers in every neighborhood in Dakar or Abidjan. They are street vendors, sidewalk painters, and popular singers. Nihilism is on the rise and is given expression in the smallest acts, as well as in art and literature. Whereas the heirs of a rigged decolonialism, now managing an as yet undigested independence, continue to tear apart Africa's societies, increasing the risk of their South Americanization, the attitude of the new nihilists holds out a hope—the will to resist the aftermath of the yoke. That is why the African imagination is, above all, a survivalist one.

Topography of the Survivalist Imagination

It is useful to approach African peoples' informal strategies of political resistance by looking at both the way they permanently try to optimize disorder in their behavior and the conceptual structure of their imagination.

Optimal Anarchy and the Aesthetics of Disorder

It all begins with the refusal to conform to what is seen as the established disorder, the old, unbearable order (compare Balandier 1988). Realistically, African peoples are in a position of weakness, hence resistance must take a subtle form. Frontal assaults are avoided. Suicidal methods that might reveal the collective strategy are proscribed. Instead, a more insidious approach is adopted, one that slowly but surely saps the foundations of the system and that may take the form of a play on words, a theory of derision, a deformation of the established rules, a refusal to follow instructions, or an irreverent attitude toward the hierarchy in place.

The other rule that African peoples follow is to avoid falling into a state of anarchy. Aware long before Proudhon of the oppressive nature of all forms of government, they part company with anarchists when it comes to formulating a strategy of insubordination. Anarchy is a sort of asymptote that they approach but never reach. Africans are well aware of the consequences of crossing the line: The resulting disorder sanctions a brutal swing of the pendulum. In other words, their common sense tells them that the absence of authority benefits only the most conservative interest groups, or the most frivolous political leaders.[5] This was one of the lessons learned from the Biafra War, which degenerated into a tragedy for the Ibo people the day that extremists believed they were strong enough to defeat the military government in Lagos. The sociopolitical use of disorder is therefore a matter of dosage, of optimal anarchy.

This technique of provoking disorder within, well, disorder, without provoking at the same time a collapse of authority, is sometimes exploited by political entrepreneurs seeking to prop up an unpopular government being pressured to step down. They proceed with subtlety. Keenly attuned to the social tensions in the air, they wait until popular resistance has begun to take on the appearance of anarchy, then they do something likely to cause chaos, which in turn justifies a "salvational" intervention on their part—for the sake of (the old) order and "peace." One such incident occurred in Madagascar in 1972, when a group of young officers led by Didier Ratsiraka interceded in political events on the pretext of maintaining the peace and preserving the unity of the country. Another occurred in Congo in 1977, when a group of officers, led by Yombi Opango and Denis Sassou Nguesso, used an "attempted coup d'état" and a political shambles to rationalize the restoration of their political authority, which was threatening to slip away. The recent, violent events in Liberia bear witness to the evolution of this technique of provocation: small, radical groups attempt to increase internal social tensions whenever they believe the political authorities have failed to redress situations in which they perceive signs of a dangerous instability, a pernicious disorder.

Aware of the dangers of derailment, African peoples have learned to play with their limited freedoms. Like certain soccer players who like to play on the touchline, where the opponent's nerves are most on edge, African peoples play with the wording of laws and rules. Official bywords, slogans, speeches, leaders' verbal tics—in short, the entire vocabulary of domination—is mimicked and mocked with a rare creativity (Toulabor 1981; Mbembe 1989).

Bipolarity of the Imagination

The African imagination in which this strategy of derision unfolds is bipolar. On the one hand, it develops a sense of self-awareness and specificity, crucial if one is to avoid unwelcome surprises in the world. On the other hand, it plants the seeds of protest linked to this awareness of the self.

By becoming conscious of who and what they are, through the exploration of the movements of the soul and the process of self-discovery, Africans weigh the infinite possibilities of resistance and their capacity to oppose, for example, political authority—notorious for its violence and injustice. Although this government of the self allows them to impress their personalities on the environment, it carries with it the risk of optical illusion and self-delusion. It can, in other words, lead to an overly rigid affirmation of identity, an insularity of consciousness that may inhibit their ability to integrate themselves into the world. Inasmuch as consciousness of Africanness stems from the desire to get even with history, it is easy to understand why it has occasionally given rise to serious crises (Bouzar 1984; Coquery-Vidrovitch 1985). More than a possible inferiority complex with regard to other peoples, this delusion best explains why Africans have had such difficulty integrating themselves into modernity.

The other pole of the African imagination today is the ever-present will to undermine the social codes promulgated by all those who claim to incarnate power in its "oldest" and hence most "legitimate" form. This explains in part why young people in sub-Saharan Africa have rejected "tradition" and have adopted a defiant attitude toward the "traditional" and administrative authorities who proudly assert that they represent the legacy of the past. In fact, this seed of protest, welling up from the very bottom of the soul, is found not only among the governed but also among the governors. Thus, as soon as Abdou Diouf came to power in Senegal, he spoke of "de-Senghorizing" the state and official ideology. In Burkina Faso, Blaise Compaoré expressed the need to "rectify" the "revolution" of his "dear friend" and predecessor Thomas Sankara. In Congo, Denis Sassou Nguesso felt the need to humiliate his predecessor, Yombi Opango, by accusing him of having gotten rich off public funds. In Cameroon, Paul Biya felt obligated to make a radical break with the old order, to "de-Ahidjoize" the nation (at least at the level of discourse) at the price of a bitter fight to the death with the shadow of his predecessor. These new leaders challenged their predecessors not only for the purpose of affirming their originality and establishing the direction of their political existence but also out of a sense of loyalty to a new philosophico-cultural constant—challenging the past. Even if the desire to overthrow the old order and to destroy the image of a burdensome predecessor stems from an egocentricity, rejection itself always involves ethical principles. We throw out the theories and methods of our predecessors because we wish to do good and do better. Of course, the imperative of change, found everywhere in official discourse, does not prohibit one from returning later to the old methods, apparatus, and system.

The governed and the governors do not express the bipolarity of the African imagination in the same way. Among the people, who are not fooled by the get-even schemes and other tricks of those in power, the bipolarity is expressed through an intense need for subversion. In the West, imagination is a process in which one first denies reality, then detaches oneself from it, and finally takes flight into the unreal in order to escape the confines of existence (Sartre 1940). In Africa, it is a matter of mocking reality, of at once appropriating and subverting it so as to be able to support its crushing weight. Human consciousness does not introduce negativity into different forms of ideology in order to bracket them; instead, it pretends to accept them so as to thwart and conquer them. The "negation" is thus positive and deliberate, in the sense that it seeks in every decision pronounced by the authorities the threshold of derision at which humor may begin to work its undermining effects upon the oppressive system.

Defined above all by the effusiveness of his emotions (laughter, dance, pleasure), the Senghorian Negro gave naive minds the justification they were seeking to label all Africans hedonists. However, laughter, dance, and even to some extent pleasure are the expressions of a state of mind that refuses to be duped by the authorities. In short, they are vehicles of dissent and insubordination.

Aspects of Downright Insubordination

Let us examine, for example, African libido. The prevailing myth of African sexuality is frequently cited as proof of "structural" inability to conceptualize freedom, said to subtend Africans' vision of the world (compare Ombolo 1991). Some authors even insinuate that there is a historical background to sexual activism in sub-Saharan Africa: Robertson and Klein assert that even during the slave trade, "male slaves often preferred the acquisition of a slave or a second wife to the purchase of their freedom" (1983:6). These myths are superficial nonsense. Indeed, the way most Africans tend to approach sexuality, at least today, has nothing to do with hedonism and very little with the victimization of women so pervasive in the feminist discourse. Let us look at what I call the popular politics of sexuality, the body, and music.

A Subversive Negotiation of Libido

Literature abounds on the African origin of AIDS. The alarming rate at which it has spread in our countries is used to support the "truth" of this argument. My purpose here is not to discuss the origin of this horrible disease—does it really matter?—but I do think that the attitude of indifference toward this danger, long exhibited by the average African, tells us several things. Beyond the mediocrity of the discourse, which limited the impact of the campaigns for the prevention of AIDS run by the ministries of public health, the instructions given by the government were so weak that few people regarded AIDS as a serious threat. In working-class bars in

Douala, for example, I heard people—not all alcoholics—say that "this AIDS thing" was "just one more invention of whites" (those in power are their agents) to keep them from fully enjoying the good things in life. Condoms? Ridiculous objects designed to take all the pleasure out of sex—"fucking without coming." Another conspiracy theory, in fact.

Of course, no one would seriously endorse this view. I merely wish to observe that the manner in which these people react to information that is supposed to terrify them is proof of their profound desire to free themselves of the dictatorship of the Other, to take responsibility for their own lives, and to affirm, without fear, what they take to be their own paradigm, their own way of life. In my judgment, this predisposition is interesting in and of itself and is indicative of real mental progress being made, however maladroit it may be. Seen as a process of self-affirmation, this attitude lies at the root of democratic production. In fact, people changed their minds very quickly as soon as the message of prevention came from opinion leaders they trusted. In 1987, for instance, the very popular Zairean artist Franco released an album called *AIDS*, raising public awareness of the scope of the disease and promoting prevention. By any account, his campaign was much more successful in central Africa than all the previous governmental actions in that domain. There is something to be learned here for policymakers who design and implement policy in countries where state officials are mistrusted.

The Body as a Space for the Expression of Freedom

This profound desire for freedom is likewise found in the African approach to the body. Travel journals and ethnological and anthropological studies on Africa often describe the "nonchalance," the "relaxed attitude," the "laxity," and the "passivity" of Africans. But few analysts have seen along with N'diaye the ethical dimension operative in the relationship to the body: "Its image is not appallingly subordinated here to the injustice of passing time," she writes. "Since the obsession with youth is not eating at one's mind, the body is at ease; it ages in peace" (1984:30).

Whereas Westerners have a tendency to feel guilty if they have neglected their bodies too long (Fedida 1977; Reichler 1983; Ceronetti 1984), Africans feel comfortable with their bodies. Regardless of its state, the body is never seen as obscene or repugnant. It is neither held in contempt nor exalted; it just is. This attitude of contentment explains why fashion trends, covered in women's magazines and eternally celebrating the cult of thinness, have never had much of an impact in African countries. Of course, young women (most notably, high school and college students) sometimes buy into the myth of the "perfect figure"—but usually not for long. The influence of this imported aesthetics transmitted through fashion magazines always loses out to the dispositions of the local imagination. In Senegal, N'diaye remarks:

> The body is clothed and it moves. Its crumbling, thick, worn flesh becomes almost lascivious beneath the fabric. It is a moving form, beautiful in its slow, forward motion. The fleshiness of the hips is a continuation of the movement, rolling above the step and softening it. The flabbiness of the relaxed flesh is completely transformed into sensuality. It dissipates into languor and forms a sort of alluring aura around this slightly ankylosed corpulence. The well-fed stomach produces a sort of expansiveness and provides a reified image of security (1984:31).

Not surprisingly, a pot belly—an "administrative stomach,"—is perceived as the first criterion of success, desired over other external signs of prosperity (the so-called three Cs: cars, castles, checkbooks).[6] Some of the biggest stars of African music disregard completely the ideology of the "perfect figure," many falling well short of any official standard of physical beauty. Zairean artists Luambo Makiadi (Franco), Tabu Ley Rochereau, and Abeti Masikini, the famous Ivoirian singer Aïcha Koné, Cameroonian Annie Disco, and many others feel comfortable living with what might be perceived as obesity. In Africa, there has never been a need to develop slogans along the lines of "Men prefer them fat" for women to feel comfortable with a few rolls of fat.

This will to live on one's own terms underscores the desire to shake up a social order in which one is not at ease, to participate, in other words, in the elaboration of an informal system of resistance. Of this emergence of a mode of democratic production, N'diaye proclaims:

> I saw there emaciated, toothless old women cover themselves in gold without shame; I saw withered skin the grain of which caught the light from beneath the powder; women deformed by multiple pregnancies transformed into Black Virgins as soon as they had donned the heavy fabrics they had chosen with care. But I also saw silly, sweet little faces change into Nefertiti through the magic of a hairstyle completed in two or three gestures. Finally, I saw mouths illuminated by a fascinating smile where two incisors of solid gold rested on a lip painted with indelible henna (1984:32–33).

One must not read these remarks as a mere celebration of the aesthetics of sensuality. One must also grasp within the attitude governing this behavior the desire of Africans to free themselves of the established discourse on beauty and choose their own look, as well as the tenacious survival of a pride demanding legitimate recognition and a better reception in the social order. In these cases, the more one's dress is nonconformist, the more one's attitude toward the body departs from the commonly accepted norms, the more one's sense of freedom and power is affirmed. The tremendous popular success of the Zairean singing duo Pépé Kallé and Emoro is largely due to the fact that one is huge and the other is tiny. Obesity and dwarfism come together here, shake up the (supposed) dogmas of the social order, and express new forms of harmony, freedom, and originality.

Music as a Vehicle for Greater Mental Welfare

One could cite endless instances of insubordination hidden behind everyday actions in black Africa. Take the example of Cameroonian soccer player Roger Milla. In the middle of the 1990 World Cup games, he executed a few dance steps after scoring the decisive goals that advanced the Cameroonian national team to a round of competition never before reached by an African team. Many commentators saw this as a typical outburst of instinctive African "emotion"—expressive gestures of pleasure, as it were, against a *makossa* backdrop (Delbourg 1991). But it ought to be seen as a noble affirmation of his dignity (Monga 1990b).

There is also the example of such singers as Nigerian Fela Anikulapo Kuti and Cameroonian Lapiro de Mbanga, who use music "as a weapon" to denounce political and social injustice. The reaction of the international media to their songs has been to regard the singers' eccentricity as nothing but showbiz, part of their image. As for social scientists, either they know nothing of this phenomenon or they perform superficial readings of the musical structure and the lyrics, lamenting all the while its hybrid modernity so little in keeping with the long and rich history of African music. It was only when Fela Anikulapo Kuti was imprisoned by the Nigerian government on the false pretext of currency smuggling that the research community began to take an interest in his work.[7] Likewise, Western musicologists began to analyze Lapiro de Mbanga's music only after he came out publicly against the government during a political trial.[8] As if the ethics of their message and the aesthetics of their music were not enough to stir up any enthusiasm for their work.

It is self-deluding to ignore the new ontology to which these artists subscribe simply because they have departed from tradition and the usual framework of exotic song. On the one hand, song in Africa has always been a vehicle of access to reality and a medium for the celebration of the possibility of a greater mental welfare. On the other, and even if one accepts the hypothetical existence of an intact cultural heritage from which each artist is to draw his authenticity, no one lives on memory alone. History is not univocal; thus, it is erroneous to believe that one can classify into neat, historically dated strata all the inspirations and tendencies that belong to the history of music. As the musicologist Haim has written: "By defining his own memory, the composer withdraws from tradition in general, before redefining himself in terms of it, before confusing it with that which it must become. It is in this sense that the composer invents his life even as his language pokes holes in the past, pierces it, selects it from the memory he has of it, from the historical unsaid that he brings up to date, the new writing he elaborates" (1990:4). The principle stated here has been applied in the West and has allowed for the sociopolitical validation of the most original forms of music. Unfortunately, those who have taken an interest in the emergence of new artistic trends in Africa's countries have failed to give it serious consideration. The evolutionist viewpoint, which holds that African music must develop in the "right direction," must be abandoned in favor of a less authoritarian type of analysis, for henceforth it is a matter of understanding what is being expressed by art's diversity and integrating the questions it raises into the general framework of society's present needs and demands.

Problematic Mixes and the Threshold of Effective Disorder

If it is true that the establishment in sub-Saharan Africa of democracy, whose minimal legal principles are far from being accepted by those in power (Toulabor 1991), cannot be limited to a simple improvement in the technical mechanisms involved in the alternation of power—a multiparty system, free elections, separation of powers, etc.—it is nevertheless necessary to point out that the emergence of modes of democratic production by way of everyday acts in everyday life is not a guarantee of their quality. In fact, it is necessary to reflect seriously on the ways and means to deal with these resistance techniques once a democratic system has been established. Policymakers must, therefore, anticipate the issue of disenchantment by both integrating the psychoaffective dimension in their strategies and adopting a dual approach to the design of the new political technology that is needed in Africa.

Integrating the Psychoaffective Dimension

The various methods of civil disobedience described earlier are effective and useful as long as authoritarian regimes are in place; however, when a democratic regime takes over, and when the time comes for people to regain the "normal" patterns of civic life, the transition to a democratic behavior might be difficult. In countries such as Mali, Niger, Benin, Congo, or Zambia, people were used to "disorder"; they enjoyed doing only what they wanted, and reluctantly agreed to return to a "regular" citizenship, that is, showing respect for the state and the democratically elected officials, complying with laws, rules, and regulations, paying their taxes, and taking care of public goods.

In Africa, more than elsewhere, it is necessary to include in the democratization process people's propensity to use the imagination for the invention of methods of resistance. There is always the risk that extremist groups, hoping to see the liberation process fail, will succeed in derailing the system. In such a case, the asymptote, the threshold of effectiveness where popular resistance takes on the appearance of anarchy, has been crossed and the mechanisms stemming from the collective will to subvert reality give way to uncontrollable disorder.

This risk exists as a result of the fact that a psychoaffective dimension is present in every social phenomenon and often fuels confusion, especially in an environment as plastic as the one in which African societies are evolving. If we wish to avoid this risk, the emergence of the democratic process must involve simultaneously the establishment of a viable institutional structure and the existence of a well-directed public consciousness. In other words, the informal systems of resistance and the modes of democratic production I have described are in no way a substitute for authentic democratic systems. Even if Africa's peoples continually invent spaces of freedom in order to arm themselves against the totalitarian impulse of the powers around them, the classical mechanisms for the protection of rights (separation of powers) and the media for the expression of dissent (freedom of the press) must retain their full credibility. Although these informal systems may be effective, they nevertheless remain palliatives of effectiveness, often problematic ones, given that they have yet to be codified and do not always succeed in transcending the emotional register in which they have developed. As Braud has said: "The now little disputed superiority of pluralist democracies over authoritarian and totalitarian regimes is not the result of the triumph of their ideological principles. If there has been an institutional consolidation (it is in fact remarkable), it is because of their superior ability to manage, without stifling them, the emotional energies that run throughout society" (1991:15)

Toward a Dual Approach

The ability of African systems of informal resistance to codify and amalgamate in a positive way the enthusiasm of African peoples—their creativity, emotions, frustrations, fears, and anger—and to generate safety valves so as to consolidate the modes of democratic production found in the microactions of everyday life is still too weak for us to content ourselves with. If we admit the necessity of conceiving democracy's progression in sub-Saharan Africa as the conceptualization of two parallel phenomena (rationalization of the operation of classical institutions and codification of the modes of informal resistance), the problem that remains to be solved is how to harmonize the aspects of this dual approach. Simultaneous to the construction of a classical democratic framework—a task that can be seriously undertaken only within the context of some kind of national forum, that is, a meeting wherein the main political actors of a country design the rules of the political game and reach a consensus on the balance of power among the main institutions—it is necessary to federate the centrifugal forces now competing in society and transform them into constructive energies.

If Africa wishes to rid itself permanently of unenlightened political systems, to come out from under the yoke of pseudoindependence and reach an optimal social equilibrium, then it will need more than politicians and jurists familiar with the intricacies of parliamentary or presidential governments. It will also require bold theorists of a new sociality capable of evaluating the positivity hidden behind the most anodyne acts and channeling this positivity into a clearly defined goal. It must produce people who will catalyze disorder, who will elaborate concepts incorporating the unsaid of the psychological environment and local culture—at once rich and in a state of ruin. This, of course, is not an easy task, for Africans are gravitating in a sphere of problematic mixes, where the threshold of effective action is particularly unstable. Theory is not linear in Africa, and every hypothesis must be relativized, in time as well as in space.

The idea is far from utopian provided Africans arm themselves with two principles: First, they must free themselves of the paradigm of collapse, which informs most prospective analyses of African societies and falsifies the terms of the debate on the future of democracy on the continent. The theme of Africa's decadence, which has loomed like a destiny in the Western press over the past few years, feeds upon the stereotypes to which lovers of ideological commodities like to refer. If it is denounced, it will allow Africa's peoples to become subjects of their own history and no longer the object of other people's generous and sordid fantasies. Next, one must abandon the intellectual mind-set of "disconnection." Though some hang on to the illusion that it is possible to "leave the world," to develop the myth of an insular African consciousness, and to isolate the continent from the rest of the world (Amin 1991), this does not correspond to the reality of the present era. Africa can and must construct its integration into the world, because the world is now a global village.

Notes

1. My view of passive resistance is similar to that of Shehadeh (1983), describing certain forms of Palestinian silent resistance in the Middle East in the 1970s and early 1980s.

2. Eboussi Boulaga, interview.

3. See also Snitow et al. (1984) and Roitman (1994).

4. Plato's equation for political decadence was: *Satiety + Immoderation = Disaster.* One can hardly use his equation to explain Africa's problem today, unless we redefine *satiety,* and we apply it to something other than material welfare.

5. Duval (1985) provides an interesting monography of a specific case of west African traditional conservatism.

6. I borrowed this phrase from the Zairean journalist Ekanga Shungu.

7. See Kpatindé (1990) for a synthetic account of Fela's struggle with the Nigerian government over foreign exchange issues in the 1980s.

8. On de Mbanga's role during my trial in Cameroon in 1991, see Chapter 3.

5

DEMOCRACY AND THE POLITICS OF THE SACRED

Etre intelligent, c'est savoir être con chaque fois que cela est nécessaire.

*

Being intelligent means knowing to act stupid whenever necessary.

—Robert Monga, Cameroon

And God in all of this?[1] No one undertaking to analyze political transformations in Africa today can fail to ask this question. The resurgence of God—"*L'enjeu de Dieu,*" as Eboussi Boulaga (1991) puts it, or, more generally, the proliferation of the sacred (Mbembe 1992)—has been one of the principal determinants of the present ferment. Its impact on society may well decide the future of fledgling democracies and economies in sub-Saharan Africa.

My purpose is not to detail the various beliefs held by the populations of Africa at the end of this millennium. Rather, I want to explore various aspects of what might be termed the explosion of the sacred throughout the continent. Some regard this as a positive phenomenon (religion energizes and unites people), others as a negative one (it may have pernicious effects during this period of political change), but no one denies its existence and importance. Whether Christians, Muslims, or animists, young or old, men or women, rich or poor, the religious now constitute the largest sector of society in Africa. Prayers, rites, and acts of atonement are the most regular activities of a significant fraction of the population.

The first section of this chapter outlines the various manifestations of the quest for meaning, which is always part of everyday life in Africa. The second section explores the main determinants of the recent explosion of the sacred in Africa. The third section highlights some of the dangers of fatalism and nihilism behind such a phenomenon. The fourth section analyzes the various ways in which African political entrepreneurs are politicizing God and the devil.

The Ever-Present Quest for Meaning

How is one to interpret the religious boom in Africa? The first problem one encounters is the scope of definition. Where does religion begin and where does it end? Is it possible to establish a line of demarcation between the political dimension and spiritual activity? And when one is dealing with Africa, where more social activity is hidden from view (the "invisible") than seen (the "visible") (Bahoken 1967; Wiredu 1980), should one analyze all the various dimensions of religious activity—what is said, done, and demanded—or confine oneself to what the naked eye observes and might eventually measure?

Some writers have rightly underscored the "puzzle" of religion's vitality in the world today (Wald 1992:2). But with respect to Africa, one may discount from the outset the rhetoric of secularization, which takes the decline of religious influence as a given and has long influenced thinking on the interplay between religion and politics in industrialized countries (Glasner 1977:chap. 2). The same goes for any "culture of disbelief" of the kind described by Carter (1993) with reference to the United States.

The idea of a religious decline in Africa is even more implausible if one considers the fact that there has been no uniform process of secularization on the continent. The notion of *differentiation*, implying the withdrawal of religion from such areas of public policy as law, education, and health, varies greatly from one country to the next. Indeed, in the largely Islamic nations of North Africa, the Sahel, or even the Horn of Africa, some politicians have promoted the idea of an identical religious and social order. The civil war in the Sudan is the most striking and painful example of this type of futile effort to use faith as a vehicle for forcibly homogenizing a recalcitrant social mix. The Djiboutian penal law code (the *Xeer* of the Issas), as well as education standards in Senegal, Guinea, Mali, or Niger, is based on leaders' interpretations of the Koran (Magassouba 1985).

Religion, moreover, is not thought of as a strictly personal matter. The religious diversity found in most countries explains why even the most cynical leaders have had difficulty imposing a state religion. The most skillful (Morocco's Hassan II, for example) have managed to elevate themselves to the legal status of "Commander of the Faithful" in order to ward off subversive interpretations of the Koran by Islamic fundamentalists. This is possible in a country where more than 95 percent of the population is Muslim. In countries where the three major monotheistic religions (Christianity, Judaism, and Islam) compete with animism and other belief systems, things prove more difficult. Politicians in such places attempt to control or seduce religious leaders, alternating between the carrot and the stick. Religious leaders are either courted by those in power—as well as by those who hope to replace them—or are fiercely attacked when they publicly express divergent opinions (Haynes 1994).

The powerful influence of the irrational (*l'enflure de l'irrationnel*) against which Etounga-Manguelle rails (1990), is not, of course, confined to Africa. As numerous writers have noted, the religious impulse is a constant of the human spirit, "a defensive reaction of nature against the dissolvant power of intelligence" (Bergson 1932). "In order that man (the individual) might not concern himself first with the burdens society imposes upon him, and might not allow the idea of death to slow down the movement of life within him, it was at once necessary for religion to impose upon him taboos and gods and to promise him life after death."[2] Humankind's desire for an intimate relationship with the gods remains one of our oldest instincts, something philosophers and anthropologists of religion have yet to "explain." If Max Weber's work (1920/1921) distinguished between ritual, salvational, and soteriological religions, it also underscored the extreme complexity and diversity of the religious phenomenon—and thus the impossibility of comprehending the multiplicity of its dimensions. Generally speaking, the difficulty of capturing the essence of the sacred and determining its root causes is consubstantial with thought on the subject. As Sarrazin has remarked, "We hesitate to utilize this worn-out concept [the sacred], which has fallen into disuse among ethnologists because, in religious phenomenology and positivist sociology, it was intimately linked to the religious, a means for the one to regard as sacred an imaginary psyche, for the other to dump into the 'rubbish bin of the irrational' everything in man that was not reducible to positivist reason—the sacred was good for the savages" (1991:11).

Even if one defines the sacred as the sum total of the social practices and actions that are tied to the range of belief systems in current practice, one is still faced with the difficulty of conceptualizing a configuration that would allow one to comprehend its various aspects.[3] To begin with, there is the problem of the age-old quest for the sacred, common to all men. As Boyer has observed, "Worship, prayer, offerings, sacrifices, thanksgiving, and commemorations may be expressed in a variety of ways in different eras and places.... It is the customs, the mentalities, and the modes of conceptualization that differ. Not their object" (1992:17).

Though they did not possess modern technical knowledge, primitive human beings also had a set of values and a need for transcendence. Africa is not the only place where veneration and sublimation are among the deepest human instincts, but their present intensity on the continent is tied to a series of crises. The traditional quest for meaning (the desire to go beyond everyday banality, to struggle against the absurd, to give purpose to life) was upset by the implosion of social structures brought on by the economic crisis. Caught in a whirlwind of structural adjustments and a chaotic process of democratization, people have turned to a pantheon of old and new gods to give meaning to their lives.

The Explosion of the Sacred: Root Causes

To explain the religious boom, leaders of religious movements generally point to the disintegration of social bonds, most notably the erosion of the family as spiritual anchor. Weakened by a tremendous loss in purchasing power and an unprecedented rate of unemployment, the African family has grown more inflexible even as it decomposes (Ngandu Nkashama 1990). Though it lacks the financial means that once made it possible to endorse and maintain a certain social order—in sum, to legitimate its existence—the family nevertheless remains totalitarian, assigning roles and responsibilities to each of its members. The collective misery and suffering have not clarified and facilitated relationships among family members; rather, they have exacerbated the overweening presence of the family clan.

Every family member seeks to escape the pressure cooker, to revolt, to find his or her own way. But insofar as freedom is always difficult to manage, the individual who cuts family ties painfully attempts to establish new relationships with others by becoming involved in social organizations. In the absence of professional associations, which might stimulate and channel the sense of belonging to the same socioprofessional group, these organizations have generally revolved around politics or religion. Part of their tremendous success may be attributed to the breakdown of lines of transmission between generations, a consequence of the crisis of the family. Having received nothing in the way of political, economic, cultural, or even symbolic capital from their parents, the young have at their disposal only vague beliefs, common mores. The fragility of their value systems allows them to fall prey easily to the allure and illusory power of religious dogma—reinforced by a well-developed marketing strategy for rallying the faithful—which helps them define themselves and put their subjectivity into some sort of perspective.[4]

At a more general level, the weakness of the individual's relationship with other members of the community has augmented the thirst for the sacred, causing more and more Africans to take the plunge into the abyss of new utopias. The crisis of the family has been further aggravated by the obsolescence of traditional forms of knowledge. The world is evolving at such a frantic pace that parents are no longer able to contribute significantly to their children's upbringing. The basics of elementary education, love, contraception, and disease appear to escape adults, who are often stuck in their ways and resistant to change.

In this environment of perpetual conceptual change, the young are not the only ones in a state of confusion. Because of their social condition and the myths that justify their marginalization, women, too, have been painfully affected by the current transformations. Forced to contend with the simultaneous omnipresence and instability of the African family, they desperately attempt to fit innumerable obligations into their schedule. They take care of the home and the housework, earn an income, deal with the budget, savings, and investments, negotiate tensions among family members, and ensure the multiple connections between city and village. They have little time for dreams and are often deprived of that minimal amount of solitude that every human being requires.

Not surprisingly, women more than men feel as if their lives are passing them by. They frequently suffer from depression and, in an effort to escape the ordeals of daily life, have enrolled in massive numbers in the fledgling sports and arts programs the leisure industry has begun to organize in large cities. More than the loneliness of the elderly in rural areas, the confusion of women, and its corollaries (emotional bankruptcy, sexual frustration), is the principal threat to the stability of social structures in sub-Saharan Africa today.

No sooner had women escaped arranged marriages and obligatory procreation than they were forced into the preestablished role of wife, mother, maid-of-all-work. Condemned to a state of economic dependency, a result of unemployment and especially of the limits society has assigned to their physical and intellectual capacities, women have had to adopt a role that does not suit them and resign themselves to their fate. They are expected to conform to a certain image and to confine themselves to the space the present sociocultural order has carved out for them. Inequitable and repressive, the African family has thus driven its principal constituents (the young, women) to seek peace and solitude elsewhere. At this moment of structural transition, the manner in which the family operates fans the flames of the collective desire for the sacred.

The need for the irrational is also fed in school and in the workplace, where the myth-making function of the sacred, which Bergson so brilliantly analyzed, blossoms. Here secret ambition, jealousy, and passion unfold. Individual energy, thought to be insufficient to achieve one's goals, is supplemented by a moral stimulant—religious fervor. In certain cases, its infinite powers break down ordinary social, ethnic, and economic barriers. Thus, every Sunday, Cameroonians are amused to find the most notorious white-collar criminals in their country seated in the front pews of churches in Douala and Yaoundé. Some of them even join the church choir, making sure their voices are heard above the rest, especially if there is a camera around, as if they feel the need to absolve themselves of their sins.

Touré and Konaté related with humor and delight how Ivoirian president Félix Houphouët-Boigny's announcement of a plan to restructure the ministries set off a serious crisis of legitimacy within the governing class, accompanied by a noticeable increase in the practice of paganism and an exponential increase in offerings: "Thursday, September 28, 1989, The Presidential Palace. After having patiently listened to twenty-three orators rooting out one by one all the evils the Ivory Coast has been made to suffer, the President proclaimed: 'On October 15, I will restructure the ministries!' The room was jubilant, the applause was thunderous, the rest of the speech was barely heard. They were looking for scape goats, they had found them. They wanted sacrifices, they were going to get them" (1990:13).

Sacrifice, an essential dimension of religion and the ultimate step in the quest for the sacred, takes on much importance here. It serves both as the foundation of a somewhat baroque system for the transfer of wealth and as the guarantor of a social order whose three functions (psychoreligious, political, and economic) have been conflated. "Between September 28 and October 15, calculations, worries, insomnia.... Even the most important state officials can't get a good night's sleep. Secret meetings, a sacrificial war: on the one side, there's the big boss who is looking for sacrificial victims; on the other, there are the little bosses who refuse to be sacrificed. Upsurge in the activities of the divinities, more than ever implored. In the intersections of Abidjan and elsewhere, the number of sacrifices offered up to them!" (1990:13).

The size of the sacrifice being directly proportional to the intensity of the entreaties and supplications, thirteen ministers were eventually let go, in spite of all their sacrifices. But in the meantime, thanks to all their offerings (animals, cereals, money, etc.), the poor would have had a feast and become accustomed to their lot. The principles that have contributed to the success of paganism and other religious syncretisms in black Africa are found here: the anchoring in the here and now and the absence of perspectives on the afterlife; the limited desire for transcendence; and the rejection of the usual dichotomies between the spirit and the body, knowledge and faith, etc. The imperative of effectiveness is the only guideline. Thus, some of the "faithful" go from one prayer group or spiritual movement to another, until they feel they have satisfied their immediate need for serenity.

Faith and the Dictatorship of Destiny

Throughout Africa, the failure of the state—once thought of as omnipotent and now incapable of offering its citizens even a minimal level of comfort—along with the general shipwreck of society, has given rise to new networks for the management of the sacred. The business of these unregulated authorities is the production of myths, symbols, and rituals packed with meaning and designed to ease the tensions of everyday life, to reduce anxiety about an uncertain future, to exorcise fears, and to chase away pain. It is a faith industry in which the dictatorship of the idea of destiny occasionally holds sway.

As Augé has aptly remarked, "Man never approaches the gods with free hands and a clear head" (1982:50). To date, the role played by religious and spiritual organizations in Africa's sociopolitical transformations has varied greatly and has sometimes proved marginal. In the future, however, their role is almost certain to grow. The interminable economic crisis and the implosion of social structures feed psychological insecurity and increase the membership of religious and parareligious organizations. Savvy politicians attempt if not to control this collective need for the irrational, then at least to exploit it to their advantage.

In the past few years, the media have called attention to the increased presence of religious leaders on the political stage—Islamic leaders in north Africa and the Sahel countries, Catholic priests in west and central Africa, and leaders of traditional religious communities in the south. The intervention of leaders of parareligious and religious communities into political life has occasionally puzzled researchers and has been interpreted in a number of ways. But Berque's analysis of the emergence of ayatollahs in Iranian politics provides a straightforward explanation of what is happening in sub-Saharan Africa today:

> Should one impute, as some have done, the fall of the Shah of Iran to the "return of the sacred" into politics? No, but to the use of religious language for the expression of demands, the same there as elsewhere, though more intense and compressed. But why such a use, one might ask, rather than a reliance on the apparently tested procedures of political parties? That is the real question. The answer to it hinges, on the one hand, upon the brutal perfection with which the classical forces of opposition had been crushed in this country. But, on the other hand, it surely hinges upon the long misunderstood or distorted possibilities of Islam (1980:61).

Berque's reading of the religious origins of the Iranian revolution is similar to Simone's analysis of political Islam in Sudan (1994). It makes two important points that may be applied to black Africa: First, it suggests that the flourishing of paganism on the continent may be attributed to authoritarianism. Second, it indicates the need for a careful analysis of the workings of belief systems in current practice.

In undertaking such an analysis, one must not be too quick to celebrate the political virtues of the rise of the sacred. The thirst for the sacred can lead not only to trivialized forms of spirituality but also to the emergence of immoral and perverted gods able to exploit a feeling of tragic fatalism. Already in Senegal, which incarnates the pseudomodel of good government that France invented for its former colonies, the mullahs of the Mourid and Tidjan sects have essentially co-opted the people's desire for freedom (Magassouba 1985). This may be explained by the fact that the quest for meaning in each citizen takes expression in a contradictory form, one in which the need for transcendence is conflated with the imperative of well-being in the here and now. As a result, religious leaders have little difficulty promoting the idea of household gods and the existence of a relationship between the lives of the faithful and the workings of the celestial powers. Credulity and suffering become a breeding ground for a populist version of spirituality.

This view of the world can have terrible consequences insofar as it risks disrupting the lines and channels of communication within society. If religious North African fundamentalism seems far away, the threat of a deliberate use of the spiritual for political purposes is present in some countries. Cameroon is the most notable example, as Fisiy (1990) and Fisiy and Geschiere (1990) have amply demonstrated. The reduction of all events to the workings of divine powers leads to fatalism. In the hands of a few religious leaders, who conflate the temporal and the spiritual and act either in their own material interest or on behalf of the urban or political elite, with whom they have formed an alliance, fear and ingenuousness become useful tools for the management of society.

Will Africans end up calling upon the power of marabouts, inspired prophets, or sorcerers to organize democratization and the education of the masses? Will the validity of public policy adopted in sub-Saharan Africa soon come to depend on the degree of spirituality it exhibits? This is the paradoxical situation in which African societies find themselves at the end of this millennium. But African politicians did not stop to answer any of these questions before taking the plunge into the religious field and making it a part of politics.

The Politics of God and the Devil

Even if every major social player has desperately tried to gain politically from the explosion of the religious and the parareligious, the grand prize for originality of goals and methods goes to the politicians in power. Their strategy is twofold. They attempt to co-opt religion itself, occupy its turf, confiscate the idea of God, and thus take over the space in which the people's quest for absolution finds expression. This is the politics of God.

When this method does not produce the desired results, they call upon the forces of evil, the powers of darkness, deeply rooted in the African imagination. This is the politics of the devil.

The Politics of God

Even in the turbulent atmosphere of the ongoing democratization process, African politicians are adept at inventing methods to maintain power. Here follow some of the ways in which they have exploited religion to this end:

1. Religion as a means of legitimation: Always and everywhere, political power has been tied to divine power and to all forms of power expressed through symbols, for power is above all representation. Thus, religion provides politicians with a host of symbols and vehicles through which they might express their power and vividly impress it on people's minds. As Kertzer has so astutely observed, "To understand the political process,... it is necessary to understand how the symbolic enters into politics, how political actors consciously and unconsciously manipulate symbols, and how this symbolic dimension relates to the material bases of political power.... Political reality is in good part created through symbolic means.... Creating a symbol or, more commonly, identifying oneself with a popular symbol can be a potent means of gaining and keeping power, for the hallmark of power is the construction of reality" (1988:2–5).

In Africa, the politics of God is above all a vehicle for reconstructing reality, a means of legitimating power that stems from brute force rather than the ballot box, a way of polishing up the tarnished image of the most brutal regimes. In short, the cult of the gods allows those in power to regenerate themselves and to restore their image in the eyes of populations generally ready to forgive them—for forgiveness is the goal of African society. Thus, dictators are quick to use religion to their advantage and to mingle with the most prominent religious leaders. This frenetic quest for sanctification sometimes borders on the grotesque. Hence, whenever Pope John Paul II visits the continent, the heads of state who receive him thoroughly exploit the event for political gain. Zaire's Mobutu Sese Seko had photos of the Holy Father blessing his family distributed worldwide in an effort to show his people that the pope approved of his regime. Deliberately dressed in the traditional formal costume of his native region, Togo's Gnassingbe Eyadema appeared everywhere with the pope and even insisted that he be "initiated" into local ritual ceremonies. Cameroon's Paul Biya carefully positioned family members around the pope, then presented him with a newborn infant from Biya's second marriage. The ceremony was broadcast on national television and received wide coverage in the press. The idea, once again, was to show to the world the Vatican's recognition of his authority, widely contested after the rigged elections of 1992. In Kenya, Daniel arap Moi did much the same thing.

2. The nourishment of fatalism: Nothing is more useful to a head of state than to divert attention from the government's incompetence and the true causes of the nation's economic and political difficulties. Studies have shown that wars are occasionally used as a means of reducing internal tensions (de Mesquita et al. 1992; Rummel 1979). But like their counterparts elsewhere, African heads of state rarely have convenient outside enemies who might serve as sparring partners in a premeditated war and provide them with the opportunity for a heroic battle for the fatherland—a battle that is worth fighting only if one is sure to win, and if it makes citizens focus on something other than the mediocre performance of their leaders. The cult of the diverse forms in which the quest for spirituality takes expression is a life buoy: Convincing the population that the world is controlled by divine powers beyond the scope of the human mind becomes an effective political strategy. In countries where public revenues come primarily from the sale of raw materials, the people are often called upon to pray to God not only to make it rain but to make the price of cocoa beans and coffee go up in international markets. In churches in Yaoundé, Abidjan, or Nairobi, the explicit aim of some sermons is to ward off the global economic crisis, the "enemy of the nation" that politicians in power never cease to rail against. By invoking supernatural forces to end the economic crisis, leaders exploit the faith of their fellow citizens and nourish a subtle form of fatalism. The responsibility for their failures is transferred to "the sinister logic of world markets," and citizens put up with their misery, return to their prayers, and wait for things to get better. In a word, this is an emotional holdup.

3. Faith as a strategy for absolution: The sacred may also serve to "rejuvenate" African politicians. Given that forgiveness is the goal of African society, a good way to obtain it is to identify oneself with God in the collective imagination. Beyond the moral authority such a position affords, there is the implicit benefit of forgiveness itself. For example, Félix Houphouët-Boigny, Côte d'Ivoire's former president, saw the construction of the world's largest basilica in his native village as the most effective means of restoring his image. His reasoning was that even if his political opponents managed to convince the population of his failures and political and economic crimes, no one could really remain angry at him, because the construction of a cathedral guaranteed him a place in heaven. What African could hold a grudge against a man who, however sinful, spent a large part of his fortune, and the rest of his life, building churches? Numerous leaders throughout the continent reason in the same way. To secure the people's forgiveness, high state officials make it a point to participate in spiritual activities. During the day, they go about their brutal business, doing whatever it takes—force, coercion, bribery—to stay in power. But at night they head for churches, mosques, and other places of prayer, stationing themselves in the front rows where they can be seen by the cameras and the people. Who could really despise the head of the secret police, responsible for the deaths of thousands of fellow citizens but regularly in attendance at all sorts of public prayer meetings? Who could be angry at the former finance minister and banker, a notorious embezzler of public funds but always at mass on Sundays? Or at the CEO of state-run television who transforms himself into an exuberant and humorous choir director after bombarding the audience with official propaganda?

4. The construction and renewal of social networks: African politicians are likewise interested in the resurgence of religion insofar as it provides them with an invaluable means of access to the souls of their constituents. In light of the ineffectiveness of such traditional organizations as political parties, unions, and socioprofessional associations, politicians have difficulty keeping abreast of the dreams, anxieties, and demands of the "electorate." Their information cannot come from major political gatherings, which celebrate the virtues of unanimity and the status quo and make hypocritical "motions of support" for the dictator in place. Not duped by their constituents' public show of admiration, politicians use the secret police and religious and parareligious organizations to stay informed of public opinion. The cult of the sacred is one of the few reliable networks in which the bottom can communicate with the top and vice versa. As such, it is an amazing source of power, a large communication network to be controlled. Priests, imams, and leaders of various sects pass on to the people the gospel from on high (not from the heavens but from the presidential palace) and bring back to the leaders the public's primary concerns.

For African leaders, putting the idea of God to good political use has a number of advantages: it allows one to sanctify one's actions, to reduce the possibility of faith being used as a vehicle for protest, and to elevate oneself to the level of director of social conscience, the best remedy against the emergence of uncontrollable forms of religious extremism.

The Politics of the Devil

African politics also allows for more violent, destructive, and perverse uses of the sacred—those that stem from politicians' cynical manipulation of the prevalent, indigenous belief in the powers of darkness. One has only to read the African press to see that the integration of the invisible realm into politics is widespread. On the one hand, illegitimate leaders attempt to appropriate the sacred not only to distinguish themselves positively but also to distinguish themselves negatively in the eyes of their constituents. On the other hand, the public, increasingly credulous as a result of the economic crisis, buys into the myths concerning the existence of supernatural forces in the political arena and, more generally, the idea that evil forces control the continent.

The current situation can be summed up in a pithy phrase: The devil is back in African politics. This pleases African leaders, for the public's belief in the devil, able to manipulate at will the powers of evil, gives them a relative advantage in the confrontation that the very act of governing implies. They are delighted to claim that they have the protection of the gods and the backing of the devil. The effectiveness of this double strategy can be measured by the extent to which the occult has penetrated the African imagination (World Values Surveys 1990–1991).

Of course, a sociopolitical analysis of the idea of the devil and, more generally, of the role played by forces of darkness in social life is a serious affair and warrants a few preliminary remarks. As Parrinder has written, "Belief in witchcraft is one of the great fears from which mankind has suffered.... In modern Africa, [it] is a great tyranny spreading panic and death" (1958:9).

It is necessary to clearly define one's terms to avoid falling into the trap of words with multiple meanings—semantic quarrels abound in studies on faith and superstition. Insofar as I am concerned with the authorities who produce and manage the idea of evil in African political life, I will adopt Evans-Pritchard's distinction between the techniques of witchcraft, which fulfills an essentially positive social function along the lines of psychiatry, and the bad magic of sorcerers per se, who engage in black magic and generally intend to do harm.

> There is much loose discussion about witchcraft. We must distinguish between bad magic (or sorcery) and witchcraft. Many African peoples distinguish clearly between the two and for ethnological purposes we must do the same (1935:22).

> A witch performs no rite, utters no spell, and possesses no medicine. An act of witchcraft is a psychic act. The sorcerer, on the other hand, may make magic to kill his neighbours. The magic will not kill them but he can, and no doubt often does, make it with that intention (1937:21).

Prudence is also in order because human history is filled with its share of witch-hunts. Works devoted to the genealogy of the idea of evil have recounted the often bloody consequences of intolerance and accusations of sorcery and black magic that people have leveled at one another since the end of the Middle Ages and the beginning of the Renaissance, a phenomenon that was exacerbated by Pope Innocent VIII's publication in 1484 of the encyclical *Summis Desirantes,* declaring war on sorcerers (Notestein 1911; Davies 1947).

Things are different in the African political scene today. The intervention of the devil and his avatars in political life (the use of occult techniques to conceptualize evil, to combat either one's ideological adversaries or one's rivals in the same camp, and to achieve political objectives) is a constant, at once desired and exploited by political players. For a number of years, one of the most influential men in west and central Africa was a marabout known as M. Cissé, who benefited from the favors of numerous high officials and was the unofficial adviser of the presidents of Benin, Mali, and Gabon. Because he had served in this capacity, he was arrested and sentenced by the new Malian government that came to power after the democratic revolution in March 1991.

The story of Nicéphore Soglo, the first democratically elected president of Benin, provides another noteworthy example of the devil's "intervention" politics. Shortly before he was to take his oath of office, Soglo was stricken with an illness his doctors were unable to diagnose. He eventually fell into a coma and was transferred to a hospital in Paris. In the meantime, his family and political allies organized a campaign against the malevolent use of sorcery in politics and accused those whom Soglo had defeated at the polls of using black magic against him. Radio programs denounced the relentlessness with which evil spirits had attacked the new head of state. "Nationalist" sorcerers were called upon to rescue democracy in Benin. If they did not save the president's life, it was implied, then the democratic process, which finally brought down former president Mathieu Kérékou, would fall by the wayside and everyone would suffer when the pendulum swung back to the other side. Group prayer meetings were organized throughout the country. And while the sick president remained under heavy guard in the hospital in an effort to ward off evil spirits, African marabouts were asked to devise a magic potion that would act as an antidote. Finally, after several months of medical care and a period of convalescence, Soglo was able to take office. When a major radio station in France questioned him about the source of his mysterious illness and asked him to comment on the political use of sorcery in his country, Nicéphore Soglo gave a cautious reply, refraining from any commentary that might strike his enemies as pompous: "I think I was poisoned, but I don't really know what happened to me."[5]

Political life in many African countries is studded with similar—if less dramatic—scenarios. Bayart related juicy anecdotes about the important role sorcerers played at the convention of Congo's former Marxist-Leninist single party, the PCT (Congolese Workers Party). According to reliable eye-witness accounts, each of the regime's principal dignitaries—Communists, mind you—arrived at the convention (the party's highest authority and the event at which the most important political decisions were made) accompanied not by his closest advisers but by the sorcerer whom he most trusted (Bayart 1989).

The democratization process begun in the early 1990s has changed nothing in this regard. Although the myth of Satan and his representatives on earth is, as a number of anthropologists have pointed out (Cohn 1970), only relatively ancient, the devil appears to have taken over the imagination of African populations and leaders these past few years. Of course, one cannot remember a time when sorcery and politics were not connected on the continent (Douglas 1963; Nadel 1952). What appears to have changed is the use to which the belief in forces of evil is now put. Twenty-six years ago, Douglas wrote: "Witchcraft beliefs are essentially a means of clarifying and affirming social definitions.... People are trying to control one another, albeit with small success. The idea of the witch is used to whip their own consciences or those of their friends. The witch-image is as effective as the community is strong" (1970:XXV).

Similarly, Willis affirmed that "in most African societies, witchcraft (here used as synonymous with sorcery) is a putative cause of what is seen by the sufferer as unmerited misfortune" (1970:129). Though they make some interesting and valid points, such analyses do not enable us to pinpoint the reasons for the irruption of sorcery in African politics today. The most remarkable aspect of the current social transformations is the implosion of communities as they have traditionally been defined. Across the board, African communities appear weaker, and individualism stronger, than ever before. Reversing Douglas's claim, one might say that in Africa today the witch image is as effective as the community is weak. Satanic cults and rituals, black masses, the celebration of the invisible, the belief in the omnipresence of the most powerful politicians, rumors of sacrifices, organ trafficking, cannibalism, and orgies, all of this is now part of the everyday landscape. The idea of being possessed traverses all social classes, all "tribes." Exorcism, as a result, is a booming business.

Is the resurgence of the occult the necessary outcome of a certain economic determinism, as Willis predicted? Are the economic crisis and the trauma of structural change the principal causes of the economic and political success of the devil in Africa? Nothing is less sure. Ardener (1970) pointed out that the Bakwéris in Cameroon retained their belief in the forces of evil despite a marked improvement in their standard of living. In other words, economic factors did not affect their cosmology. The absence of a correlation between the two has been confirmed by Horton (1967, 1982), who stresses that the religious and parareligious beliefs of Africans, based on the real and immutable power of the invisible, go much further than purely symbolic, superficial rituals.

If African politicians have been able to exploit the public's credulity—that is, manipulate, at a subconscious level, the belief in the forces of evil for the purpose of gaining and maintaining power—it is because this belief exhibits its own rationality. The irrational here has a coherence and internal logic that allow for the harmonious integration of phenomena that might strike an observer as bizarre, horrible, and unjustifiable. However obvious it might seem that the success of sorcery, for example, is related to subjectivity, political analysts must attempt to define the objective functions of such practices. That is what Appiah invites us to do when he writes: "Concentrating on the noncognitive features of traditional religions not only misrepresents them but also leads to an underestimation of the role of reason in the life of traditional cultures" (1992:134).

Indeed, one has only to interview political actors to see how they exploit belief in the supernatural. First, it allows them to introduce the elements of fear and respect into the construction of their image. The collective imagination easily accepts the idea that power needs a little black magic to solidify itself and affirm its superiority over its opponents, and that leaders need to shield themselves against the hatred, jealousy, and violence of evil spirits. The conversations between political activists are often studded with remarks such as: "The leader of our party is very strong. He is shielded by all the sorcerers" or "Your president is off to a bad start! Even the spirits of our ancestors are against his policies, which is why they haven't had good results." Various cults are involved in political campaigns. Discussions at political meetings often revolve around magico-religious themes: legendary tales of famous opposition leaders who escaped numerous assassination attempts thanks to the powerful force of their gris-gris; epics of the supernatural powers of beloved leaders, who made banana trees grow overnight, were untouched by gunshots fired at point-blank range, and transformed themselves into winged creatures to escape the wrath of their enemies. In fact, one essential criterion of political popularity seems to be mastery over the occult. No one wants a naive leader who could be blown away like a leaf by the most insignificant sorcerer working for the opposition. To receive the confidence of the public, a leader must be solid, powerful, able to vanquish the forces of evil on their own satanic turf.

The public acceptance of the use of the occult in politics has various implications. Many politicians now believe that it is necessary to use sorcery to advance their political ideas. Their logic is simple: To win the support of the electorate, it is best to monopolize its imagination. Any means may be used to achieve this end: seduction, fear, or threats. That is why a number of sects and religions have sprung up within political networks in almost every country in Africa.

As long as this frenzy is limited to mind games involving the idea of the devil, these rituals are harmless. Rituals, in themselves, are not the problem: all powers throughout the world validate themselves through the institution of networks of legitimation (ideological, religious) in which they have faith. Within the machinery of the state, Gabon's president, Omar Bongo, informally established a sect—the bwiti—dedicated to his worship. Anyone hoping to move up the ladder in his administration knows that it is advisable to be a member of this sect, for competence alone or even "ethnic representation," used not so long ago to achieve "regional balance," is not enough. The president of Cameroon, Paul Biya, has turned membership in the Rose-Croix, of which he is a member, into a litmus test for legitimacy and a pledge of loyalty for high government officials. Most other heads of state have acted in like manner, vesting various religious and parareligious sects with full rights over the management of the political sector.

The real problem lies in the degree to which the use of occult forces is limited: A total absence of control opens the way to various abuses. For example, the violence of the state, which, as Foucault (1979) has demonstrated, often provokes the irreparable, is increasingly transferred to private groups outside the administrative hierarchy. These groups answer only to the heads of state, who, for the most part, no longer trust the military. This perverse "privatization" of violence has occurred in Mobutu's Zaire, where "uncontrolled soldiers," who are nevertheless loyal to the Zairean dictator, terrorize poor areas of Kinshasa. It is likewise found in Somalia, where the state has ceased to exist in any form whatsoever, and where the international community has rehearsed one of the main diplomatic principles of the post–Cold War era: silent abdication of responsibility.

In his well-known preface to the English edition of Weber's *Sociology of Religion,* Parsons suggested we take seriously the belief in the supernatural:

> Every society possesses some conceptions of a supernatural order, of spirits, gods or impersonal forces which are different from and in some sense superior to those forces conceived as governing ordinary "natural" events, and whose nature and activities somehow give meaning to the unusual, the frustrating and the rationally impenetrable aspects of existence. The existence of the supernatural order is taken seriously, in that many concrete events of experience are attributed, in part at least, to its agency, and men devote an important part of their time and resources to regulating their relations with this order as they conceive it (1963:xxvii–xxviii).

I have attempted to follow his advice, without, however, giving in to the temptation of adapting Weber's evolutionist models. Beyond the fact that such an approach allows access to the hidden dimension of certain myths, it opens up new perspectives on the manner in which the "religious" segment of African civil society is organized and operated today. A serious analysis of the quest for the sacred among Africans likewise helps one understand better the misadventures and complexities of current sociopolitical transformations. It sheds light on the unwritten rules of African politics.

Notes

1. This simple question is a well-known phrase used by French journalist Jacques Chancel for several years to revive his famous interviews on Radio France Internationale.

2. That is how Augé (1982:49) explains Bergson's justification of the origins of religion.

3. Besides the "classical" religions, such a definition includes all kinds of new sects, which, in some African cities, are the main technostructure through which the relationship between people and the sacred takes place. Thus, my definition is broader than the one suggested by Durkheim: "Système de croyances et de pratiques relatives à des choses sacrées, c'est-à-dire séparées, interdites, croyances et pratiques qui unissent en une même communauté morale, appelée Eglise, tous ceux qui y adhèrent [A religion is a unified system of beliefs and practices relative to sacred things, that is to say, things set apart and forbidden—beliefs and practices that unite into one single moral community, called a church, all those who adhere to them.] (1979:65).

4. There seems to be no distinction related to social class, gender, or socioprofessional status. Rich and poor people, literate and illiterate, all are potential customers for marabouts, sorcerers, and other agents of spiritual racketeering.

5. I personally spoke with President Soglo about these matters during an interview in August 1995.

6

Civil Society and Public Sphere: The New Stakeholders

Un peuple ne tombe jamais en faillite totale.

*

A people never becomes totally bankrupt.

—Were-Were Liking, Cameroon

When analyzing the implosion of political space and the rupture of social stability that have characterized the course of African history in recent years, there has too often been a tendency to focus attention on institutions, structures, and politicians. Though these are obviously important, such an approach tends to obscure the groundswell of new and yet barely understood social changes. Because politicians seem unable to advance the process in which so many people have invested so much, many observers feel the need to explore alternative sources of dynamism. This is largely the reason for the current interest in the notion of *civil society,* which has become fashionable in the cloistered world of African studies.

One of the first problems with the term *civil society* is determining exactly what it means. Although there is evidently a need to define the nature and sphere of political parties' activities in Africa, any attempt to define the forces hastily grouped under the label *civil society* appears problematic and doomed to failure. This is principally due to the diversity of political situations and the inherent inadequacy of using tools designed for understanding the workings of Western democracies to analyze the situation elsewhere in the world, which raises the general problem arising from the transfer of sociological concepts across space and time.[1]

Yet an attempt to define civil society is essential if our study of recent political movements in Africa is to be more than a superficial commentary. We are now witnessing a complete transformation of the conditions in which politics emerge, not least because new popular ambitions have created an upsurge in the aspirations and dreams cherished by Africans. This has manifested itself in the movements of social protest that appear to have been amplified by the huge challenges posed by this fin de siècle. Africans sense these opportunities all the more acutely, as they have fewer economic resources than others with which to ensure the survival of their species in the emerging world order. New social frontiers are being traced, new networks of solidarity are being established, new mentalities are taking shape. Values believed to be lost have reappeared, supplanting and replacing the ideologies whose limits have been exposed by thirty years of single-party rule. In this flux we are witnessing a diversification of political activities: Pressure groups emerge from the shadows, lobbies spring into broad daylight, and no one knows either the main actors or their ambitions, let alone their scope for action.

An empirical examination of the sociopolitical situation in most of the countries caught up in this democratic vortex reveals the emergence of new social mechanisms and the discovery of what one might call public opinion. People are becoming more and more aware of belonging to specific, defined groups and increasingly express the desire to create interest groups in both civil and political arenas. From political courtiers to financial marabouts, from unemployed youths of the suburbs to the intellectual and religious elites, there is hardly a social group that has not felt the need for its members to communally articulate their daily concerns.

For example, in both public and private companies the void due to the absence of structures of collective organization—notably, unions, works committees, employers associations—is being filled by a multiplicity of increasingly dynamic informal groupings, even if these are often established along Weberian lines of sex, age, kinship, and religion. For Africans, these groupings are a way of reclaiming the right of self-expression, long confiscated by the official institutions of power. In establishing their members as full participants in the political game, these groups expand the arena of association, stealthily influencing the ongoing multifaceted transformation. By blurring the rules of the game, they represent a disruptive force in the sociopolitical environment, what Ilya Prigogine would call a "structure dissipative" structure.[2]

The upsurge of informal groupings has the potential to overturn not just the existing political order but also the surrounding moral order—assuming that such a thing exists. The emergence of such dominant players on the national stage brings both virtues and the risk of distortions. Their strength lies in the fact that their collective conscience is greater and sharper than the sum of the citizens who participate. Many of the new organizations are rooted in a popular base, supporters are recruited from the lower classes, and they are flexible in their operations and efficient in their lobbying. Their presence means that the social game has become even more complex.

Although the fact that broader sections of African societies are speaking out on and reappropriating major issues is a welcome change, a swift sociology of the diverse systems emerging and a close look at the behavior of the principal actors raise a series of worrying questions. Beyond the obvious risks inherent in new movements, such as leaders rapidly stagnating and/or settling into new hierarchical systems, one must ask how these social structures, until recently unknown, will fit into the "national project" of each country and whether their ideas and actions will draw them into or distance them from the official discourse. Are they centrifugal forces that will stimulate and enhance the construction of the state, or will they be swept into centralization and squabble over the remains of the ruined state? Do they aim to embody the earnest proclamations of democracy or to establish alternative spiritual values and impose radically different modes of social exclusion and violence? Does their tendency to refer to tradition have any substance?

With so many things changing, researchers face new difficulties. The numerous reforms undertaken in the name of political and economic adjustment, the new and diverse modes of producing freedom analyzed in Chapter 4, and the intense social creativity have generated new cultural phenomena and the ballooning of the informal economy. Thus analysts must first to grapple with the problems of precisely defining civil society, then interpret the multitude of evolution, and, most important, offer a reading of the changes that will help identify and evaluate the scale of the current dynamic for democratization.[3]

In this chapter, I present some elements of a study based on the premise that most political authorities in Africa do not have a grip on the actual mechanisms of society. I suggest that rather than historical, institutional, or economic factors, psychological and emotional aspects of everyday life determine the main social phenomena that continue to be experienced. Needless to say, the work of others has long demonstrated the importance of the subconscious in the psychology of social groups in general.[4] My own findings highlight the emotional dimension of the protest movements that have been shaking Africa's political stage. I believe that these movements cannot be understood unless they are seen within the perspective of what might be termed an *anthropology of anger.* This chapter is therefore a study of cumulative frustrations and an analysis of collective modes of expression and discontent, including the informal attempts to use them as vehicles for political action.

How to Define a Phantom Concept

There is little doubt that African civil society cannot be fully comprehended, let alone assessed, by the classic instruments of analysis. Most institutions that make up African society cannot be compared to those we see working in Europe, where elected local, regional, and national structures meet regularly to decide policy and choose leaders. In Africa, the leadership, membership, and functioning of such structures are often shrouded in mystery.

Of course, most associations have a constitution that provides, inter alia, information about their aims, membership, finance, and internal rules. In reality, the officers are frequently changed to suit the circumstances, particularly as there are often no selection procedures. Although the decisions made can have a decisive effect on society, the most important meetings happen only irregularly, have no formal agenda, and are held in closed session, frequently in secret locations. We cannot define a specific African civil society without referring to its peculiarities or the context in which it has emerged.

Inflation of Politics and the Civic "Deficit"

Thirty years of authoritarian rule have forged a concept of indiscipline as a method of popular resistance. In order to survive and resist laws and rules judged to be antiquated, people have had to resort to the treasury of their imagination. Given that life is one long fight against the state, inventiveness has gradually conspired to craftily defy everything that symbolizes public authority. Once politics has been opened up, any collective recalcitrance can only lead to a profound civic deficit. Decrees cannot change overnight patterns of behavior patiently refined over many decades of quasi dictatorship.

That the existing structures of social management are inefficient is obvious to all observers. In general, it was not political parties that initiated the protest movements. With very few exceptions, trade unions, often the most easily organized of mass movements, did not play a determining role in the course of events, and those content to act as a mouthpiece for the ruling single-party were hardly likely to oppose the status quo.[5] Still, violent social disturbances frequently forced the established authorities to climb down and triggered a process of democratization. This is proof that, despite apathy from opposition parties and unions, African societies were able to generate their own networks of communication and forums for discussion within which it was possible to express collective fears and dreams. For me, the term "civil society" refers to those birthplaces where the ambitions of social groups created the means of generating additional freedom and justice.

Geographic Variables

Any definition of civil society will be different on opposite sides of the Sahara, since from a political point of view, the problems are not identical.

Sociologists in the Maghreb, for example, include only "the parties and associations which, despite their divergences of opinion on many issues, share the same values of human rights and individual freedoms."[6] Such a definition excludes movements laying claim to fundamentalist Islam, even if they have a dominant role in the sociopolitical plan. South of the Sahara, things are different. The mullahs do not, at least for the moment, have a determining role on the course of events, although this statement needs qualifying. The mobilizing potential of religious communities is clear in Nigeria, where the smallest clash between their members may result in hundreds of deaths. The chaotic and violent history of the building of a mosque in Cameroon revealed a well-established "Muslim force" in the capital. In Senegal, the chief of the Mouride community has for many years dominated the country's business affairs (Magassouba 1985). Nevertheless, religious organizations capable of influencing politics as much as the Islamic movements do in Algeria, Tunisia, Egypt, or Morocco do not yet exist in Nigeria, Cameroon, or Senegal.

That is why my definition of civil society south of the Sahara incorporates the churches and religious movements that, until now, have contributed in their own way to the birth of democratic power. It includes all organizations and individuals whose actions have helped amplify the affirmations of social identity and the rights of citizenship, often in opposition to those in power, whose natural tendency is to repress such identities and rights. It obviously does not exclude the interactions among the state, the political parties, and leading personalities. In a nutshell, civil society in Africa is formed by all those who are able to manage and steer communal anger.

I am well aware that I shall not escape the criticism of those who reject the notion of civil society in states that are not democratic in the Western sense, such as the Tunisian sociologist Mohammed Kerrou (1989). Although my formulation of the concept differs significantly from the eighteenth-century European definition, it has the advantage of clearly emphasizing the significance of historicity and the capacity of African societies to evolve within their own unique trajectory.[7]

Preponderant Role, Mysterious Organization

The opening up of politics in Africa has prompted a quasi-anarchic multiplication of parties, yet in almost all countries, the new political leaders have almost immediately revealed their limitations. Thus, to avoid the risk of being deprived democratization, society has had to invent alternative structures to manage and express its dissatisfaction by creating informal networks of communication.

The Discrepancy Between Political Supply and Demand

The weakening of authoritarian regimes has triggered an implosion of politics and an extraordinary rise in individuals claiming to be the leaders of so many new parties; in 1991, 19 political parties were legalized in the space of just a few months in the Central African Republic, 27 in Gabon, 70 in Cameroon, and over 200 in Zaire. This turmoil is a response to the demand of representation in each country, but these parties generally have neither a clearly defined program nor any effective organization. Their capacity to make an impact on the political stage and to promote change seems limited. The multiplication of parties has not increased the civil rights of ordinary citizens. Public discourse is still unidimensional because too many leaders are content to proclaim slogans and pledges of faith during the meetings to which people flock in the hope of hearing real solutions to their daily hardships.[8]

Most embryonic organizations are inevitably characterized by a lack of trained cadres and strategies. Faced with many grievances and demands from poor social groups, the supply of ideas from the political leaders has remained limited. This is the source of widespread disillusionment with politics and the inversely proportional eruption of alternative groupings through which large segments of the population try to express their views and demands.

Reappropriating Symbolic Goods

Given the prevailing circumstances, it is not surprising that public discontent manifests itself in terms of anger. The proliferation of privately owned newspapers and magazines, the growth of efforts to create independent trade unions, the multiplication of private media, cooperatives, professional bodies, youth organizations, and academic groups, all serve to promote the demand for rights that conventional organs and institutions seem unable to understand or satisfy.

Everywhere, the emerging civil society tends to be self-managing as its leaders attempt to rekindle social consciences. Four influential social groups have emerged in the leadership role: (1) the students in all countries, who have been at the forefront of protest; (2) the clergy (notably in Benin, Zaire, Gabon, and Mali); (3) the lawyers (Algeria, Tunisia, Central African Republic, Cameroon, Togo, and Mali); and (4) the intellectuals and journalists (Cameroon, Côte d'Ivoire, Kenya, and Zambia). By their commitment to the democratic struggle, they have amplified the collective dream.[9] One of their principal demands concerns the symbolic commodities of recognition and dignity.

The leaders of these new social groups are motivated by a thirst to express themselves, to participate and be represented in the crucial cabals so that they may influence the choices made by politicians. They demand their share of the "national cake," although this is not always their main aim. Occasionally, their links with elements of the political class cast suspicion on their position; hence, in the minds of some, they are assimilated into the opposition movements, lending a partisan connotation to their struggle to reestablish certain values. In Mali, Togo, and Cameroon, the decision by human rights organizations to join antigovernment alliances means that their leaders have become frustrated politicians.

It is difficult to make categorical judgments about what is happening in Africa. Does an organization designed to defend human rights compromise its critical stance if it joins a group of opposition political parties in the struggle against an authoritarian power? Should it remain always neutral to conserve its impartiality? A similar question applies to the private press. On the pretext of objectivity, should rulers whose illegitimacy is well established be treated in the same manner as opponents who are struggling to change their country? It is interesting to note that these types of questions were not raised about social organizations in Eastern Europe after the collapse of Communist regimes.

The Discovery of New Means of Communication

In practice, the leaders of the most active elements of civil society could not afford to dither over such existentialist questions. Having decided not to wait for international public opinion to come to their rescue, they set themselves up in opposition, establishing informal channels of information to get their message across to the people. In fact, they did not really have a choice. Access to public media in Africa has always been denied to any group challenging the existing authorities. Professional organizations and student groups, for example, knew that it would be dangerous, if not impossible, to criticize those in power in state-owned television, radio, and publications. In most countries the press laws either implicitly or explicitly allow censorship—perhaps by a paragraph surreptitiously introduced into the text adopted by the assembly or by a proregime committee installed in the offices of a newspaper. Necessity is the mother of invention, and thus killing two birds with one stone became a preoccupation for those who wished to earn money while discreetly undermining the authorities that they at best half-heartedly supported.[10]

Oral communication in the political arena, whether by word of mouth and/or *radio trottoir,* has been reestablished. Numerous organizations in Senegal, Burkina Faso, and Cameroon, for example, have used the ebb and flow of people between large towns and villages as a means of effectively distributing critical messages. Orders for strikes have been transmitted from one area to another by family visits and day trips. Word of mouth can be distinguished from rumor by the fact that the information communicated in the former is generally precise and unusually specific. Such modes of expression have an authority that allows the emerging civil society to free itself from the shackles of official propaganda and to define the image of its own evolution.

Is Civil Society Civilized?

Many African countries have recently witnessed both the intensity of public wrath and the desire of emerging social institutions to direct actively the sense of public frustration. The absence of fear and the growing dynamism of these institutions have established them as forces with whom the public authorities are obliged to talk and thus render obsolete the remarks of John Dunn, who noted that there is "good reason to see in the internal domination of state power, the relative inconsistency of civil society, (the low) degree of viable and sustainable institutionalization of social forces outside the sphere of the state" (1978:15).

The aim of the new stakeholders is to assume control of the collective anger in order to intensify the momentum for political change. This poses numerous problems, notably that the more voluntarist view of the relationship between fragile or even moribund states and their societies encourages the emergence of rival factions and rebellious leaders. One can also question the efficiency and goals of these new groupings whose actions are still unclear. Having abruptly established themselves as the driving force behind current political changes, they find themselves center stage. In the process, they have altered the structures of civil society, changing the sociological space to such a degree that their organization requires further study. Other issues worth investigating are the perverse effects of the extraordinarily large scope of action that various groups have created for themselves. On what basis do they form alliances and promote solidarity, and how do they determine their objectives?

The Standards of Solidarity

What is the best way to analyze the civil society that is developing in Africa? Antonio Gramsci suggested a method of evaluating three distinct dimensions: the organization, the normative space, and the "private" nature of the groups involved in the process (1977: 606–607).

Organization

Whether it be trade unionists, journalist, intellectuals, students, or the unemployed, many in Africa today are no longer content to wear the labels of social origin, tribe, or age. Rather, they increasingly choose to adhere to a particular social group according to individual ideas of solidarity based on religious, philosophical, or spiritual criteria. Numerous popular religious organizations, active notably among urban youth, are now able to recruit members from throughout society, not just from one segment or tribe, as was the case twenty or thirty years ago. However, it is a slow process and is more sucessful in some areas than others. It does not necessarily represent a radical change in the way Africans participate in associations; many people still follow traditional forms of solidarity.

Normative Space

Whereas socioprofessional bodies tend to disregard the primary affiliations of their members, even within each social class, these are reinforced by organizations with an ethnic or regional basis. Nevertheless, they all attempt to inculcate a sense of communal solidarity in place of individual identity, which seems to have been the guiding principle for the majority of citizens. Some associations believe that membership of tribes and/or parties help create the conditions for their more effective role in society. This idea is worrisome, particularly to those who agree with Habermas that the democratic process is linked to the ability of individuals to free themselves from the dictatorship of groups, whether they are based on family, ethnicity, or religion, and that access to freedom is proportionally linked to the affirmation of individualism, because "the new conflicts do not arise from problems of redistribution but from questions which are linked to the very grammar of forms of life" (1987:432).

One can question the validity of the morals that govern the ambition of opinion formers within the new social groups. In many countries, powerful associations openly affirm their tribalist affiliations in the name of ethnic groups that they claim have been marginalized in the distribution of the national cake.[11]

Private Aspect of Civil Society

The drive to create voluntary organizations does not stem from the so-called crisis in the African state—notably, the state's inability to manage society—as some theoretical models would have predicted (Thériault 1992; Melucci 1985). To the contrary, the popular will to create spaces of freedom for new groups is an attempt to fill the social void that the absence of the state represents for so many of the inhabitants.

Choosing a Framework of Analysis

Apart from looking at the operation of civil society in Africa, we need to analyze the way in which opinions and decisions are made within this emerging entity. The motivations underlying the choice of a particular set of beliefs and references follow a subtle evolution. Collective social representations—the way in which most Africans reappropriate daily events by translating them into commonsense terms—transcend individual subjectivity and are imposed on each member of the community as an inescapable constraint. This occurs all the more easily for populations in revolt because of the injustices they have suffered, which strengthens their tendency to return to the tribe as a point of reference and deemphasizes the role of the individual.

Impatient observers may feel that tribalism is both an imperative of and a key to understanding civil society. In reality, most men and women interpret issues in daily life in diverse ways. The "success" of the constraints operating within sub-Saharan social organizations can be explained by the fact that representations have both a psychic and a cognitive structure, having been theorized by the leading personalities of each social group. Evidently, this is true even if the a priori logic rests on a purely imaginary base. This does not mean that the choice of a cognitive framework is necessarily an act imposed by the groups. As it is anywhere else, the fundamental motivation in Africa is the expansion of individual interests. The ideas articulated by pressure groups have the possibility of taking root in the collective imagination if they obey this imperative.[12] Citizens make decisions on the basis of the quality of their information and their ability to manage anxiety. They will either follow or disobey the orders of their social group according to the intensity of their anger and the scope of their competing social identities. When tribalism and xenophobia become the official ideologies of certain factions, their fear will lead to troops being mobilized, whether they want to carve out an electoral domain, govern, or maintain themselves in power. The structures of civil society are particularly receptive to leaders who adopt slogans in line with populist illusions. In Africa, the misery for so long suffered by ordinary citizens tends to increase society's receptiveness to such ideas.

All of these observations raise legitimate concerns. Is the form of civil society being constructed in Africa democratic? Are its leaders motivated by ethical ambitions or by a desire for revenge against the state and those elements of society that oppose their interests? Do they know how to adapt their demands to the socioeconomic issues and imperatives of the market economy? Will they abide by the rules of the political game if these rules legitimate their marginalization and appear unfavorable to certain interest groups?

How to Deal with the Process of Social Fragmentation?

The theoretical issues raised by the ongoing sociopolitical adjustment are as serious as the threats to the future stability and viability of each African state posed by the anarchic emergence of an ill-defined civil society. Faced with the weakening of law and order and a decaying state, the fragmentation of society due to the rise of tribalism and regionalism, and the absence of politicians with clear plans, the African population tends to react by rejecting all forms of authority. After decades of resistance to the brutalities of power, people's behavior has come to be inspired primarily by personal interests. This autistic tendency, which marks the end of unanimity, is simultaneously welcomed and worrying; although it frees the citizen from group discipline, which we know can be detestable, it legitimizes a private universe as the principal reference point for every social leader.[13]

How should this problem be studied? This constant risk of barbarism that African civil society carries could interfere in the ongoing reappropriation of freedom. On this precise point, how can the West assist the process of democratic construction in Africa?

Issues of Conceptualization

In order to react positively to current political developments, we must first decipher the notion of *civic duty,* or *socialité.* Hence, we need to presuppose that civil society is sufficiently strong to contain and channel its collective anger and that it is desirable to steer the socialization of the state toward some kind of optimal equilibrium. This means taking a closer look into the issues raised by the way civil society works in Africa today, notably, the extent to which many policymakers now tend to adjust their decisions according to the degree of legitimacy enjoyed by certain groups in each country (Monga 1994a).

Diamond (1994) has suggested an interesting framework for assessing what he calls the ten democratic functions of civil society. The theoretical considerations emphasized in his analysis include the educational virtues of a dynamic civil society, the numerous advantages of social mobilization and participation, the adoption of transparent rules in the political game, and the recognition and institutionalization of lobbies, which means the emergence of a new type of political culture focusing on cooperation, bargaining, and accommodation rather than on conflict and violence.

However, in order to comprehend fully the significance and implications of the rediscovery of civil society in Africa, we must also study a number of disturbing developments. The first is the cult of nihilism and cynicism that is a feature of many religious and civic groups; indeed, in countries whose protagonists are primarily animated with revenge and anger, the dissemination of despair and violence seems to be the main feature of informal political markets. In Senegal, Mali, and Cameroon, for example, some of the most popular slogans used by the new social leaders have to do with organizing public trials of those who were in charge of the country since independence—in other words, they are promoting retaliation, punishment, and various witch-hunts. Such discourse sets a negative tone for political debate, not least by limiting the types of issues that are brought to the forefront.

The second major threat stems from the informalization of the political markets. Indeed, it is clear that some of the most vocal trade unionists and civil rights activists in francophone Africa have taken advantage of the relative freedom that they have as social leaders to engage in subtle strategies of political entrepreneurship. Given the inflexible structures of government and administration in most of these countries, as well as the fact that political parties are increasingly mistrusted by the general public, many mysterious associations have been created by people who are really running for office. These leaders simply argue that they have found a way of circumventing the current renewal of authoritarianism since those in power are much less willing to crack down on a "human rights league" than on a political party.

A third issue concerns the political role assigned to international nongovernmental organizations (NGOs). In Senegal, for instance, Oxfam has become so powerful that one cannot dismiss the need for scrutiny, regardless of the staff's commitment to ethics. I do not claim that NGOs always have a hidden agenda, but it would be naive to believe that there is no political price to be paid for the charity business in Africa.

Policy Recommendations

For any given country, the policy recommendations emerging from my analysis can be classified as follows.

Restoring the Idea of a Common Destiny

There is an obvious need to restore hope and a sense of common destiny in the hearts of people who hardly believe in the relevance of any kind of public authority. The aim must be to convert what appears as violent collective anger against the state into a source of energy for a more dynamic process of social engineering. As the key political event of the past five years, the uprising of civil society has been due to the failure of governments to provide a moral foundation for the principle of "togetherness." While disillusion about the goals of the nation-state is not an issue per se, it is necessary to emphasize that people are bound to live together, and that any policy ignoring that premise is likely to lead to a "no win–win" situation and possible bloodshed—unless countries deliberately choose ethnic cleansing as a means for solving disputes. So it is urgent to reinforce the message that the members of all groupings in any given country share the same destiny, regardless of their tribe, status, or religion. It may sound obvious, but past and ongoing tragedies in Africa remind us of the necessity to insist on some banal truths. This can be done through very well-designed communication strategies.

Building a Better Leadership

There is an urgent need for strong, responsible, unselfish new leaders who are committed to pursuing ethical values. Their paucity, so apparent throughout the continent, requires that we look beyond the elites that recycle the same old tactics, using ethnicity and violence as their main political tools. To paraphrase West, Africa needs leaders who can situate themselves within the continent's larger historical narrative, grasp the complex dynamics of its people, and imagine new political strategies grounded in the best of its past, yet who are attuned to the frightening obstacles ahead. "Quality leadership is neither the product of one great individual nor the result of odd historical events. Rather, it comes from deeply bred traditions and communities that shape and mold talented and gifted persons" (1990:37). The new leaders must place their trust in today's grassroots initiatives and traditional African philosophy that highlights democratic accountability and perceives negotiation as a fair and honorable way of making decisions.

Expanding Social Capital Beyond Geographic Borders

The literature on civil society usually emphasizes the necessity of strengthening civic communities by supporting NGOs and by providing them with various forms of aid. But one must go beyond such requests. A much more powerful way of tackling the pervasive issue of urban nihilism, for example, and of encouraging the feeling and reality of "brotherhood" would be to build links not only within but also among social groups and across countries. The term *social capital* has been used by some authors when referring to "features of social organization, such as trust, norms, and networks, that can improve the efficiency of society by facilitating coordinated actions."[14] In fact, in the case of most African countries, there is little or no lack of such social capital; the problem is its limited scope in the absence of formal or informal links between the various components of civil society. Expanding the network of existing groups beyond their geographic and regional limits means that more people with similar interests and concerns can be connected, not least so that they can perceive how similar their fears and dreams are.

Linking Civil Society and the Legislature

It is essential that the marginalized social groups—from which the new organizations are currently attracting support—be gradually eased out of their ghettos. The equilibrium necessary to the functioning of political institutions cannot be maintained unless full democratic citizenship is restored to all those who feel marginalized. This raises the problem of the linkage between economics, politics, and society.[15] Social stability cannot be established if political gains are not accompanied by parallel economic improvements. In particular, these must meet the basic needs of the poorest sections of society, who often form the majority. New bodies may need to be created to inculcate a moral ethos into the leadership of the nascent social groups.

A new political apparatus must limit the potential for conflict between the diverse groups of civil society, and constructive links need to be established with the legislature. There are numerous judicial ways in which this might be achieved. For example, the most influential sociopolitical organizations could be directly represented in parliament. Even those societies that operate secretly could be given opportunities to express their views about laws and rules drafted by the political power. This would be sensible given the determinant role that such groups have always played, notably during the resistance to all forms of colonialism, as well as during the struggle to create the state in Africa.[16]

Adopting a New Scale of Interests

The rupture of social bonds currently under way is likely to continue. People's heightened awareness of their own personal interests could hasten the erosion of the primary family, ethnic, and regional ties that have been dominant until now. Already one can see what Merton (1965) called "the paradigm of anticipated socialization," according to which individuals tend to assume the values and behavior of the groups to which they aspire to belong rather than those to which they are assumed to belong. The shift in the scale of values against which Africans measure their interests implies the demolition of the powerful myth of the tribe or ethnic group as the dominant social factor.[17]

Numerous studies have demonstrated that the nature of the bonds between state and society, what some writers have called "penetrative interdependence," is one of the specific characteristics of democratic countries.[18] A number of analyses have established the existence of a correlation between the phenomenon of the state's penetration of society and the proportion of the state budget allocated to social spending. Yet this observation is of no use in Africa, where macroeconomic aggregates do not have the same meaning and social problems are very different. Although the scale of public spending allocated to social needs might increase substantially, the state simultaneously refuses to root itself in the society it is ostensibly representing.

It is small wonder that African societies aim to take their revenge on the state and to establish only a symbolic relationship with public authorities. Having been at their mercy for so long, society now seeks a radical shift in the balance of power. This ambition is expressed through the operation of informal groupings and the multiple strategies of resistance to public authority, including infiltration into areas of responsibility normally reserved as the domain of the state. (This infiltration can explain why in some villages and towns in Africa, people have never waited for governmental subsidies to build schools, roads, and other public works.) Studies of social dynamics must henceforth look beneath the violent disturbances and analyze the issues that have created this collective anger.

The problem is to find an optimal equilibrium point in this process of "socializing the state"[19]—namely by defining limits to society's revenge without repudiating the state or stripping it of any legitimacy, as is too often the case. By appropriating territory normally under the control of the public authorities, civil society is locked in a struggle that, eventually, can only weaken all concerned. Take, for example, the fact that in almost all African countries the collection of taxes is falling. For most citizens, not paying taxes is an act of civil defiance, a way of reducing the amount of national wealth that has been salted away in Swiss banks (compare Monga 1990a).

Some Conclusions

How can a reciprocal contract between the state and civil society be defined so that democratic governance in Africa is more likely? How can communal anger be steered so as to avoid its degeneration into an anarchic cacophony behind the mask of an amorphous civil society? How can the credibility of the state be reestablished, providing firmer foundations for private society while achieving a better rate of democratic citizenship per person? How can we ensure that the social rights won from the state through the struggle of NGOs correspond to new political obligations for the electorate?

My hypothesis is that civil society will acquire moral objectives only through a better-educated middle class, since its members are at the forefront of those fighting for political space. Of course, their associations are still young and vary from one region to another, yet they represent those segments of the population that are the most engaged in the struggle for change and that have the greatest influence with the poorest urban and peasant households. Better information and training among targeted groups could be designed for much wider transmission and might be the most efficient way of spreading a message of hope for all social classes.

Obviously, the efficient regulation of informal political markets cannot be resolved by theoretical analysis, hence the need for practical suggestions aimed at reinforcing the components of civil society in Africa. I believe that the lack of material resources is not the biggest obstacle to democratization in Africa. Far more important than money, the sub-Saharan states need to benefit from the knowledge, experience, and savoir faire of others, particularly social engineering and the political apparatus. By this I mean that all the mechanisms, rules, and institutions should be dedicated to the best possible regulation of relations between the state, the market, and the society.

The social fabric of Africa has to be strengthened in a variety of ways, not least by helping the independent mass media play a more effective role, as was suggested in May 1991 by the UN/UNESCO seminar for African journalists held in Windhoek, Namibia (Martin 1992). Before the end of the Cold War in Europe, when the Polish trade union Solidarity was fighting to free the nation from the dictatorship of General Wojciech Jaruzelski, the publishers of *Le Monde* donated their old printing machines to Lech Walesa's organization. This soon proved to be one of the most significant acts of Western assistance, and the private press in a number of African countries would greatly benefit from this kind of imaginative support. Campaigns on civil rights and duties must be arranged, with adequate funds for television and radio programs, books, pamphlets, cartoons, and advertisements. Journalists would obviously gain from seminars, conferences, and courses organized by leading practitioners, from Africa and elsewhere, who want to share their expertise and experiences.

The multiplication of human rights groups in Africa has not necessarily meant a better cataloguing of violations and abuses. The assorted organizations often appear to be structures of power in the hands of certain individuals who are more concerned with personal advancement than with public investigation. None of these groups have published precise, verified information on the violent incidents that have shaken the continent in recent years! However, there are many associations outside Africa that could train human rights observers to perform this essential task.

We must explore other possibilities if we do not want the political inflation accompanying current social upheavals to transform into a deeper communal disenchantment with a wholesale loss of civil values. There is no question of transferring ready-made solutions in the North to the South, but the leaders of African civil society should be offered the means of avoiding the errors, delays, and catastrophes that marked the democratic process in the West—and that have already occurred in Rwanda and Burundi.

Notes

1. The difficulty in using the term *civil society* in applied research is not restricted to Africanists. The history of the concept is littered with queries and skepticisms; useful surveys are Ferguson (1996) and Keane (1988). See also the philosophic synthesis of Gourdon (1991).

2. See Prigogine and Stengers (1988) and Prigogine and Nicolis (1989). It is also worth mentioning the retrospective of Gleick (1989), which synthesizes the numerous attempts to use the methodology and theories of physical sciences in the social sciences.

3. The notion of *dynamism* is taken here from the psychoanalytic theory that analyzes psychological principles of change. See Lewin (1948) and Fischer, et al. (1993).

4. See Le Bon (1963) and Tarde (1901) for the oldest frameworks available in social sciences.

5. This is not true for the countries of North Africa, where unions have always been very active. They played a key role in the evolution of politics in Congo and Southern Africa in 1989 and 1990 but have had virtually no presence in Cameroon, Central African Republic, or Mali.

6. See Zghal (1991). For a good understanding of the fears of Maghrebian intellectuals on this issue, see the lively pamphlet by the Algerian Mimouni (1992), as well as Boudjedra (1991).

7. Here I mean historicity in the Gramscian sense. After World War I and the victory of the Russian Communist party, Gramsci used the ideas of civil society to analyze the specificity of the Communist parties of Western Europe.

8. This partially explains the fact that while the demonstrations organized by opposition parties in Abidjan and Douala in 1990 and 1991 attracted hundreds of thousands, in 1992 they were attended by only tens of thousands. Such indications, still provisional, suggest real disenchantment.

9. Personalities such as Monsignor Ernest Kombo (Congo), Laurent Mossengo (Zaire), Demba Diallo (Mali), Nicolas Tiangaye (Central African Republic), Christian Tumi, Bernard Muna, and Charles Tchoungang (Cameroon) have all become familiar to those who follow political news in Africa.

10. In francophone Africa, a popular newspaper normally sold at FCFA 200 may fetch FCFA 500–2,000 on the black market. Hence, there is clearly a temptation, especially in those countries where the average monthly pay of a police officer is around FCFA 70,000 to make ends meet by organizing illegal sales of certain publications, especially as there is no record of the number seized.

11. A highly instructive survey is given in Collectif Changer le Cameroon (1992).

12. These processes, termed *objectification* or *anchoring*, are well described by Aebischer and Oberlé (1990).

13. Authors who have examined this issue, which in Europe is one of the traits of postmodernity, include Rosanvallon (1981), Mendel (1984), and Lipovestky (1983). For a synthesis of such ideas, see Jalbert (1992).

14. See Putnam et al. (1993:167). The concept of *social capital* was introduced by Loury (1977).

15. Researchers are increasingly agreeing on this point; see Lefort (1981).

16. See Augé (1982), especially chap. 7, "Signes du corps, sens du social: sorcier imaginaire, sorcellerie symbolique," pp. 211–280. See also Mbokolo (1990).

17. Although one needs to question the authority of these terms, Amselle and Mbokolo (1985) began such a task in their excellent work.

18. The term comes from Banting (1986:14).

19. A process that Daniel C. Bach provocatively called "the cannibalization of the state by civil society." See his comments at the conference on "European-African Relations: Challenges in the 1990s," Ebenhausen, Stiftung Wissenschaft und Politik, May 24–27, 1992.

7

A Theory of Disenchantment and Violence: Rwanda and Other Tragedies

Le pouvoir est plus fort que tout, hormis le péché.

*

Power is stronger than anything, except sin.

—Bamanan proverb, Mali

Washington, D.C., July 1995. A Cameroonian businessman now living in Maryland as a political refugee told me his bitter tale. Although he had once enjoyed a prosperous existence in Yaoundé and been considered a darling of the Biya administration, he had had to leave his country abruptly after the rigged 1992 presidential election. He had "compromised" himself with opposition parties, and the government would not forgive him for having betrayed his friends in the upper echelons of the regime, for having bitten the hand that had fed him for years. Ill-prepared for his new life as a nomad, he said what bothered him most was his friends' and family's lack of understanding concerning his decision to join the fight for democracy. Over and over again, people told him: "Why on earth would you risk your fortune, your important political connections, your reputation, and maybe even your life to become an opposition party activist? Business doesn't mix well with politics. You stand to lose a lot more than the intellectuals and the unemployed who are lining the streets. Don't get involved! We're all in favor of democracy. But why should some people have to sacrifice themselves for the cause? When democracy comes, we'll all rejoice. In the meantime ..." Comments like these were especially disturbing to him because they often came from people in the lower ranks of society, from the very disenfranchised whose plight had sparked his desire to rebel and who stood to benefit the most from democracy.

My friend's words reminded me of the advice I myself had received from the Cameroonian authorities, who had tried to put a lid on my political activism. "Who would think that a man like you, a young executive, the director of central Africa's largest commercial bank, with a great career ahead of him, would sacrifice both his own future and that of his family by getting involved in politics?" Albert Ekonno Nna, governor of the Littoral province in Douala, asked me in 1991. "I'm speaking to you now," he continued, "not as a political opponent but as a father, or an older brother. Don't you see that your so-called supporters are pushing you into a suicidal trap? You're the one who's sleeping in a prison cell. The machinery of the state is going to come down hard on you, not them. Does it give you pleasure to destroy your own future? Are you a masochist? What about your wife? Your children? Your family? I can't believe they let you do so many reckless, unnecessary things. Stop opposing the government. Beware of all your friends who are encouraging you to commit suicide. You're an intellectual. You know all about the French Revolution. You've heard Georges Brassens's song, 'Die for ideas, yes, but die a slow death,' because dying for the sake of ideas is what all those people who are exploiting your enthusiasm and naïveté live for!"

*

* *

These anecdotes illustrate the two most serious types of problems threatening the democratization process now under way in most African countries: disenchantment with democracy and the possible eruption of naked violence, which can only complicate an already delicate process of social restructuring. They also suggest a paradox as well as questions that might be raised at the end of this work: Why has African inventiveness, which has been celebrated in the preceding chapters, not yet had a positive impact on the social dynamics of the day? How will Africa survive its at once complex and ephemeral democratic dreams? How will Africans avoid becoming like Nitu Dadou, the protagonist in the novel by Congolese Sony Labou Tansi, *l'Anté-peuple,* who, in his relentless search for a better world, ends up drowning in his own desire for freedom?

In this final chapter, I propose several theoretical frameworks for an understanding of the pervasiveness of disenchantment and the tendency to resort to violence. The first section explores the problem of disaffection with the new political actors: Some populations come to terms with this painful emotion, managing as well as they can their fears and disappointments and directing their energy and creativity away from politics and toward other goals; in so doing, they reinvent uses for disillusionment. Others are less fortunate: Led by unscrupulous or unimaginative political entrepreneurs, they pervert political disenchantment, transforming their disappointments in the political field into cynicism toward society in general. Citizens attempt to profit from the democratic idea but are not willing to pay the price for it, treating it as one might a public good. The second section presents an anatomy of conflicts in Africa. Recommendations on how to solve the problem of violence are offered in the third section.

Interpreting Disenchantment

Numerous scholars and journalists fear that democratization may derail because there is no popular support for the human, material, financial, and other sacrifices that are required to obtain institutional and political concessions from ruling autocrats. Notice, first of all, the sadomasochistic nature of the implicit assumption that African peoples ought to accept collective flagellation stoically in order to prove to the world their allegiance to the democratic idea. Not only is such an argument politically unrealistic and intrinsically incompatible, the ethical imperative around which it is constructed is selective: It expects of African peoples that which would never be asked of others. Disenchantment with democracy is found not only in Russia, former Soviet bloc countries, and Latin America but also in the "great industrial democracies" such as France, Japan, the United States, and Germany. But African societies, far from systematically resigning themselves to the disillusions of democracy, attempt to reinvent and recreate the spaces of political transformation outside the political arena. The real problem facing them in this new adventure is their capacity to engage in a collective ethical pursuit in these uncertain times. To understand this, it is necessary to see democracy for what it is at bottom, that is, a public good. Economic theory elucidates these new challenges: When freedom and social well-being are conceived as public goods, this necessarily leads to the emergence of free riders, who use the goods but do not pay for them. Their existence, in turn, may increase the risk of disenchantment.

The Pervasiveness and Reinvention of Democratic Disillusionment

Let us suppose that the anecdotes related at the beginning of this chapter are representative of a general disaffection toward the democratic idea—a tremendous supposition to which I will later return. Even if this is so in the absolute, the phenomenon is in no way confined to Africa. Empirical research on the subject looks like a transnational kaleidoscope of political disaffection. Numerous signs of skepticism toward democracy are found in all of the world's industrialized nations.

In a recent report, the *New York Times* summed up the situation in Japan:

> Politics in Japan in recent decades has mostly been a struggle for power among factions, rather than a competition among people with different ideas. That has added to the perception that Japan is really being run by bureaucrats, and that politicians are a kind of second-tier imperial family—granted fine titles and lots of television time, but entrusted with little power.... Polls find comparatively low satisfaction in Japan in the way their democracy works. Only 35 percent of Japanese say they are satisfied with their democracy, one of the lowest figures in any industrialized country (Kristof 1996).

A journalist's account is by definition impressionistic. But the deep feeling of collective disillusionment with democracy that Kristof captures is confirmed in the writings of numerous scholars, notably Johnson (1995).

In the United States, although a greater number of citizens say they are satisfied with the democratic system (64 percent according to Kristof), empirical studies substantiate the prevalence of disillusionment. Statistics on voter turnout show that, of all countries considered to be democratic, the United States is at the bottom of the list in the area of political participation (Wolfinger et al. 1990). Powell (1986) has linked this phenomenon to class: The poorest and most numerous members of society are disproportionately excluded (the unemployed and those with the lowest incomes vote the least). According to Powell, this phenomenon is explained by U.S. political culture, which privileges active involvement by the individual in the voting process (voter registration, the act of voting itself) and sanctions gerrymandered voting districts (and hence structural inequality in the intensity of political competition), as well as superficial relationships between the political parties that dominate the political game and the social groups whose interests they are supposed to defend. The political system also allows for institutional conflicts (acknowledged or implicit) that weaken in the end the sentiment of democratic legitimacy.

Though he does not share Powell's view that a correlation exists between political culture and voter turnout, Jackman stresses the importance of political institutions and the electoral technostructure (political parties, voting laws, fair competition): "Where institutions provide citizens with incentives to vote, more people actually participate; where institutions actually generate disincentives to vote, turnout suffers. Thus, the meaning of national differences in voting turnout is rather clear: turnout figures offer one gauge of participatory political democracy" (1987:419).[1]

The same debate exists in Germany—which Carr (1984) sees as a country on the verge of becoming "a society of conditioned reflexes," and where Habermas (1984) addressed political modernity and its discontents—France, and many other countries with a long democratic tradition. Even the shortest trip across any of the world's great democracies reveals political disillusionment and causes one to raise two essential questions:

"How much nonparticipation can a democratic system tolerate? Does participation fundamentally affect the quality of representation?" (Crotty, 1991:19). Before addressing the specific question of democratic disenchantment in Africa, let us recall how the general debate has been framed and interpreted by scholars in the social sciences.

Numerous hypotheses have been advanced to explain disenchantment with society. Among the most compelling is Bell's (1960) thesis concerning the end of ideology. In his assessment, liberalism and socialism, the principal ideologies of the nineteenth and twentieth centuries, each conceived as "a set of beliefs, infused with passion, and seek[ing] to transform the whole way of life," finally lost their power to mobilize the masses during the 1950s. Bell cites two main reasons for this: (1) their failure to prevent world wars, economic depression, and the emergence of dictators; and (2) structural changes in capitalism, summed up in the expression "the welfare state." Bell also contended that the overall rise of ideology during this period was a phenomenon geographically limited to Africa and Asia—in the West only "'piecemeal' change in the social-democratic direction" occurred.

The logic of this thesis, in reality a rather old one, caused some writers to applaud, others to lament, the idea of a social order stripped of great ideological struggles and dominated by what might be called an ideologically transparent technological fervor devoid of true political substance.[2] Other writers such as Lipset (1960) and Aron (1966) expressed concern about the ravages of unchecked industrialization, which they saw as leading to the creation of a society based upon an apolitical, administrative consensus among elites. They predicted that the West would henceforth be immune to ideological frenzies and that "pragmatic" utopias (that is, adapted to reality) and an ethics of responsibility would alone guide politicians in industrial democracies.

Repeating Max Weber's words of caution in *The Ethics of Capitalism*, Birnbaum (1975) warned us twenty years ago about the dangers of such a reductive, linear approach to the history of humankind. The debate over the "end of ideology" thesis, which I shall not discuss in detail here, led some to conclude that the end of ideology was no more than the end of certain ideologies and a way to legitimate U.S. ideological dominance (Meynaud 1961), that is, the emergence of a new ideology that preferred to disguise its name (Haber 1968). Providing an explanation for the decrease in political participation, the end-of-ideology hypothesis foresaw a depoliticization of society, a uniformization of political programs, and a decline in ideological debates, hampering the emergence of coalitions. Let us now discuss these predictions within the African context.

Is this paradigm borne out south of the Sahara? Has disillusionment with democracy caused nameless freedom fighters in Dakar or Djibouti to adopt the types of behavior described by Bell and Aron? The answer varies from one country to the next, sometimes from one region to the next in the same country. True enough, a slackening of political involvement has occurred in large African cities—either because the sacrifices the population made between 1990 and 1995 did not succeed in toppling the authoritarian regimes (in Senegal, Côte d'Ivoire, Cameroon, Zaire, Kenya, etc.) or because the change in government did not bring the hoped-for increase in political, economic, and social well-being. But beyond the feeling of discouragement, there is a surprising reinvention of everyday ways of being—as if political disenchantment had been a socioeconomic and cultural wake-up call to African peoples.

In some regions, it would be a hasty generalization to say that a depoliticization of the electorate had occurred, as the classical view on political disenchantment predicted, because Africans are much more likely to vote than people in Europe and the United States. African authoritarian regimes are so very aware of this tendency that they do their best to discourage people from voting, by manipulating the size of the electorate, by passing laws limiting the eligibility and rights of voters, or even by blocking access to the polls (Monga 1995b). Though voting habits sometimes appear to reflect membership in a social group rather than an ideological choice, the social groups with which citizens wish to associate themselves are dynamic. The notion of ethnic voting blocs, for example, does not withstand scrutiny, for, like all group labels, ethnicities are not monolithic entities: Voters are, of course, Yorubas, Bamilekes, Kikuyus, or Zulus, but these labels represent only a part of their civic identity, which also includes their professional and religious affiliations as well as their philosophies on life. In addition to being Yorubas, Bamilekes, Kikuyus, or Zulus, African voters are taxpayers, employed or unemployed, Catholics or animists, inhabitants of large cities or small towns; the competition between the multiple aspects of their identity make them less likely to vote automatically with their ethnic group, which may not represent their self-interests. The results of the Nigerian presidential election, nullified by the army in 1993, confirm the absence of polarization along ethnic lines. In the words of Nobel Prize winner Wole Soyinka:

> The "robust detonation" of the myth of the North-South dichotomy took place finally on 12 June 1993.... On that occasion, Nigerians voted across so-called ethnic divides and declared themselves a nation. We cannot ignore the treason represented by the annulment of that election, for it was more than the election of an individual. It was the annulment of Nigeria's declaration that it wants to be one nation (1995:8).

Neither does the uniformization of political programs correspond to the end of the right-left ideological debate, as one might have thought. For one thing, there have never been ideological struggles per se in African nations, because independence has rarely been synonymous with freedom on the continent. For another, political parties have only recently become the framework in which public discourse is developed and alternative ideas are legitimated: The political parties created during the colonial era were embryonic, belonging to those "culturally premature institutions" the colonists bequeathed to Africa (Michalon 1995). The uniform quality of the few political programs published by certain parties is attributable to the single economic agenda international monetary institutions have forced upon most African nations (the infamous structural adjustment programs proposed by the World Bank and the International Monetary Fund). Their uniformity reflects the reality of international politics and the incompetence of opposition party leaders, not the exhaustion of thought or a breakdown in the production of new ideas.

Another feature of the paradigm of disenchantment fails to apply to Africa, namely, the sociocultural aspects of depoliticization described by Lavau (1962). Literature, music, painting, and film on the continent have not disengaged themselves from politics; rather, they have increasingly become a platform for the expression of political demands. Artists have invented so many new and subversive political languages suggestive of another possible reality that African governments have sometimes had to commission artists to create "political" works of literature, music, or even sculpture celebrating their regimes.[3]

Finally, the emergence of urban and rural elites is neither the consequence of disenchantment nor the result of a clash of sterile doctrines held by various camps: This phenomenon has always existed, even under single-party rule. What we are witnessing now is an actualization of the practice of negotiating political power, which long allowed autocrats to present themselves to the people as representing all ethnicities and regions in the country (the former president of Côte d'Ivoire, Félix Houphouët-Boigny, was a master of this method of governing). What has changed is the more inclusive and unstable nature of political coalitions, which bring together many more people exhibiting a greater range of sociological profiles—those who yesterday fiercely opposed the government align themselves with it tomorrow in order to get a piece of the national cake. Notable examples of this are Abdoulaye Wade, who, overnight, swapped his status as public enemy number one for that of chief sycophant to President Abdou Diouf; Bernard Zadi Zaourou, who, after having symbolized for decades intellectual rebellion against single-party rule in Côte d'Ivoire, suddenly and remorselessly joined the Henri Konan Bédié administration; and Dakolé Daïssala, a Cameroonian political prisoner who, after having undergone state-sponsored torture, exchanged his filthy jail cell for a luxurious ministerial office located within a few yards of his former prison. Examples such as these are endless and demonstrate that today's coalitions are modeled after an old practice and in no way derive from but rather contribute to public disenchantment with politics.

If the end-of-ideology thesis is not a valid or sufficient explanation for the disenchantment of African peoples, who deal with their disillusionment as well as they can and daily reinvent other spaces of political contestation, then what accounts for the deceleration of the democratization process between 1993 and 1995?

My thesis is that beyond disenchantment there is another, more important factor that has weakened democratization in Africa: the thankless nature of the democratic idea itself. However appealing that idea may be, it is nevertheless a collective pursuit, an endless fight that must be of concern to the largest social groups. By its very nature, it elicits the tendency toward discouragement. A paradigm borrowed from economics helps explain why: the concept of public goods.

Democracy as a Public Good: Implications

The social scientific definition of *public goods* or *collective goods*, when applied to democracy, helps illustrate the tendency toward discouragement that I view as consubstantial with the idea of citizenship itself.[4] It inhabits citizens in all parts of the world, notably those who are fighting against authoritarianism. As opposed to a private good, which is supposed to be consumed individually, a public good is a good whose consumption by person A does not affect its consumption by person B (Samuelson 1954). This definition, which borders on tautology, nevertheless has some important features that economists have found useful.[5] I describe two of these features, both of which may seem obvious and useless, and subsequently apply them to the analysis of democracy in order to demonstrate more clearly their theoretical and practical implications.

- By nature, a collective good is *nonexclusive*, which is to say that the fact that it is consumed or used by person A does not prevent it from being consumed at the same time by person B. This is what primarily differentiates public goods from private or individual goods. As soon as public goods are produced, the number of consumers or users may increase or decrease without leading to increased costs and without affecting the well-being of the initial consumers.
- A collective good is also *indivisible*: It cannot be produced, bought, or sold in small quantities. Thus, for each user of a public good, it is virtually impossible to determine the fraction of the cost corresponding to his or her consumption.

This framework may also be used to understand the internal contradictions within the dynamics of the democratization process in Africa. If each African citizen living under a dictatorial regime is seen as a political *agent* who is seeking to maximize his or her political well-being while limiting the costs it implies (the risk of police reprisals, brutality of all kinds, etc.), the problems involved in the pursuit of any collective good are made clear:[6]

• Democracy is a *nonexclusive* good. When it exists, a given citizen's "consumption" of it does not affect the quantity available to others. If Senegal, for instance, were a democratic country, it would not suffer from the fact that people from Casamance or any other region would "use" too much of the "national production" of democracy.

• Democracy is also an *indivisible* good: It may not be satisfactorily acquired in small doses; it may not be cut up into pieces. A citizen in Kinshasa could not accept a "piece" of voting right or a tad of freedom of expression. Similarly, the Zairean state oppressing him or her could not decide to "produce" only a limited quantity of democracy, in the form of a selective lifting of oppression or a reduced level of torture. It is likewise impossible to calculate the cost incurred by each citizen in the struggle for democratization.

In the early 1960s, Olson proposed an elegant mathematical model based on these features and on the behavior of social groups composed of individuals seeking to maximize their self-interests. It elucidates the intrinsic problems of collective goods. Summing up the main lesson of his model, Olson writes:

> The necessary conditions for the optimal provision of a collective good, through the voluntary and independent action of the members of a group, can ... be stated very simply. The marginal cost of additional units of the collective good must be shared in exactly the same proportion as the additional benefits. Only if this is done will each member find that his own marginal costs and benefits are equal at the same time that the total marginal cost equals the total or aggregate marginal benefit. If marginal costs are shared in *any* other way, the amount of collective good provided will be *sub*optimal [or inefficient] (1965:30–31).

If we assume that the citizens who are pursuing freedom behave rationally, and that democracy is a collective good with a cost (if only in terms of the punishment those fighting for change stand to suffer at the hands of the autocratic regime), one may extrapolate from Olson's theory of groups a theorem of the political efficiency of democratic movements in Africa: When the marginal political benefit of democratization (that is, the hard-fought additional gain in freedom and social justice) is not shared in the same proportion as the marginal cost (the additional pain and deprivation suffered daily by those fighting for change), then there is a possibility of inefficiency in the social dynamics at work. But by its very nature, the democratic idea necessarily educes such distortions: Given that its cost and its benefits per citizen are not quantifiable or measurable, it necessarily gives rise to mixed feelings. It is therefore to be expected that even those who are fighting for democracy greet its arrival with ambivalence or even rejection.

Applying Olson's model to the study of democracy as a collective good, the obvious "scientific" explanation for political disenchantment is the perception of a poor distribution of the political benefits of freedom. To this I would add another reason: the various ways in which well-being is experienced by the citizens and main political actors, even within the same country. These different political utility levels (Monga 1996) explain the differences in behavior and internal contradictions in social groups whose members all face the same problems. The different levels increase the likelihood that there will be disagreement over the estimated costs of achieving democracy and the expected benefits of democracy once it has been won. The fundamental incompatibility of the various methods and premises advocates of democracy use to calculate its risk-return ratio explains why democratization appears to have stalled in certain African nations: Many citizens who, between 1990 and 1995, fought hard against authoritarianism and made physical, financial, and psychological sacrifices "now prefer to concern themselves with other things and to let time take care of things" (Nantang Jua 1995). They figure that democracy will come sooner or later—others will take care of it and everybody will benefit, so why should they make sacrifices?

This is known as the free-rider problem. As Frey puts it:

> The basic problem of public goods is that the prospective consumers have no incentive to reveal their preferences for such a good and are thus not ready to contribute towards financing the provision of the good. In the extreme case this incentive to act as [a] "free rider" leads to no supply of the public good at all, although everyone would potentially benefit from its provision (1988).

The following example, drawn from recent political events in Côte d'Ivoire, is a good illustration of the problem. Only a few weeks before the presidential and legislative elections, President Henri Konan Bédié prohibited opposition parties from organizing public rallies in the streets of the capital and other large cities. "Fear of the disorder" that mass demonstrations might cause in a tense political climate was the official reason for the ban—the real reason was the possible mobilization of a majority of the urban population against his regime. For the opposition parties, the measure was all the more capricious and unjust in that it took effect right before an important election and did not apply to the president's own party. Thus, opposition leaders decided to ignore the ban and organized demonstrations in various parts of the country, instructing activists to participate in the marches in Abidjan. The decision of whether or not to participate was difficult for every activist. To take the risk of publicly revealing one's convictions by following party instructions was to confront, head on, a brutal administration well versed in punishment techniques. The Bédié government's reaction could range from professional and administrative harassment to imprisonment, physical torture, and even assassination (unauthorized demonstrations in Côte d'Ivoire have always led to violent clashes with the police and armed forces, generally resulting in bloodshed). Figure 7.1 shows how the situation presented itself to each opposition activist.

Let us call our activist Mr. Kouassi, a member of the Ivoirian Popular Front, one of the main opposition parties to the Konan Bédié regime. Let us assume that under ordinary circumstances it is possible for the opposition to mobilize 500,000 people in the capital. There are four possible outcomes:

• If Mr. Kouassi joins in the protest, he may be subject to punishment from the government (he will pay, if you will, the price of the collective good that democratization represents), but this risk lessens if all opposition activists participate in the demonstration. In that case, the demonstration is likely to succeed—if only in terms of media attention. If Mr. Kouassi is

Figure 7.1

	If Mr. Kouassi participates in the protest	*If Mr. Kouassi does not participate in the protest*
If all opposition activists participate in the protest	• There will be 500,000 people in the streets of the capital. • The demonstration will be a huge success.	• There will be 499,999 people in the streets of the capital. • The demonstration will be a huge success.
If no opposition activists participate in the protest	• He will be the only one in the street. • The demonstration will be a fiasco. • The wrath of the government will come down on him alone.	• There will be no one in the streets. • The demonstration will be a fiasco. • No one will suffer the consequences.

the only one who takes part, not only will the demonstration be a total failure, but he alone will pay the price for his courage.

• If Mr. Kouassi does not take part in the demonstration, he runs no risk (he will not have to pay the price of democratization). His absence will not affect the success of the operation if he is the only one who decides not to participate: If 499,999 people show up rather than 500,000, the media will not notice the difference. But if all activists follow suit, each one assuming that his or her presence will not make any difference and that it is not worth taking such an enormous, unnecessary risk, no one will be in the streets and the result will be a fiasco.

The incentive to act as a free rider is clear: In a situation such as this, Mr. Kouassi and other opposition activists tend to analyze the possible outcomes in a self-interested way; they want to reap the benefits of democracy without helping to finance its costs, without paying the price for it.

Figure 7.1, based upon the principles of game theory, provides a rough sketch of the different hypothetical scenarios and payoffs from which our opposition activist has to choose. Roughly speaking, these are the four possible outcomes from which Ivoirians had to choose in 1995. Many chose not to take the risk of participating. Large numbers of people did show up at some demonstrations, but these numbers did not reflect the mobilization potential of the opposition parties.

The same is true for many other African countries in the past few years. Far from being a childish display of ill humor or discouragement, the political disenchantment that many Africanist political scientists have noticed is above all attributable to a reshuffling of individual preferences, a reevaluation of probable collective behavior, and a cost-benefit analysis (sometimes instinctive, of course) of the desire for freedom.

Is it possible to alter the determinants of individual attitudes in such a way as to change the terms of the equation that people living under a dictatorship and dreaming of freedom must work out for themselves? Here again, economics provides a host of techniques that open onto diverse possibilities. The most obvious solution would be to change the structure of the political game in each country so that the outcomes of the four possible scenarios listed in Figure 7.1 would advantage risk takers. The idea would be either to diminish the the authoritarian regime's capacity to do harm or to give citizens more incentives to take risks in order to win their freedom—or a combination of both.

Taking our Ivoirian example, the idea would be to arrive at a matrix like that shown in Figure 7.2.

How does one arrive at a political game structured in this way? The current balance of power in African political markets obviously does not allow for such an arrangement. Authoritarian regimes still have a solid grip

Figure 7.2

	If Mr. Kouassi participates in the protest	*If Mr. Kouassi does not participate in the protest*
If all opposition activists participate in the protest	• There will be 500,000 people in the streets of the capital. • The demonstration will be a huge success. • He will not be in any danger. • The international community will take note of the event.	• There will be 499,999 people in the streets of the capital. • The demonstration will be a huge success. • The international community will take note of the event.
If no opposition activists participate in the protest	• He will be the only one in the street. • The demonstration will be a fiasco. • Nevertheless, he will not be in any danger. • Pressure from backers and the international community will keep the government from retaliating against him.	• There will be no one in the streets. • The demonstration will be a fiasco. • No one will suffer the consequences. • The opposition will nevertheless lose its credibility.

on the reins of power, thus disequilibrating political competition. The democratization process, which in many respects resembles the transition from a controlled economy to a market economy, takes place in the context of a monopoly on state power held by an elite who does not wish to introduce competition. African citizens are rational and fairly well informed—despite governmental control over the media. The missing ingredient is acceptance of the principle of competition—the adoption of and adherence to commonly agreed upon rules as well as "market" (that is, voter) approval.[7] In advanced industrial nations, it is generally the role of the administration (which is neutral despite the fact that it is composed of individuals with their own political convictions) to ensure respect for the political process. Pope John XXIII uttered words to this effect, basing his argument on the implications of the inherent properties of public goods: "There exists an intrinsic connection between the common good on the one hand and the structure and function of public authority on the other. The moral order, which needs public authority in order to promote the common good in human society, requires also that the authority be effective in attaining that end" (quoted in Rosen 1988:62).

But in African countries where the state is both the arbiter of and a major player in the political game and is often the principal obstacle standing in the way of democracy, there is little hope of seeing an improvement in the efficiency of the political market in the short term. This necessitates the endorsement of any foreign intervention that might alter the balance of power between democrats and advocates of the status quo. I am well aware that this proposition will ignite the indignation of some theorists, who consider that Africa's current political and economic impasse is due exclusively to the weight of history and to the interventionism of foreign powers. From this point of view, it would be naive to think that foreign intervention, whatever form it might take (diplomatic or military), could be carried out without harming the interests of African peoples. My own view is structurally less pessimistic, because I do not believe that African interests are automatically opposed to the interests of foreign powers. Furthermore, I do not subscribe to a static view of world history: The balance of power between great powers and small countries evolves over time in unpredictable ways.[8]

The postcolonial African state serves to reveal and catalyze social tension rather than acting as a buffer or arbiter. It might thus be said that it has disqualified itself from spearheading the democratization process in sub-Saharan Africa—and this for a number of years. Often partisan, actively engaged in the political battle (generally siding with the autocrats in power), the postcolonial state was unable to foresee and forestall the political consequences of social disenchantment and the sometimes horrifying implications of the avenues into which African peoples have channeled their disillusionment.

The international community has also failed to shoulder the moral and political responsibilities it has taken on in other parts of the world. By refusing to regard human rights violations in Zaire as equivalent to those that occurred in Romania, by refusing to treat Nigeria's General Sani Abatcha in the same manner as Poland's General Jaruzelski, the UN, international organizations, and Western political chancelleries have left African peoples to their own devices, to a chaotic handling of their disenchantment. The growing intensity and multiplication of forms of political violence, witnessed of late in Rwanda and elsewhere, derives from the abdication of responsibility on the part of the state and the so-called developed world.

Anatomy of Political Violence

Oddly enough, the eruption of violent conflicts in Africa always seems to take the world by surprise. Whereas the existence and evolution of social tensions are well documented in other parts of the world, it appears that people are invariably astonished by the turn of events in Africa. As a result, and in spite of the good will and sincere compassion of international opinion, foreign intervention is more a function of media coverage (what might be termed the "CNN Curve") than of policy considerations.

Generally speaking, internal disputes (such as those in Cameroon, Togo, and Kenya) rarely pique the interest of the international community. Even when these disputes involve significant loss of life and property, the great powers and international institutions do not always become involved. The Congolese 1992–1995 civil war, for example, elicited little reaction from the UN. As a rule, it is only when the media turn on their cameras that international opinion begins to put pressure on Western policymakers to act. And, of course, no sooner are the cameras turned off than interest begins to wane; this is presently the case for Rwanda and Somalia. The programming directors of large television networks such as CNN have become some of the most influential actors on the international scene.

Figure 7.3 illustrates the "CNN curve," the indifference and slow reaction time of the international community, which, even when it perceives the emergence of a serious social problem in Africa, generally contents itself with short-term solutions until social unrest paralyzes the country and causes the economy to collapse. When such countries are no longer able to make foreign-debt payments or to absorb, through importation, production surpluses that the West could not sell elsewhere, they become

Figure 7.3

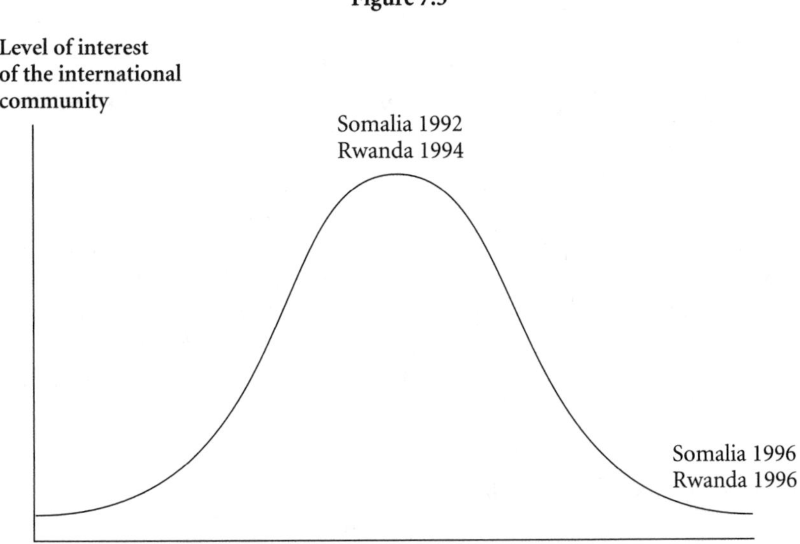

problem cases. The World Bank and the International Monetary Fund are then charged with the task of "adjusting" them, not developing them over the long term but reducing the size of the budget and the government, which artificially stimulates economic growth and makes them "solvent" again (Tchundjang Pouémi 1980). Figure 7.4 may be used to illustrate the Western reaction to African conflicts.

Figure 7.4

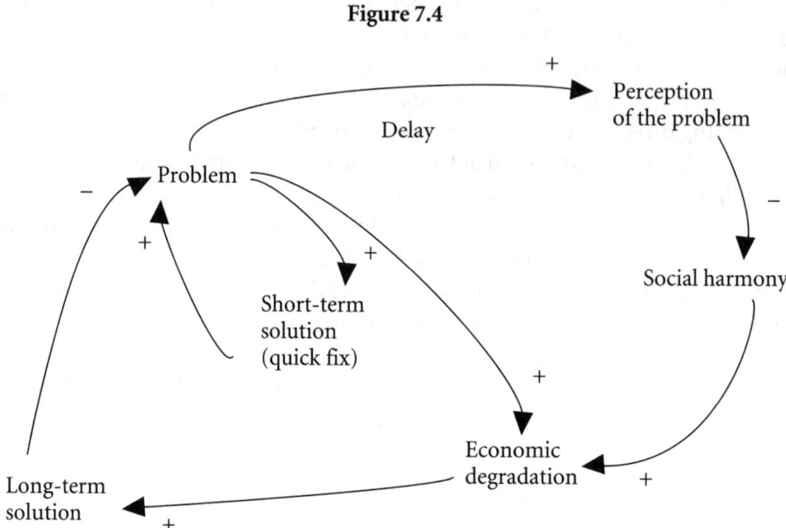

Note: The diagram is based on the principles of systems dynamics. The + and – signs indicate: X positively affects Y if $\partial Y/\partial X > 0$, and vice versa.

Before offering a few suggestions on the possible uses of economic means to resolve the problem of community violence in Africa, I will first examine the mechanisms triggering the disputes, which will help explain why disenchanted citizens express themselves collectively through acts of political violence. I will then analyze the soundness of theories on violence in Africa and conclude by proposing another approach to conflict resolution.

In the Beginning Was the Alibi

There are "objective" conditions—historical precedents, political maneuvers that play on "philosophical" disagreements between neighboring peoples, cultural differences, economic and social injustice, etc.—that cause conflicts to grow in scale. But however intense a conflict may be, there are always clearly identifiable harbingers of it before it erupts. Most often local media—including the most powerful of all, public rumor—give a clear account of its existence, but the international community does not pay attention. Then the opposing parties start engaging in psychological manipulation, informal information and disinformation campaigns, and mudslinging and insults, which increase tension and strengthen bonds within social groups, divided not along class lines but along those of the tribe, of the clan, of religion, etc.

It is at this moment, when the troops for the future conflict are being assembled, that the international community should intently focus on the situation and intervene in some way. It might attempt to catalog the types of situations that give unscrupulous political entrepreneurs the dynamite they need to ignite a conflict. The World Bank employs doctors, sociologists, and anthropologists; it might ask a few of them to conduct socioeconomic studies on the risk of turmoil in countries and regions of Africa where the clash of cultural identities or different itineraries tends to erode the social fabric. They might also examine the distribution of public utilities, roads, schools, clinics, etc. Tremendous holes exist in the economic and social infrastructure of certain communities and regions, whereas others have an overabundance of underutilized resources. A case in point is the small Ivoirian village of Yamoussoukro, where, among other grandiose public works projects, six-lane expressways, which no one ever uses, crisscross the town. Countless other examples could be cited.

Similarly, the fact that legislation is passed in some countries favoring certain social groups (in such areas as taxation, credit, regulation of commerce, and tariffs) and harming others creates tensions that can lead to vendettas between these groups. The resurrection of past injustices that few even remember appears incomprehensible, yet this is exactly what happened in Ethiopia, Chad, Rwanda, Nigeria, and Kenya. The memory of the pain and suffering one social group suffered at the hands of another suddenly comes to the fore and the "victims" discover that their exploitation dates back several decades or more. When this happens, we have on our hands the makings of a lengthy conflict.

Unfortunately, the Western backers who discuss and finance public works projects are not interested in these sorts of problems. For institutional and political reasons, it is no doubt understandable that they do not wish to decide for the government of a sovereign state, which has the right to define its own priorities and plan its own development. It is nevertheless clear that an effort to take account of the economic and social disparities in the budget, fiscal and credit policies, and investment codes would weaken the argument of warmongers who play on the social misery of their communities and the "normalization" of injustices to increase their political clientele.

The prevention of conflicts through the use of economic instruments may take various forms: setting up projects, creating exchanges and markets between opposing groups, and financing information campaigns and civic education programs. Such readily financed microprojects designed to fight misery, disenfranchisement, and ignorance would help channel the energies of civil society in positive directions. One might try to take advantage of the fact that the intensity of a conflict ebbs and flows over time (Kriesberg 1991:5) by implementing some new strategies. For example, if international monetary institutions sponsored a civics program on the rights and responsibilities of citizens, underwriting the design, publication, and distribution of a pamphlet in comic book form, their advice on good governance and democratization would appear more credible and reach more people.

But what should one do when latent conflicts explode and degenerate into civil wars, as they did in Rwanda, Burundi, and Liberia? The first priority should be to set in motion emergency mechanisms. (The absence of structures allowing for the implementation of community violence "stabilization" measures was painfully obvious when the crises in Rwanda and Burundi broke out.) Though the role of international monetary institutions is somewhat limited at this stage, they still have some room to maneuver. Numerous studies have shown that lulls in fighting most often occur when there is a shift in the balance of forces. Zartman and Aurik argue that in the case of a "stable and intense" conflict, the chances for a successful settlement or deescalation of the conflict are greatest when the two sides have equal military capabilities—otherwise, the stronger has no incentive to negotiate (1991:152). This observation underscores how important it is for the international community—notably, international aid agencies—to adopt a less partisan position and to refuse to take sides in a conflict, which they invariably do either directly or indirectly. For example, when institutions operating under the Bretton Woods system grant a warring country credits known as "balance of payment support" even though they are aware, on the one hand, that the money goes to finance the political battle in which the leaders are engaged and, on the other, that they have no control over the use of the funds, they implicitly take part in the conflict and de facto finance violent operations. In so doing, they tilt the balance of forces to one side and effectively torpedo the chances for a sustained negotiation. They also alienate leaders in the opposition and civil society, who then find it necessary to take a more radical position and cease to trust the international community, which only further complicates the search for a compromise.[9]

Do Theories of Violence Apply to Africa?

The preceding remarks underline the necessity of reexamining the theoretical framework that shapes thinking on the prevention of conflicts. The literature on the subject is voluminous. A brief look at the present state of knowledge in the field allows one to pinpoint both the main causes of conflicts and the determinants of sustainable peace.

Causes of War

The use of quantitative methods to analyze systematically the structure of conflicts and the mechanisms for their resolution is a burgeoning area of research in the social sciences.[10] The interest of researchers has grown since the end of the Cold War has given rise to new tensions in the Balkans and in the former Soviet bloc, but which has elsewhere ushered in an era of peace that has presented new challenges to public policymakers in various parts of the world.[11] Recent studies allow one to understand better the dynamics of social violence and to identify which types of economic interaction may be engaged in in wartime to promote peace.

What is known as the realist paradigm dominates thinking on the causes of international conflicts. The various models of this paradigm fall into two main categories: structural realism, which attributes war between nations to the structure of the international system, and deterrence theory, whose variants are based on an evaluation of the distribution of power (the military capabilities of each nation).

Combining variables from each of these two theories, Huth, Gelpi and Bennett (1992) have developed a model designed to test the hypotheses underlying both arguments. They studied ninty-seven great-power militarized disputes between 1816 and 1984 and decisively concluded that the evolution of the international environment contributes less to the emergence of a conflict than do changes in the military and deterrent capabilities of the parties involved. In other words, monitoring the military power of nation-states and social groups allows one to predict with a high degree of accuracy whether a conflict is likely to break out.

At the individual level, the decision to wage war is often motivated by what specialists in systems dynamics call "obstacles to the understanding" of real-world phenomena. Leaders who advocate violence are generally unable either to sift through and comprehend the various levels of information they are receiving or to extricate themselves from the whirlpool of complex systems. In Figure 7.5, Sterman (1994) provides a graphical representation of the complexities of our time:

Figure 7.5

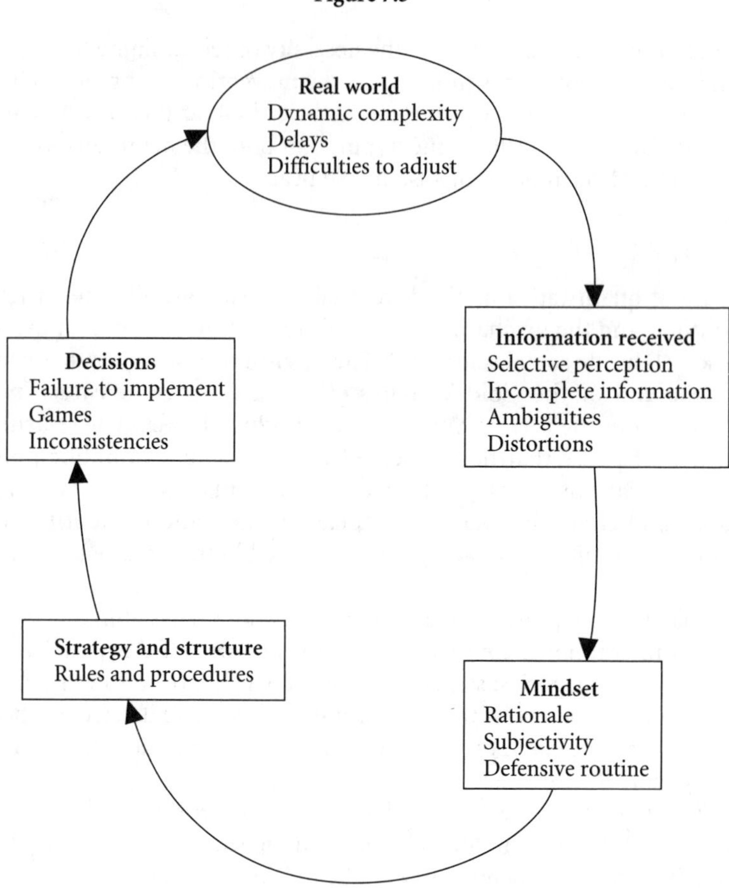

Causes of Peace

Does the nature of a political regime affect its propensity to wage war? Empirical studies have shown that a strong correlation exists between peace and democracy. The fact that a regime is democratic does not automatically prevent it from waging war; however, the intrinsic properties of democracy contain stabilizing mechanisms and tend to reduce the probability of war. As Maoz and Russett put it, "There is something in the general makeup of democratic states that prevents them from fighting one another despite the fact that they are not less conflict-prone than nondemocracies" (1993:624).

Which factors precisely account for this peculiarity of democratic regimes? Researchers generally answer this question in one of two ways. Those who rely on normative models argue that democratic countries tend to export their political principles, such as the regulation of political competition; the settlement of conflict by peaceful means; the almost systematic recourse to compromise; the maintenance of spaces of freedom and power for all, including the conquered; the refusal to annihilate physically opponents and minorities; and the perspective of future victories for the losers.[12] Such norms ensure the psychological stability of all political actors, at the personal level as well as at the local, regional, and national levels. A virtuous circle is thereby created: The more citizens adhere to democratic norms, the more it is in their economic and financial interest to adhere to them and to avoid violent disputes. "Dependence on democratic norms tips rational cost-benefit calculations toward further support of those norms" (Maoz and Russett 1993:625).

Those who have devised structural analysis models contend that it is difficult for elected leaders to engage in militarized disputes.[13] Democratically elected leaders only rarely become warmongers because they must garner tremendous support (public opinion, institutions, dominant interest groups) for the war. As a rule, this is possible only in situations that are widely perceived as emergencies.

Both schools arrive at the same conclusion: democracies are better able to negotiate disputes than are other forms of government (Maoz and Abdolali 1989). As Dixon has reaffirmed in a recent study, "Democratic states locked in disputes are better equipped than others with the means for defusing conflict situations at an early stage before they have an opportunity to escalate to military violence" (1994:14).

The Myth of the African Exception

Can these theories be applied to African conflicts? Some writers think not. The *exceptionality* paradigm appears to be the dominant framework for understanding conflicts in sub-Saharan Africa. Indeed, most available works on the subject tend to stress the specificity of Africa's historical background, invoking such notions as the "historicity proper" to African societies (Bayart 1989) so as to provide authenticity and a raison d'être to the conflicts and violent phenomena that have erupted over the past four decades. Yet this literature rests on questionable assumptions and shaky epistemological foundations.

True, it is not easy to classify the African continent. Its narrow, eccentric markets, which fall outside the confines of what Braudel (1979) has termed the "world-economy," look like veritable fortresses. They are paradoxical: Regulations are endless but are not based on actual norms; networks are invariably aleatory; unstable structures and places abound. The complexity of the decisionmaking process, the multiplicity of social codes, and the mysterious designs of the governors quickly lead one to give up. The coarse exoticism of this indecipherable otherness lies at the heart of the cult of a mythical exceptionality and has disturbing overtones: The racism sometimes present in the celebration of the "virtues" of African specificity is all the more subtle in that it is inverted.

In spite of its strange rituals, Africa is not always resistant to theories; there are no particular ingredients conducive to a bellicose spirit in Africa (Deng and Zartman 1991). The aforementioned determinants of war and peace apply in all parts of the world. The social dynamics that create conflicts and lead to revolution (Brinton 1965; Brown 1994) are virtually identical to those described in this study.[14] Consequently, conflict resolution and prevention measures should be based on general principles that promote peace: real support for democratization processes and a better assessment of the balance of power between each country's social actors. African heads of state endorsed such principles themselves in the Document de Kampala, adopted in 1991. One important passage reads:

> The concept of security goes beyond military considerations; it encompasses all aspects of social life, notably the economic, political and social dimensions of individual, familial, community, local, and national life. The security of a nation must be interpreted in terms of the security of its citizens, of the satisfaction of their essential needs.... The absence of democracy that alone allows populations to participate freely in the management of public affairs, the denial of individual liberties, the abuses of religion, the preeminence given to military expenditures to the detriment of other sectors of national life, and the absence of appropriate administrative mechanisms to control the management of public funds are some of the deep-rooted causes of insecurity (O.U.A. 1992:8).

One can only regret that these accurate observations were not followed up with concrete actions.

Surviving Dreams and Nightmares

What can the international community do to help redirect disenchantment and resolve conflicts in Africa? How can the West help lighten the burden of broken dreams and unforgettable nightmares that incited poor peasants in Rwanda and elsewhere to follow blindly political opportunists who led them toward the brink? How can social disenchantment be reinvented positively? This section presents a few concrete measures to prevent violence that might be implemented by the international community.

I see several areas in which the intervention of international development agencies could prove effective. This intervention, however, requires that certain preconditions be met. First, policymakers must be willing to go beyond economism pure and simple, which until now has prevented them from exploring new avenues and methods of intervention. Second, the stated objective must not be to co-opt a few local elites into a so-called unified national government, but rather to convince ordinary citizens that peace is a strong economic asset and that the visible and invisible costs of violence go against their self-interests. Third, the prevention of conflicts must be placed within the larger framework of political and economic reforms aimed at consolidating democratic processes and affirming all dimensions of citizenship.

Of course, a separate methodological framework must be devised for each specific situation, but the seven following points should guide one's course of action:

- Better understanding the motivations and impulses that cause communities to tear themselves apart
- Emphasizing the common values and interests of social groups
- Creating an institutional and political framework that energizes civil society and clearly defines its scope of action
- Restoring to favor negotiation as a fundamental political tool, for it is often seen as a sign of corruption, weakness, or capitulation
- Pursuing equity in the choice of public works projects; instructing people about the costs of potential violence to individual and collective interests
- Giving priority to investments that facilitate freedom of movement, thereby putting people in contact with one another and creating markets and business opportunities (roads, railways, tourism projects)
- Adopting laws and regulations that protect property rights and stimulate creativity and the entrepreneurial spirit

It is important to take into account the immediate and distant causes of conflicts:

Causes of conflicts in Africa

- Historical misunderstandings and religious clashes;
- Mismanagement of social conflicts;
- Politics as a zero-sum game;
- Ethnic economic inequalities (whether this is real or simply a collective illusion);
- Poverty and lack of opportunities;
- Improper functioning of the structure of repression;
- Ill-conceived division of territory;
- Illegitimate governments and centralized states;
- Dangerous use of mass media;[15]
- Political racketeering (populism, tribalism, fatalism);
- Intellectual vacuum and absence of public debate over the main issues;
- Overblown reactions of leaders[16]

Given the diversity of causes, it is essential to develop both short- and long-term prevention strategies. I propose a few measures that might be taken by international organizations involved in the prevention of conflicts in Africa. These measures seek to forestall the usual causes of escalation.

Strategies for prevention

Short-term actions:

- Socioeconomic studies, polls, surveys to identify subjects of dispute;
- Identification of the main political actors in each country;
- Organization of debates, conferences, and forums over key issues;
- Creation of institutional frameworks for permanent interaction of social forces;
- Media campaigns aimed at consciousness raising;
- National campaigns on the rights and responsibilities of citizens;
- Training seminars on leadership, and renewal of confidence in negotiated settlements;
- Demilitarization, demobilization, and reintegration of former members of the armed forces;

Long-term actions:

- Education and training, including conflict-prevention courses in school curricula;
- Media productions to raise awareness of the consequences of violence and war;
- Political engineering (administrative reforms and decentralization);
- Building communications infrastructure;
- Improvement of intraregional infrastructure;
- Symbolic actions for managing collective memory in a positive way;
- Valorization and reinforcement of the private sector to increase economic opportunity for the poor;
- Development of an effective financial system.

The tremendous challenge of dealing with disenchantment and potential violence in Africa has caused some analysts to question the effectiveness of all measures of "preventive diplomacy." Stedman typifies this view: "Violent conflict of the type found in Somalia, Bosnia, and Rwanda is a combination of the predictable fault lines in societies and the unpredictable world of individual and group decisions. The former adheres to the mechanical world of clocks; the latter, the complex world of clouds" (1995:16). Of course the present state of knowledge in the social sciences offers few certainties and does not allow one to venture into the realm of predictions: which is what conflict prevention theories implicitly do. Furthermore, the linear and teleological view of the world that is contained in some of these theories invites caution. But if it is true that hastily devised prevention measures may aggravate the very conflicts they are supposed to forestall, then it would be pure fatalism to accept calmly the prospect of the worst.

Empirical research devoted to the study of conflicts has shown that violent disputes erupt under certain precise conditions. The speed with which the military capabilities of potential belligerents evolve and the absence of stabilizing mechanisms to defuse the explosive rhetoric flowing from different sources of authority are among the most important (Kim and Morrow 1992). This confirms what Olson (1993) and others have written about the importance of democracy: Far from being a by-product of economic development, as recent theorists of authoritarianism have affirmed, democracy is an important factor in economic growth.[17] As such, it is a powerful tool for resolving social antagonisms.

Conclusion

Having reached the end of this study, I would say, somewhat surprisingly, that the old debate on how effective Western democratic models are in Africa is beside the point: the U.S. presidential system or the British parliamentary government could easily be transferred to any African nation provided the social actors involved in implementing these models were truly committed to setting up the proper institutional framework. Conversely, no system of government, however just or well suited to the cultural environment and historical background it may be, has a chance of succeeding in Africa as long as the various elite factions spend most of their time undermining institutions in order to serve the exclusive interests of the networks they claim to represent.

The success or failure of an imported model depends foremost on the will of those charged with its implementation. The pursuit of the balance of powers that legitimated and validated the presidential system in the United States and the parliamentary system in Great Britain is not fundamentally incompatible with the various social structures, modes of collective action, philosophical systems, or need for justice found in African societies today. This is all the more true in that "the [legal] principle of state sovereignty," according to Badie, "does not hold up well to empirical evidence" (1992:17). Nations, peoples, and systems of thought are not discrete chemical substances—interdependence is now an obvious political and ideological reality.

Whether it is a matter of the political, the economic, or the social, the real issue is the capacity of the current elements of social change to increase the public's involvement in political process. On the political chessboard, urban elites attempt to confiscate the democratic project, writing rules of the game guaranteeing that representatives of only the most turbulent groups will attain to positions of power. Everywhere there seems to be a consensus that the exercise of government belongs exclusively to elites who are chosen by co-optation. One of the reproaches leveled against leaders who are truly popular in Africa is that they draw in the masses: Not only is popularity suspect, it is said to constitute populism and to contain the seed of fanaticism and violence. The foreign decisionmaking bodies that heavily influence the pace of political change may "forgive" new African leaders their political ideas and gradually come to tolerate their presence on the political chessboard they have long controlled. However, new African leaders are harshly condemned by these bodies if their actions lead more citizens to take an interest in the management of state affairs. This is yet another paradox of contemporary Africa, where leaders have a greater need for legitimacy than do leaders elsewhere in order to alert their peoples to urgent problems as they arise.

The fact that the real power to generate ideas and manage society is held by a small group of people limits the cognitive framework in which solutions may be devised. Given the implosion of the state, the globalization of difficulties, and the effects of transnationalization, decisions concern all the more directly the fundamental levers of the economy (international commerce, capital flow, interest and exchange rates, etc.). The gulf between the political realm and the rest of society is so large that the concept of citizenship remains a slogan. The tendency to resort to violence in numerous countries is a simultaneous reflection of the people's desire for revenge against illegitimate governments and of the governing elite's inability to see what is really at stake. Recognizing this simple truth would be enough to move things forward, for Africa is no more cursed than any other part of the world.

Notes

1. Basing his beliefs on statistical estimates, Powell thinks that institutional problems and the party system account for 13 percent of voter abstention in the United States and that 14 percent is attributable to administrative formalities.

2. Birnbaum (1975) traces the beginning of this idea to the early 1940s, when Karl Mannheim proclaimed "the crisis of values," and shows how Raymond Aron's hypothesis concerning the "suppression of the ideological debate" contributed to its development and how it began to be articulated clearly in the mid-1950s, when Edward Shils spoke of the end of the ideological age in Western industrialized nations. The same types of arguments are used in the less compelling "end of history" thesis put forth by Fukuyama (1992).

3. See Chapter 3.

4. Mishan (1981) and others think that the expression *collective goods* should be used in place of *public goods* because it is more accurate and precise.

5. See, e.g., Miller (1982:107–109) and Rosen (1988), especially chs. 5–7.

6. This premise overgeneralizes somewhat, for it assumes that political well-being is conceived of and structured in the same way in all areas of the world, an idea I have elsewhere refuted (compare Monga 1996).

7. In Wittman's view, the absence of monopolies, agents with good information, and limits on rent-seeking are the three main factors contributing to the success of the market economy. He writes: "Political and economic markets both work well. I show that democratic political markets are organized to promote wealth-maximizing outcomes, that these markets are highly competitive, and that political entrepreneurs are rewarded for efficient behavior" (1989:1395–1396). Stigler (1972) also held that political markets function in the same way as economic markets.

8. Twenty years ago, who would have thought that countries such as Singapore and Korea would figure among the most important in the world? Both Botswana and Côte d'Ivoire have the means to make the same politico-economic leap if the main local political actors decide to focus on this objective. Economic theories dealing with convergence (Barro and Sala-i-Martin 1992) and economic backwardness (Gerschenkron 1962) amply demonstrate that this is not a utopian idea.

9. One of the most popular election campaign themes in Africa is fierce criticism of international monetary institutions. This is explained not only by the social costs of structural adjustment programs but also by the widely held view that the World Bank and the International Monetary Fund support the sitting authoritarian government, despite all their words about "good governance," which strike people as nothing but demagoguery.

10. A substantial body of literature on this question exists in English. Researchers use, most notably, models drawn from game theory. See, e.g., Huth, Bennett, and Gelpi (1992); Morrow (1989); Levy (1983); Gurr (1980); and Stohl (1976).

11. See, e.g., Fischer, Hausman, Karasik, and Schelling (1994); and Fischer, Rodrik, and Tuma (1993).

12. Normative models date back to Kant. For an overview, see Doyle (1986).

13. See de Mesquita and Lalman (1986) and Rummel (1979).

14. See, e.g., Deng's (1995) superb monograph on the war in Sudan.

15. Radio des Mille Collines, for example, was frightfully successful in igniting Rwanda in 1994 (compare Willame 1995). In many African countries today, tribal hatred and calumny are propagated by the "private" newspaper industry the government has set up as a defense against the other private press, the one they cannot control. Examples of such newspapers are *Le Témoin* and *Le Patriote* in Cameroon and *Le Démocrate* in Côte d'Ivoire.

16. Here again, the example of Rwanda is instructive. It is now clear that the reaction of the leaders of various factions to the assassination of President Juvénal Habyarimana poisoned the political climate. For a succinct account of this, see Awwad (1994). Conversely, the call for calm and moderation by Cameroon's chief opposition leader, John Fru Ndi, no doubt allowed Cameroon to avoid bloodshed when the results of the rigged October 1992 presidential election were announced.

17. Wade (1990), for example, maintains that the Taiwanese government's success in restructuring the economy is above all attributable to the inability of public opinion to influence and possibly block the implementation of necessary reforms. Przeworski and Limongi (1993) see no correlation between the type of government and economic growth, even though political institutions clearly affect the latter.

References

Adotevi, Stanislas Spéro K. (1972), *Négritude et négrologues,* Paris, U.G.E., 10/18.

Aebischer, Verena, and D. Oberlé (1990), *Le groupe en psychologie sociale,* Paris, Dunod.

African Agenda (1995), "Daddy, Buy Me What I Saw on MTV" (Johannesburg), vol. 1, no. 7, p. 51.

Ahidjo, Ahmadou (1973), "Discours d'ouverture du Conseil National de l'Union Nationale Camerounaise," Yaoundé, November.

Akendengue, Pierre (1973), "Le chant du coupeur d'okoume," on the album *Nandipo,* lyrics by Pierre-Edgard Moudjegou, Paris, Saravah.

Almond, Gabriel, and Sidney Verba (1963), *The Civic Culture: Political Attitudes and Democracy in Five Nations,* Boston, Little, Brown.

Amin, Samir (1991), *L'empire du chaos—La nouvelle mondialisation capitaliste,* Paris, L'Harmattan.

Amondji, Marcel (1993), *L'Afrique noire au miroir de l'Occident,* Paris, Editions Nouvelles du Sud.

Amselle, Jean-Loup, and Elikia Mbokolo (1985), eds., *Au coeur de l'ethnie: ethnies, tribalisme et etat en Afrique,* Paris, La Découverte.

Appiah, Kwame Anthony (1992), *In My Father's House: Africa in the Philosophy of Culture,* New York, Oxford University Press.

Apter, David E., and Carl G. Rosberg (1994), eds., *Political Development and the New Realism in Sub-Saharan Africa,* Charlottesville, The University Press of Virginia.

Ardener, E. (1970), "Witchcraft, Economics, and the Continuity of Belief," in: M. Douglas (ed.), *Witchcraft: Confessions and Accusations,* London, Tavistock Publications, pp. 141–160.

Aron, Raymond (1966), *Trois essais sur l'rige industriel,* Paris, Plon.

———(1972), *Etudes politiques,* Paris Gallimard.

———(1973), *Histoire et dialectique de la violence,* Paris, Gallimard.

Attali, Jacques (1977), *Bruits: Essai sur l'économie politique de la musique,* Paris, PUF.

Augé, Marc (1982), *Génie du paganisme,* Paris, Gallimard; especially chap. 7, "Signes du corps, sens du social; sorcier, imaginaire, sorcellerie symboliques," pp. 211–280.

———(1985), *La traversée du Luxembourg,* Paris, Hachette.

———(1986), *Un ethnologue dans le métro,* Paris, Hachette.

Awwad, E. (1994), "Les mécanismes de gestion des conflits en Afrique: bilan," *Défense nationale,* December, pp. 153–166.

Ayittey, George B. N. (1992), *Africa Betrayed,* New York, St. Martin's.

Bach, Daniel C. (1992) "Comments," Conference on European-African Relations: Challenges in the 1990s. Ebenhausen, May 1992. Typescript.

Badie, Bertrand (1988), *Culture et politique,* Paris, Economica.

———(1990), "'Je dis Occident': démocratie et développement. Réponse à 6 questions," *Pouvoirs,* no. 52, pp. 43–64.

———(1992), *L'Etat importé: l'occidentalisation de l'ordre politique,* Paris, Fayard.

Bahoken, J.-C. (1967), *Clairières métaphysiques africaines,* Paris, Présence Africaine.

Bahoken, J.-C., and E. Atangana (1975), *La politique culturelle en République Unie du Cameroun,* Paris, Presses de l'UNESCO.

Balandier, Georges (1955), *Sociologie actuelle de l'Afrique noire,* Paris, Armand Colin.

———(1971), *Sens et puissance,* Quadridge, PUF.

———(1972), *Political Anthropology,* Harmondsworth, Penguin.

———(1984), interview in *Entretiens avec Le Monde,* vol. 4, *Civilisations,* Paris, La Découverte.

———(1985), *Le détour. Pouvoir et modernité,* Paris, Fayard.

———(1988), *Le désordre—Eloge du mouvement,* Paris, Fayard.

Banting, Keith (1986), "Points de vue sur l'Etat contemporain: introduction," in: K. Banting (ed.), *L'Etat et la société: le Canada dans une optique comparative,* vol. 31, Ottawa, Etudes de la Commission Royale.

Barkan, Joel D. (1992), "The Rise and Fall of the Governance Realm in Kenya," in: G. Hyden and M. Bratton (eds.) *Governance and Politics in Africa,* Boulder, Colo., Lynne Rienner Publishers, pp. 167–192.

———(1993), "Kenya: Lessons from a Flawed Election," *Journal of Democracy,* vol. 4, no. 3, July, pp. 85–99.

Barley, Nigel (1983), *Symbolic Structures: An Exploration of the Culture of the Domwayos,* Cambridge, Cambridge University Press.

Barro, Robert J., and Sala-i-Martin (1992), "Convergence," *Journal of Political Economy,* vol. 100, April, pp. 223–252.

Barry, B. (1978), *Sociologists, Economists, and Democracy,* Chicago, University of Chicago Press.

Bates, Robert H. (1981), *Markets and States in Tropical Africa,* Berkeley, University of California Press.

———(1994), "The Impulse to Reform in Africa," in: J. A. Widner (ed.), *Economic Change and Political Liberation in Sub-Saharan Africa,* Baltimore, Johns Hopkins University Press, pp. 13–28.

Bayart, Jean-François (1989), *L'Etat en Afrique: La politique du ventre,* Paris, Fayard.

Bebey, Francis (1981), interview in *Paroles et Musique,* no. 15, pp. 25–38.

———(1983), "King of Pygmies," on the album *Superbebey,* Paris, Ozileka Records.

Bell, Daniel (1960), *The End of Ideology: On the Exhaustion of Political Ideas in the Fifties,* Glencoe, Ill., Free Pree Press.

Bemba, Sylvain (1984), *50 ans de musique du Congo-Zaïre,* Paris, Présence Africaine.

Bender, Wolfgang (1991), *Sweet Mother: Modern African Music,* Chicago, University of Chicago Press.

Bennett, S. E., and L. L. Bennett (1986), "Political Participation," *Annual Review of Political Science*, pp. 157–204.

Bergson, Henri (1932), *Les deux sources de la morale et de la religion*, Paris, Alcan.

Bernal, Martin (1987), *Black Athena: The Afroasiatic Roots of Classical Civilization*, vol. 1, New Brunswick, N.J., Rutgers University Press.

Berque, Jacques (1980), *L'islam au défi*, Paris, Gallimard.

Beti, Mongo (1993), "Ecrivain africain, qu'est-ce que c'est?," *Europe*, October, pp. 156–162.

Birnbaum, Pierre (1975), *La fin du politique*, Paris, Editions du Seuil.

Bloch, Ernst (1988), *The Utopian Function of Art and Literature*, Cambridge, MIT Press.

Bloch, Marc (1970), *French Rural History*, trans. Janet Sondheimer, Berkeley, University of California Press.

Bobbio, N. (1987), *Which Socialism?* Cambridge, Polity Press.

Boudjedra, Rachid (1992), *FIS de la haine*, Paris, Denoël.

Bouzar, Wadi (1984), *La mouvance et la pause*, 2 vols., Algiers, Editions SNED.

Boyer, R. (1992), *Anthropologie du sacré*, Paris, Editions Mentha.

Brady, Henry E., Sidney Verba, and Kay Lehman Schlozman (1995), "Beyond SES: A Resource Model of Political Participation," *American Political Science Review*, vol. 89, no. 2, June, pp. 271–294.

Bratton, Michael, and Beatrice Liatto-Katundu (1994), *Political Culture in Zambia: A Pilot Survey*, MSU Working Papers on Political Reform in Africa, no. 7, January, East Lansing, Michigan State University.

Bratton, Michael, and Nicolas van de Walle (1992), "Toward Governance in Africa: Popular Demands and State Responses," in: G. Hyden and M. Bratton (eds.), *Governance and Politics in Africa*, Boulder, Colo., Lynne Rienner Publishers, pp. 27–55.

Braud, Philippe (1991), *Le jardin des délices démocratiques*, Paris, Presses de la Fondation Nationale des sciences politiques.

———(1992), *La vie politique*, 3d ed., Paris, PUF.

Braudel, Fernand (1979), *Civilisation matérielle, économie et capitalisme, XVé-XVIIIéme siécle*, tome 2, *Les jeux de l'échange*, Paris, Armand Colin.

Brinton, Crane (1965), *The Anatomy of Revolution*, revised and expanded edition, New York, Vintage Books.

Brown, Seyom (1994), *The Causes and Prevention of War*, 2d edition, New York, St. Martin's Press.

Bwaenga, Bolya (1991), *L'Afrique en kimono*, Paris, Editions Nouvelles du Sud.

Callaghy, Thomas (1994), "State, Choice, and Context: Comparative Reflections on Reform and Intractability," in: D. E. Apter and C. G. Rosberg (eds.) *Political Development and the New Realism in Sub-Saharan Africa*, Charlottesville, University Press of Virginia, pp. 184–219.

Callinicos, Alex (1991), *The Revenge of History: Marxism and the East European Revolutions*, Cambridge, Polity Press.

Carr, Wolf-Dieter (1984), "Toward a Society of Conditioned Reflexes," in: Habermas (1984), pp. 31–66.

Carruth, Hayden (1993), *Sitting In: Selected Writings on Jazz, Blues, and Related Topics,* Iowa City, University of Iowa Press.

Carter, Stephen L. (1993), *The Culture of Disbelief: How American Law and Politics Trivialize Religious Devotion,* New York, Basicbooks.

Castoriadis, Cornelius (1987), *The Imaginary Institution of Society,* trans. Kathleen Blamey, Cambridge, MIT Press.

Ceronetti, Guido (1984), *Le silence du corps,* Paris, Albin Michel.

Changer le Cameroun (1992), *Le Cameroun éclaté? Une anthologie des revendications ethniques,* Yaoundé.

Chege, Michael (1993), "The Kenya December 1992 General Elections: Opposition Leaders Play into the Hands of the Ruling KANU Party," CODESTRIA Bulletin no. 1.

———(1994), "Swapping Development Strategies: Kenya and Tanzania After Their Founding Presidents," in: D. E. Apter and C. G. Rosberg (eds.) *Political Development and the New Realism in Sub-Saharan Africa,* Charlottesville, University Press of Virginia, pp. 247–290.

Chinweizu, Onwuchekwa Jemie, and Ihechukwu Madubuike (1980), *Toward the Decolonization of African Literature,* Enugu, Nigeria, Fourth Dimension Publishing.

Chomsky, Noam (1987), "Language and Freedom," in: James Peck (ed.), *The Chomsky Reader,* New York, Pantheon, pp. 139–155.

Cohen, Jean L., and Andrew Arato (1992), *Civil Society and Political Theory,* Cambridge, MIT Press.

Cohn, N. (1970), "The Myth of Satan and His Human Servants," in: M. Douglas (ed.), *Witchcraft: Confessions and Accusations,* London, Tavistock Publications, pp. 3–16.

Coleman, James S. (1990), *Foundations of Social Theory,* Cambridge, Harvard University Press.

Coleman, James S., and C. R. D. Halisi (1983), "American Political Science and Tropical Africa: Universalism Versus Relativism," *African Studies Review,* vol. 26, nos. 3/4, September–December, pp. 25–62.

Collier, Paul (1991), "Africa's External Economic Relations, 1960–90," *African Affairs,* vol. 90, no. 360, July, pp. 339–356.

Compaoré, Blaise (1995), "Mon ambition pour le Burkina Faso," interview in *Jeune Afrique Economie,* no. 202, September 4, pp. 52–57.

Comte, Gilbert (1988), *L'empire triomphant 1871–1936. L'aventure coloniale de la France,* Paris, Denoël.

Conrad, Peter (1991), "Prometheus and His Creatures," *The Observer,* September 15.

Coquery-Vidrovitch, Cathérine (1985), *Afrique noire, Permanences et ruptures,* Paris, Payot.

Crotty, William (1991), "Political Participation: Mapping the Terrain," in: William Crotty, ed., *Political Participation and American Democracy,* New York, Greenwood Press, pp. 1–22.

Crystal, David (1987), *The Cambridge Encyclopedia of Language,* Cambridge, Cambridge University Press.

Dabezies, Pierre (1992), "Vers la démocratisation de l'Afrique," *Défense nationale,* May, pp. 21–33.
Dahl, Robert A. (1971), *Polyarchy: Participation and Opposition,* New Haven, Yale University Press.
———(1985), *A Preface to Economic Democracy,* Cambridge, Polity Press.
———(1992), "The Problem of Civic Competence," *Journal of Democracy,* vol. 3, no. 4, October, pp. 45–59.
Davidson, Donald (1977), "The Method of Truth in Metaphysics," *Midwest Studies in Philosophy,* vol. 2, pp. 244–254.
Davies, Reginald Trevor (1947), *Four Centuries of Witch Beliefs,* London, Methuen.
de Certeau, Michel (1984), *The Practice of Everyday Life,* trans. Steven F. Rendall, Berkeley, University of California Press.
de Heutsch, Luc (1986), *Le sacrifice dans les religions africaines,* Paris, Gallimard.
de Mesquita, Bruno, et al. (1992), *War and Reason,* New Haven, Yale University Press.
de Mesquita, Bruce Bueno, and David Lalman (1986), "Reason and War," *American Political Science Review,* vol. 80, no. 4, December, pp. 1113–1129.
de Tocqueville, Alexis (1945), *Democracy in America,* 2 vols., New York, Vintage Books.
Delbourg, Patricce (1991), "Milla-Noah: Match au sommet," *L'Evénement du Jeudi,* no. 339, May, pp. 96–97.
Delli Carpini, M. X., and S. Keeter (1993), "Measuring Political Knowledge: Putting First Things First," *American Journal of Political Science,* vol. 37, no. 4, November, pp. 1179–1206.
Déloye, Yves (1993), "L'élection au village: le geste électoral à l'occasion des scrutins cantonaux et régionaux de mars 1992," *Revue française de science politique,* vol. 43, no.1, February, pp. 83–106.
Deng, Francis M. (1995), *War of Visions: Conflict of ldentities in the Sudan,* Washington, D.C., The Brookings Institution.
Deng, Francis M., and William I. Zartman (1991), eds., *Conflict Resolution in Africa,* Washington, D.C., The Brookings Institution.
Descartes, René (1962), *Discourse on Method,* trans. John Veitch, La Salle, Ill., Open Court Publishing Company.
Diamond, Larry (1990), "Three Paradoxes of Democracy," *Journal of Democracy,* vol. 1, no. 3, Summer, pp. 48–60.
———(1992), "Economic Development and Democracy Reconsidered," *American Behavioral Scientist* vol. 35, nos. 4/5, March/June, pp. 450–499.
———(1994), "Rethinking Civil Society: Toward Democratic Consolidation," *Journal of Democracy,* vol. 5, no. 3, July, pp. 4–17.
———(1995), *Promoting Democracy in the 1990s: Actors and Instruments, Issues and Imperatives,* A report to the Carnegie Commission on Preventing Deadly Conflict, New York, Carnegie Corporation.
Dibango, Manu (1991), interview in *Le courrier de l'UNESCO,* March, pp. 4–7.
Diop, Cheikh Anta (1979), *Nations nègres et culture,* 2 vols. (originally published in 1954), Paris, Présence Africaine.
Diop, Momar Coumba, and Mamadou Diouf (1990) *Le Sénégal sous Abdou Diouf,* Paris, Karthala.

Dixon, William J. (1994), "Democracy and the Peaceful Settlement of International Conflict," *American Political Science Review*, vol. 88, no. 1, March, pp. 14–32.

Douglas, M. (1963), "Techniques of Sorcery Control in Central Africa," in: John Middleton and E. H. Winter (eds.), *Witchcraft and Sorcery in East Africa*, London, Routledge & Kegan Paul.

———(1970), "Introduction: Thirty Years After *Witchcraft, Oracles and Magic*," in: M. Douglas (ed.), *Witchcraft: Confessions and Accusations*, London, Tavistock Publications, pp. xiii–xxxviii.

Doyle, Michael W. (1986), "Liberalism and World Politics," *American Political Science Review*, vol. 80, no. 4, December, pp. 1151–1169.

Dunn, John (1978), "Comparing West African States," in J. Dunn, (ed.), *West African States, Failure and Promise, a Study in Comparative Politics*, Cambridge, Cambridge University Press, 1978, p. 1–21.

Durkheim, Emile (1968), *The Elementary Forms of the Religious Life*, (originally published in French in 1912, trans. Joseph Ward Swain), London, Allen and Unwin.

Duval, M. (1985), *Un totalitarisme sans Etat—Essai d'anthropologie politique à partir d'un village burkinabé*, Paris, L'Harmattan.

Duvignaud, Jean (1991), *Fêtes et civilisations*, Paris, Actes Sud.

Eboussi Boulaga, Fabien (1976), *La crise du Muntu*, Paris, Présence Africaine.

———(1991), *A contretemps: l'enjeu de Dieu en Afrique*, Paris, Karthala.

Ekani, André-Vincent (1990), "Portrait of John Fru Ndi," *Cameroon Tribune*, May 30.

Ela, Jean-Marc (1982), *L'Afrique des villages*, Paris, Karthala.

———(1990), *Quand l'Etat pénètre en brousse—Les ripostes paysannes à la crise*, Paris, Karthala.

———(1994), *Restituer l'histoire aux sociétés africaines—Promouvoir les sciences sociales en Afrique*, Paris, L'Harmattan.

Elmandjra, Mahdi (1990), interview in *Sud-Ouest*, March 12.

Etounga-Manguelle, Daniel (1990), *L'Afrique a-t-elle besoin d'un programme d'ajustement structurel?* Paris, Editions Nouvelles du Sud.

Euba, Akin (1989), *Essays on music in Africa (2), Intercultural perspectives*, Elekoto Music Centre (Lagos), Bayreuth African Studies.

Evans-Pritchard, E. (1935), "Introduction," *Africa* (quarterly), October, pp. 22–24.

———(1937), *Witchcraft, Oracles and Magic Among the Azande*, Oxford, Clarendon Press.

Eyinga, Abel (1978), *Mandat d'arrêt pour cause d'elections: de la démocratie au Cameroun, 1970–1978*, Paris, L'Harmattan.

Fedida, Pierre (1977), *Corps du vide et espace de séance*, Paris, Delarge.

Ferguson, Adam (1996), *An Essay on the History of Civil Society*, New York, Cambridge University.

Fischer, G. N. (1993), *La dynamique du social, violence, pouvoir, changement*, Paris, Dunod.

Fischer, Stanley, L. J. Hausman, A. D. Karasik, and T. C. Schelling (1994), eds., *Securing Peace in the Middle East: Project on Economic Transition*, Cambridge, MIT Press.

Fischer, Stanley, Dani Rodrik, and Elias Tuma, (1993), eds., *The Economics of Middle East Peace,* Cambridge, MIT Press.

Fisiy, Cyprian (1990), "Le monopole juridictionnel de l'Etat et le règlement des affaires de sorcellerie au Cameroun," *Politique africaine,* no. 40, pp. 60–72.

Fisiy, Cyprian, and Peter Geschiere (1990), "Judges and Witches, or, How Is the State to Deal with Witchcraft? Examples from South-East Cameroon," *Cahiers d'Etudes Africaines,* 118, XXX-2, pp. 135–156.

Fonkoué, Jean (1985), *Différence et identité: Les sociologues africains face à la sociologie,* Paris, Silex.

Fontanier, P. (1968), *Les figures du discours,* rev. ed., Paris, Flammarion.

Foucault, Michel (1966), *Les mots et les choses,* Paris, Gallimard. (*The Order of Things,* 1973, New York, Pantheon.)

———(1969), *L'archéologie du savoir,* Paris, Gallimard. (*The Archeology of Knowledge,* 1982, New York, Pantheon.)

———(1976), *Histoire de la sexualité,* tome 1 (*The History of Sexuality,* vol. 1, An Introduction, 1978, New York, Pantheon.)

———(1979), *Surveiller et punir,* Paris, Gallimard.

French, Howard (1995a), "An African Nation's Path to Democracy Takes a Detour," *New York Times,* October 13.

———(1995b), "Africa's Ballot Box: Look Out for Sleight of Hand," *New York Times,* October 24.

Frey, Bruno S. (1988), "Public Goods," in: Phyllis Deane and Jessica Kuper, eds., *A Lexicon of Economics,* London, Routledge, pp. 320–321.

Fukuyama, Francis (1992), *The End of History and the Last Man,* New York, Free Press.

Gastil, Raymond D. (1991), "The Comparative Survey of Freedom: Experiences and Suggestions," in: Alex Inkeles (ed.), *On Measuring Democracy,* New Brunswick, N.J., Transaction.

Gautier, Claude (1993), *L'Invention de la société civil: lectures anglo-ecossaises, Mandeville, Smith, Ferguson,* Paris, PUF.

Geisler, Gisele (1993), "Fair? What Has Fairness Got to Do with It? Vagaries of Election Observations and Democratic Standards," *The Journal of Modern African Studies,* vol. 31, no. 4, pp. 613–637.

Gellner, Ernest (1991), "Civil Society in Historical Context," *International Social Science Journal,* vol. 129, pp. 495–510.

Gerschenkron, Alexander (1962), *Economic Backwardness in Historical Perspective,* Cambridge, Harvard University Press.

Glaser, Antoine, and Stephen Smith (1992), *Ces messieurs Afrique, Le Paris-Village du continent noir,* Paris, Calmann-Lévy.

Glasner, P. E. (1977), *The Sociology of Secularization: A Critique of a Concept,* London, Routledge & Kegan Paul.

Gleick, James (1989), *La Théorie du chaos,* Paris, Albin Michel.

Gould, Carol C. (1988), *Rethinking Democracy: Freedom and Social Cooperation in Politics, Economy, and Society,* Cambridge, Cambridge University Press.

Gourdon, H. (1991), *Trois comptines à propos de la société civile,* in: M. Canau (ed.), *Changements politiques au Maghreb,* Paris, Editions du CNRS, pp. 191–205.

Gramsci, Antonio (1977), *Gramsci dans le texte,* Paris, Editions Sociales.

Gurr, Ted Robert (1970), *Why Men Rebel,* Princeton, Princeton University Press.

———(1980), ed., *Handbook of Political Conflict: Theory and Research,* New York, The Free Press.

Gurr, Ted R., and R. Duvall (1976), "Introduction to a Formal Theory of Conflict Within Social Systems," in: L.A. Coser and O.N. Larsen (eds.), *The Uses of Controversy in Sociology,* New York, Free Press.

Haber, Robert (1968), "The End of Ideology as Ideology," in: F. Lindenfeld, ed., *Reader in Political Sociology,* New York, Funk and Wagnals.

Habermas, Jurgen (1984), ed., *Observations on "The Spiritual Situation of the Age,"* Cambridge, MIT Press.

———(1987), *Théorie de l'agir communicationnel, vol 2, Pour une critique de la raison fonctionnaliste,* Paris, Fayard.

Hagège, Claude (1985), *L'homme de paroles,* Paris, Fayard.

Haim, Philippe (1990), "Musiques vivantes...," *Libération,* October 11, p. 4.

Harbeson, John W., Donald Rothchild, and Naomi Chazan, (1994), eds., *Civil Society and the State in Africa,* Boulder, Colo., Lynne Rienner Publishers.

Harriss, J., and M. Moore (1984), eds., "Development and the Rural-Urban Division," *The Journal of Development Studies,* vol. 20, no. 3, April, special issue.

Hayek, F. A. (1960), *The Constitution of Liberty,* London, Routledge & Kegan Paul.

———(1976), *The Road to Serfdom,* London, Routledge & Kegan Paul.

Haynes, J. (1994), *Religion in Third World Politics,* Boulder, Colo., Lynne Rienner Publishers.

Hegel, G. W. F. (1975), *Aesthetics,* trans. T. M. Knox, 2 vols., Oxford, Clarendon Press.

Held, David (1987), *Models of Democracy,* Stanford, Stanford University Press.

———(1994), ed., *Prospects for Democracy: North, South, East, West,* Stanford, Stanford University Press.

Hermet, Guy (1983), *Aux frontières de la démocratie,* Paris, PUF.

Hobsbawm, Eric J. (1973), "Peasants and Politics," *Journal of Peasant Studies,* vol. 1, no. 1, pp. 3–22.

Holmquist, Frank, Michael Ford, and F. Weaver (1994), "The Structural Development of Kenya's Political Economy," *African Studies Review,* vol. 37, no. 1, April, pp. 69–105.

Horowitz, Donald L. (1985), *Ethnic Groups in Conflict,* Berkeley, University of California Press.

———(1993), "Democracy in Divided Societies," *Journal of Democracy,* vol. 4, no. 4, October, pp. 18–38.

Horton, R. (1967), "African Traditional Religion and Western Science," *Africa,* vol. 37, nos. 1/2, pp. 50–71 and 155–187.

———(1982), "Tradition and Modernity Revisited," in: S. Lukes and M. Hollis (eds.), *Rationality and Relativism,* Oxford, Basil Blackwell, pp. 201–260.

Houtondji, Paulin (1983), *African Philosophy: Myth and Reality* (originally published in French in 1976), Bloomington, Indiana University Press.

Huntington, Samuel P. (1968), *Political Order in Changing Societies,* New Haven, Yale University Press.

———(1991), *The Third Wave: Democratization in the Late Twentieth Century,* Norman, Oklahoma University Press.

———(1993a), "The Clash of Civilizations?" *Foreign Affairs,* vol. 72, no. 3, Summer, pp. 22–49.

———(1993b), "If Not Civilizations, What? Paradigms of the Post–Cold War World," *Foreign Affairs,* vol. 72, no. 5, November/December, pp. 186–194.

Huth, Paul, Christopher Gelpi, and Bennett D. Scott (1993), "The Escalation of Great Power Militarized Disputes: Testing Rational Deterrence Theory and Structural Realism," *American Political Science Review,* vol. 87, no. 3, September, pp. 609–623.

Huth, Paul, Bennett D. Scott, and Christopher G. Gelpi (1992), "System Uncertainty, Risk Propensity, and International Conflict Among Great Powers," *Journal of Conflict Resolution,* vol. 36, pp. 478–517.

Hyden, Goran, and Michael Bratton (1992), eds., *Governance and Politics in Africa,* Boulder, Colo., Lynne Rienner Publishers.

Imbert, Claude (1984), *Ce que je crois,* Paris, Grasset.

Inglehart, Ronald (1988), "The Renaissance of Political Culture," *American Political Science Review,* vol. 82, no. 4, December, pp. 1203–1230.

Inglehart, Ronald, and P.R. Abramson (1994), "Economic Security and Value Change," *American Political Science Review,* vol. 88, no. 2, June, pp. 336–354.

Jackman, Robert W. (1987), "Political Institutions and Voter Turnout in the Industrial Democracies," *American Political Science Review,* vol. 81, pp. 405–423.

Jalbert, Lisette (1992), "L'Etat ancré ou les frontières de la démocratie," in: G. Boismenu, P. Hamel, G. Labica, *Les formes modernes de la democrtie,* Paris and Montreal, L'Harmattan and Presses de l'Université de Montreal, pp. 83–112.

Jary, David, and Jean Jary (1991), eds., *The HarperCollins Dictionary of Sociology,* New York, Harper Perennial.

Johnson, Chalmers A. (1995), *Japan, Who Governs?: The Rise of the Developmental State,* New York, Norton.

Joseph, Richard (1983), "Class, State, and Prebendal Politics in Nigeria," *Journal of Commonwealth and Comparative Politics,* vol. 21, no. 3, pp. 21–38.

Kabou, Axelle (1991), *Et si l'Afrique refusait le développement?* Paris, L'Harmattan.

Kamto, Maurice (1987), *Pouvoir et droit en Afrique noire,* Paris, LGDJ.

Karl, Terry L. (1990), "Dilemmas of Democratization in Latin America," *Comparative Politics* vol. 23, no. 1, October, pp. 1–21.

Keane, John (1988), ed., *Civil Society and the State, and Democracy and Civil Society,* London, Verso.

Kerrou, Mohammed (1989), "A propos de la société civile," *Outrouhat* (Tunis), vol. 15, pp. 26–29.

Kertzer, David I. (1988), *Ritual, Politics, and Power,* New Haven, Yale University Press.

Kim, W., and James D. Morrow (1992), "When Do Power Shifts Lead to War?" *American Journal of Political Science,* vol. 36, no. 4, November, pp. 896–922.

Klossowski, Pierre (1969), *Nietzsche et le cercle vicieux,* Paris, Mercure de France.

Kom, Ambroise (1983), ed., *Dictionnaire des oeuvres littéraires négro-africaines, des origines à 1978,* Sherbrooke, Quebec, ACCT/Naaman.

———(1991a), "Mongo Beti Returns to Cameroon: A Journey in Darkness," *Research in African Literature,* vol. 22, no. 4, pp. 147–153.

———(1991b), "Writing Under Monocracy: Intellectual Poverty in Cameroon," *Research in African Literature,* vol. 22, no. 1, pp. 83–92.

Konan Bédié, Henri (1993), interview in *Jeune Afrique Economie,* no. 163, January, pp. 20–33.

Kotto Essome (1985), "Du tribalisme comme stratégie à la tribu comme fiction," *Nouvelles du Sud,* no. 1, August, pp. 33–42.

Kpatindé, Francis (1990), "Fela, un saxophoniste au violon," in: *Grands procès de l'Afrique contemporaine,* Paris, Editions Jeune Afrique Livres, pp. 49–63.

Kriesberg, Louis (1991), "Introduction," in: L. Kriesberg and S.J. Thorson, *Timing the De-escalation of International Conflicts,* Syracuse, N.Y., Syracuse University Press.

Kristof, Nicholas D. (1996), "For Many Japanese, Change in the Government Seems to Bring No Real Change," *New York Times,* January 14.

Kroeber, A. L., and C. Kluckhohn (1952), *Culture: A Critical Review of Concepts and Definitions,* New York, Vintage Books.

Krueger, Anne O. (1974), "Political Economy of the Rent-Seeking Society," *American Economic Review,* vol. 64, no. 3, June, pp. 291–303.

Krugman, Paul (1995), *Development, Geography, and Economic Theory,* Cambridge, MIT Press.

Kwabena Nketia, J. H. (1990), "Dimensions esthétiques des instruments de musique africains," in: M. T. Brincard, ed., *Afriques, formes sonores,* Paris, Editions de la Réunion des Musées Nationaux.

Lancaster, Carol J. (1993), *United States and Africa: Into the Twenty-First Century,* policy essay no. 7, Washington, D.C., Overseas Development Council.

Lavau, Georges (1962), "Les aspects socio-culturels de la dépolitisation," in: *La dépolitisation, mythe ou réalite'?* Paris, Armand Colin, pp. 182–186.

Le Bon, Gustave (1963), *La Psychologie des foules* (1895), Paris, Presses Universitaires de France.

Lefort, Claude (1981), *L'invention démocratique: les limites de la domination totalitaire,* Paris, Fayard.

———(1986), *Essais sur le politique XIX–XXème siècle,* Paris, Seuil, Esprit.

Lévi-Strauss, Claude (1958), *Anthropologie structurale,* Paris, Plon.

Lévi-Strauss, Claude, and Didier Eribon (1990), *De près et de loin,* Paris, Points Odile Jacob.

Levy, Jack S. (1983), *War in the Modern Great Power System, 1495–1975,* Lexington, University Press of Kentucky.

Lewin, Kurt (1948), *Resolving Social Conflicts,* New York, Harper & Brothers.

Lijphart, Arend (1977), *Democracy in Plural Societies: A Comparative Exploration,* New Haven, Yale University Press.

Lipovestky, Gilles (1983), *L'ère du vide,* Paris, Gallimard.

Lipset, Seymour Martin (1960), *Political Man: The Social Bases of Politics,* Garden City, N.Y., Doubleday.

———(1990), "The Centrality of Political Culture," *Journal of Democracy,* vol. 1, no. 4, Fall, pp. 80–83.

Lipton, Michael (1977), *Why Poor People Stay Poor: Urban Bias in World Development,* Cambridge, Harvard University Press.

Loury, Glenn C. (1977), "A Dynamic Theory of Racial Income Differences," in: Phillis A. Wallace and Annette La Mond (eds.), *Women, Minorities, and Employment Discrimination,* Lexington, Mass., Lexington Books, pp. 153–186.

Lugan, Bernard (1989), *Afrique, l'histoire à l'endroit,* Paris, Perrin.

Lyotard, Jean-François (1993), "Musique, mutique," in Christine Buci-Glucksman and Michaël Levinas (eds.), *L'idée musicale,* Saint-Denis, Presses Universitaires de Vincennes, pp. 111–124.

Macpherson, C. B. (1977), *The Life and Times of Liberal Democracy,* Oxford, Oxford University Press.

Magassouba, Moriba (1985), *L'islam au Sénégal: Demain les Mollahs?* Paris, Karthala.

Mana, Ka (1991), L'Afrique va-t-elle mourir? Paris, Editions du Cerf.

Maoz, Zeev, and Bruce Russett (1993), "Normative and Structural Causes of Democratic Peace, 1946–1986," *American Political Science Review,* vol. 87, no. 3, September, pp. 624–638.

Maoz, Zeev, and Nasrin Abdolali (1989), "Regime Types and International Conflict: 1815–1976," *Journal of Conflict Resolution,* vol. 33, no. 1 , March, pp. 3–35.

Marshall, Gordon (1994), ed., *The Concise Oxford Dictionary of Sociology,* New York, Oxford University Press.

Martin, Guy (1995), "Continuity and Change in Franco-African Relations," *The Journal of Modern African Studies,* vol. 33, no. 1, pp. 1–20.

Martin, Robert (1988), *The Meaning of Language,* Cambridge, MIT Press.

———(1992), "Building Independent Mass Media in Africa," *The Journal of Modern African Studies,* vol. 30, no. 2, June, pp. 331–340.

Mayer, Nona, and Pascal Perrineau (1992), *Les comportements politiques,* Paris, Armand Colin.

Mbembe, Achille (1988), *Afriques indociles: Christianisme, pouvoir et Etat en société post-coloniale,* Paris, Karthala.

———(1989), "Notes (provisoires) sur le pouvoir en postcolonie," paper presented at the Annual Meeting of the African Studies Association, Atlanta, Ga., November.

———(1992), "La prolifération du dîvin en Afrique noire," in: Gilles Kepel, *Les politiques de Dieu,* Paris, CERI-Seuil, pp. 177–201.

Mbock, Charly-Gabriel (1985), *Cameroun: l'intention démocratique,* Yaoundé, SOPECAM.

Mbokolo, Elikia (1990), ed., *Résistances et messianismes, L'Afrique centrale au XIXème siècle,* Paris, ACCT/Présence Africaine.

———(1992), ed., *Afrique noire: histoire et civilisations,* Paris, Hatier-AUPELF.

Médart, Jean-François (1994), "La patrimonialisation des relations franco-africaines," paper presented at Brazzaville + 50, Boston University, Francophone Africa Research Group Conference, October 7–8.

Melucci, Alberto (1985), "The Symbolic Challenge of Contemporary Movements," *Social Research,* no. 52 (4), pp. 789–816.

Mendel, Gérard (1984), *Cinquante-quatre millions d'individus sans appartenance,* Paris, Robert Laffont.

Merton, Robert K. (1965), *Eléments de théorie et de méthode sociologique,* Paris, Plon.
Meynaud, Jean (1961), *Destin des idéologies,* Lausanne.
Michalon, Thiérry (1993), "Légitimité de l'Etat et solidarités ethniques," *Le Monde diplomatique,* November, p. 26.
———(1995), "A la recherche de la légitimité de l'Etat," paper presented at conference, La création du droit en Afrique, Bordeaux, October 27–28.
Midiohouan, Guy Ossito (1991), "Modern Literature and Flourishing of Culture in Black Africa," *Research in African Literature,* vol. 22, no. 1, pp. 93–99.
Miller, Roger Leroy (1982), *Economics,* 4th edition, New York, Harper & Row.
Mimouni, Rachid (1992), *De la barbarie en général et de l'intégrisme en particulier,* Paris, Le Pré au Clercs.
Ministère de l'Information et de la Culture (1974), *Rapport du Conseil National des Affaires Culturelles,* December 18–24 session, Yaoundé, MINFOC.
———(1985), *Actes du colloque sur l'identité culturelle camerounaise,* Yaoundé, MINFOC.
Mishan, Edward J. (1981), *Introduction to Normative Economics,* New York, Oxford University Press.
Mitterrand, François (1993), interview in *Le Monde,* September 22.
M'nteba, Metena (1992), "Afrique: 'A quand la fin des indépendances?'" *Etudes,* vol. 376, no. 6, June, pp. 725–732.
Mobutu, Sese Seko (1994), "On a voulu me diaboliser," interview in *Jeune Afrique Economie,* no. 180, June, pp. 16–27.
Mofchie, M. F. (1994), "The New Political Economy of Africa," in: D. E. Apter and C. G. Rosberg (eds.), *Political Development and the New Realism in Sub-Saharan Africa,* Charlottesville, University Press of Virginia, pp. 145–183.
Monga, Célestin (1983), "Hors la musique, point de salut," *Jeune Afrique,* no. 1184, September 14, pp. 66–69.
———(1988), *Têtes d'affiche. Ces Africains qui font l'Afrique,* Paris, Silex.
———(1990a), *Esquisse d'une approche plurielle de la crise des finances publiques au Cameroun,* December, Yaoundé, Friedrich Ebert Foundation.
———(1990b), "Roger Milla est-il l'intellectuel africain de la décennie ?" *Afrique 2000,* no. 3, pp. 121–125.
———(1990c), *Un Bantou à Djibouti,* Paris, Silex.
———(1993a), "Computing a Democratization Index for Africa," unpublished research paper, Cambridge, John F. Kennedy School of Government, Harvard University.
———(1993b), *La recomposition du marché politique camerounais, 1991–1992,* Douala, GERDES.
———(1994a), "La problématique de la légitimité collective," paper given at conference, Droits de la personne et droits de la comunauté, Université d'Avignon, November.
———(1994b), "Coffins, Orgies, and Sublimation: Mismanaging the Economy of Death," paper presented at the African Studies Seminar, University of Chicago, February.
———(1995a), "Dollars, francs CFA et démocratisation—Symbolisme politique et fonctions économiques de l'argent en Afrique francophone," paper presented

at conference,Retour du pluralisme politique et perspectives de consolidation de la démocratie en Afrique, Université Laval, Quebec, May 5–6.

———(1995b), "L'indice de démocratisation: comment déchiffrer le nouvel aide-mémoire de l'autoritarisme," *Afrique 2000,* no. 22, July–September, pp. 63–77.

———(1996), *Measuring Democracy: A Comparative Theory of Political Well-Being,* working papers in African Studies, Boston University, forthcoming.

Morrow, James (1989), "Capabilities, Uncertainty, and Resolve," *American Journal of Political Science,* vol. 33, pp. 941–972,

Mosley, Paul, et al. (1991), *Aid and Power: The World Bank Policy Based Lending in the 1980s,* London, Routledge.

Moulton, John Fletcher (1925), *Laws and Manners,* reprinted from *Atlantic Monthly,* July 1924, Boston.

Mouralis, Bernard (1984), *Littérature et développement,* Paris, Silex.

Mudimbe, Valentin Y. (1988), *The Invention of Africa: Gnosis, Philosophy, and the Order of Knowledge,* Bloomington and London, Indiana University Press and James Currey.

Muhando Mlama, Penina (1990), "Creating in the Mother-Tongue: The Challenges to the African Writer Today," *Research in African Literature,* vol. 21, no. 4, pp. 5–14.

Muller, Edward N., and Mitchell A. Seligson (1994), "Civic Culture and Democracy: The Question of Causal Relationships," *American Political Science Review,* vol. 88, no. 3, September, pp. 635–652.

Nadel, S. F. (1952), "Witchcraft in Four African Societies: An Essay in Comparison," *American Anthropologist,* vol. 1, no. 54, pp. 18–29.

Naipaul, V. S. (1980), "A New King for the Congo: Mobutu and the Nihilism of Africa," in: *The Return of Eva Peron, with the Killings in Trinidad,* New York, Alfred Knopf, pp. 205–228.

———(1984), "The Crocodiles of Yamoussoukro," in: *Finding the Center: Two Narratives,* London, André Deutsch, pp. 87–189.

Nantang Jua, Ben (1995), "Beyond the Crisis: Comments," roundtable discussion at the workshop *Prospects for Peace in Africa: The State, Civil Society, and the International Conmmunity,* Amherst College, November 9–11.

N'diaye, Cathérine (1984), *Gens de sable,* Paris, P.O.L.

Ndiaye, Jean-Pierre (1976), *Monde noir et destin politique,* Paris, Présence Africaine.

New York Times (1995), "Zambian Government Plans to Deport Kaunda as Illegal Alien," October 19.

Ngandu Nkashama, Pius (1984), *Littératures africaines,* Paris, Silex.

———(1985), "La culture et son nouvel ordre: ordre et désordre," *Nouvelles du Sud,* no. 1, August, pp. 59–67.

———(1990), *Eglises nouvelles et mouvements religieux,* Paris, L'Harmattan.

Ngiman, Zacharie (1993), *Cameroun: la démocratie emballée,* Yaoundé, SOPECAM.

Notestein, Wallace (1911), *A History of Witchcraft in England,* Washington, D.C., American Historical Association.

Nozick, R. (1974), *Anarchy, State and Utopia,* Oxford, Basil Blackwell.

Ntsama, Etienne (1993), interview in *La Nouvelle Expression* no. 105, 4–8 November, Douala.

Nzete, Paul (1991), "Le lingala de la chanson zairo-congolaise de variétés," *Afrique 2000,* no. 4, IPRI, Brussels, January–March, pp. 95–101.

Obiang Nguéma, Theodoro (1994), "Quel dommage que mon pays soit méconnu!" interview in *Jeune Afrique Economie,* no. 186, December, pp. 100–105.

Olson, Mancur (1965), *The Logic of Collective Action: Public Goods and the Theory of Groups,* Cambridge, Harvard University Press.

———(1993), "Dictatorship, Democracy and Development," *American Political Science Review,* vol. 87, no. 3, September, pp. 567–576.

Ombolo, Jean-Pierre (1991), *Sexe et société en Afrique noire,* Paris, L'Harmattan.

Onfray, Michel (1989), *Le ventre des philosophes—Critique de la raison diététique,* Paris, Grasset.

Organization of African Unity (1992), *Document de Kampala,* New York, Africa Leadership Forum.

Ouologuem, Yambo (1968), *Le devoir de violence,* Paris, Seuil. Translated by Ralph Mannheim under the title *Bound to Violence,* 1971, London, Heinemann.

Owomoleya, Oyekan (1994), "With Friends Like These ... A Critique of Pervasive Anti-Africanisms in Current African Studies Epistemology and Methodology," *African Studies Review,* vol. 37, no. 3, December, pp. 77–101.

Owona, Joseph (1991), "Biyidi Bi Awala, l'albatros," *Le Patriote,* no. 63, March 11, p. 2.

Owusu, Maxwell (1992), "Democracy and Africa—A View from the Village," *Journal of Modern African Studies,* vol. 30, no. 3, pp. 369–396.

Pambou Tchivounda, Guillaume (1982), *Essai sur l'Etat africain post-colonial,* Paris, LGDJ.

Parrinder, G. (1958), *Witchcraft: European and African,* London, Faber and Faber.

Parsons, Talcott (1963), "Introduction," in: Max Weber, *The Sociology of Religion,* Boston, Beacon Press, pp. xix–lxvii.

Pateman, C. (1985), *The Problem of Political Obligation: A Critique of Liberal Theory,* Cambridge, Polity Press.

Péan, Pierre (1983), *Affaires africaines,* Paris, Fayard.

———(1988), *L'argent noir: Corruption et sous-développement,* Paris, Fayard.

Plato (1977), *Plato in Twelve Volumes,* vol. 1, Cambridge, Harvard University.

Poliakov, Léon (1981), "Mise au point," *Le Débat,* no. 13, June, p. 104.

Powell, G. Bingham Jr. (1986), "American Voter Turnout in Comparative Perspective," *American Political Science Review,* vol. 80, no. 1, pp. 17–43.

Powers, John (1995), "The Splintering of America," *Boston Globe Magazine,* November 12.

Prigogine, Ilya, and Grégoire Nicolis (1989), *Exploring Complexity: An Introduction,* New York, W. H. Freeman.

Prigogine, Ilya, and Isabelle Stengers (1988), *Entre le temps et l'éternité,* Paris, Fayard.

Przeworski, Adam (1991), *Democracy and the Market: Political and Economic Reforms in Eastern Europe and Latin America,* New York, Cambridge University Press.

Przeworski, Adam, and F. Limongi (1993), "Political Regimes and Economic Growth," *Journal of Economic Perspectives,* vol. 7, no. 3, Summer, pp. 51–69.

Putnam, Robert D., Robert Leonardi, and Raffaella Nanetti (1993), *Making Democracy Work: Civil Traditions in Modern Italy,* Princeton, Princeton University Press.

Quisumbing, M.A.R., and L. Taylor (1990), "Resource Transfers from Agriculture," in: K. Arrow (ed.), *The Balance Between Industry and Agriculture in Economic Development,* London, Macmillan.

Reichler, Claude (1983), *Le corps et ses fictions,* Paris, Editions de Minuit.

Richardson, John (1991), *A Life of Picasso,* vol. 1, 1881–1906, New York, Random House.

Roberts, A. (1990), ed., *The Colonial Moment in Africa: Essays on the Movements of Minds and Materials, 1900–1940,* New York, Cambridge University Press. The essays were originally published in *The Cambridge History of Africa,* vol. 7, 1986.

Robertson, Claire C., and Martin A. Klein (1983), eds., *Women and Slavery in Africa,* Madison, University of Wisconsin Press.

Robinson, Pearl T. (1994), "The National Conference Phenomenon in Francophone Africa," *Comparative Studies in Society and History,* vol. 36, no. 3, July, pp. 575–610.

Rohrschneider, R. (1994), "Report from the Laboratory: The Influence of Institutions on Political Elites' Democratic Values in Germany," *American Political Science Review,* vol. 88, no. 4, December, pp. 927–941.

Roitman, Janet L. (1994), "Lost Innocence: The Production of Truth and Desire in Northern Cameroon," *Critique of Anthropology,* vol. 14, no. 3, pp. 315–334.

Rosanvallon, Pierre (1981), *La crise de l'Etat-providence,* Paris, Seuil.

Rosen, Harvey S. (1988), *Public Finance,* 2nd ed., Homewood, Ill., Irwin.

Rousseau, Jean-Jacques (1762), *The Social Contract,* 1968 edition, Harmondsworth, Penguin.

Rufin, Jean-Christophe (1982), *L'empire et les nouveaux barbares,* Paris, Editions Jean-Claude Lattès.

Rummel, R. J. (1979), *Understanding Conflict and War,* vol. 4, Beverly Hills, Sage Publications.

Rustow, Dankwart A. (1970), "Transitions to Democracy: Toward a Dynamic Model," *Comparative Politics,* vol. 2, no. 3, April, pp. 337–363.

Said, Edward W. (1993), *Culture and Imperialism,* New York, Alfred A. Knopf.

Samuelson, Paul A. (1954), "The Pure Theory of Public Expendirure," *Review of Economics and Statistics,* XXXVI, November, pp. 387–390.

Sarrazin, Bernard (1991), *Le rire et le sacré,* Paris, Desclée de Brouwer.

Sartre, Jean-Paul (1940), *L'imaginaire—Psychologie phénoménologique de l'imagination,* Paris, Gallimard.

———(1947), *Existentialism,* trans. Bernard Frechtman, New York, Philosophical Library.

———(1964), *Les mots,* Paris, Gallimard.

Schmitter, Philippe C., and Terry L. Karl (1991), "What Democracy Is … and Is Not," *Journal of Democracy,* vol. 2, no. 2, pp. 75–88.

Schneider, Mark, and Paul Teske (1992), "Toward a Theory of the Political Entrepreneur: Evidence from Local Government," *American Political Science Review,* vol. 86, no. 3, September, pp. 737–747.

Scott, James C. (1985), *Weapons of the Weak: Everyday Forms of Peasant Resistance,* New Haven, Yale University Press.

Seligman, Adam (1992), *The Idea of Civil Society,* New York, Free Press.

Servan-Schreiber, Jean-Louis (1985), *L'art du temps,* Paris, Fayard.

Shehadeh, Raja (1983), *Tenir Bon,* Paris, Seuil.

Sheridan, Alan (1985), *Discours, sexualité et pouvoir. Initiation à Michel Foucault,* Paris, Pierre Mardaga Editeur.

Shils, Edward (1991), "The Virtue of Civil Society," *Government and Opposition,* vol. 26, no. 1, winter, pp. 3–20.

Simone, T. Abdou Maliqalim (1994), *In Whose Image? Political Islam and Urban Practices in Sudan,* Chicago, University of Chicago Press.

Sklar, Richard (1986), "Democracy in Africa," in: Marion E. Doro and Newell M. Stultz (eds.), *Governing Black Africa,* New York, Africana.

———(1993), "The African Frontier for Political Science," in: R. H. Bates, V. Y. Mudimbe, and J. O'Barr (eds.), *Africa and the Disciplines: The Contribution of Research in Africa to the Social Sciences and Hunanities,* Chicago, University of Chicago Press, pp. 83–110.

Snitow, A., et al. (1984), eds., *Powers of Desire: The Politics of Sexuality,* London, Virago.

Snowden, F. M. (1970), *Blacks in Antiquity,* Cambridge, Harvard University Press.

Soglo, Nicéphore (1995), "La maturité politique du peuple béninois a eu raison des injures," interview in *Jeune Afrique Economie,* no. 197, June 5, pp. 58–65.

Southall, A. (1970), "The Illusion of Tribe," *Journal of Asian and African Studies,* vol. 5, no. 1, pp. 28–50.

Soyinka, Wole (1995), "On the 12 June 1993 Election," in: *Nigeria's Political Crisis: Which Way Forward?* Conference report by the International Forum for Democratic Studies, Washington D.C., National Endowment of Democracy, February, p. 8.

Spengler, Oswald (1926), *The Decline of the West,* trans. Charles Francis Atkinson, New York, Alfred A. Knopf.

Stedman, Stephen John (1995), "Alchemy for a New World Order: Overselling 'Preventive Diplomacy,'" *Foreign Affairs,* May–June.

Sterman, John D. (1994), *Learning In and About Complex Systems,* Cambridge, MA, MIT—Sloan School of Management, typescript.

Stigler, George J. (1972), "Economic Competition and Political Competition," *Public Choice,* vol. 13, Fall, pp. 91–106.

Stiglitz, Joseph E. (1993), *Economics,* New York, W. W. Norton and Co.

Stohl, Michael (1976), *War and Domestic Political Violence,* Beverly Hills and London, Sage Publications.

Stubos, George (1993), "Consent and Consensus in Emerging Democracies: The Case of Eastern Europe," in: B. Berman and P. Dutkiewicz (eds.), *Africa and Eastern Europe: Crises and Transformations,* Kingston, Ont., Queen's University Centre for International Relations.

Suberu, Rotimi T. (1993), "The Travails of Federalism in Nigeria," *Journal of Democracy,* vol. 4, no. 4, October, pp. 39–54.

Tarde, Gabriel (1901), *L'opinion et la foule,* Paris, Alcan.

Tchundjang Poumi, Joseph (1980), *Monnaie, servitude et liberté. La répression monétaire de l'Afrique,* Paris, Editions J.A. Conseil.

Thériault, J.-Yvon (1992), "La société civile est-elle démocratique?" in: Gérard Boismenu, Pierre Hamel, and Georges Labica (eds.), *Les formes modernes de la démocratie,* Paris and Montréal, L'Harmattan, Presses de l'université de Montréal, pp. 67–79.

Tibbetts, Alexandra (1994), "Mamas Fighting for Freedom in Kenya," *Africa Today,* vol. 41, no. 4, pp. 27–48.

Timmer, C. P. (1988), "The Agricultural Transformation," in: H. Chenery and T. N. Srinivasan (eds.), *Handbook of Development Economics,* vol. 1, London, Elsevier Science Publishers, pp. 275–331.

———(1992), "Agriculture and Economic Development Revisited," in: P. Teng and F. P. De Vries (eds.), *Agricultural Systems,* London, Elsevier Science Publishers, pp. 1–35.

———(1993), "Why Markets and Politics Undervalue the Role of Agriculture in Economic Development," B. H. Hibbard Memorial Lecture Series, University of Wisconsin–Madison, July 1993.

Todorov, Tzvetan (1982), *La conquête de l'Amérique: la question de l'autre,* Paris, Seuil.

———(1993), *On Human Diversity: Nationalism, Racism, and Exoticism in French Thought,* Cambridge, Harvard University Press.

Toulabor, Comi M. (1981), "Jeux de mots, jeux de vilains—Lexique de la dérision politique au Togo," *Politique africaine,* no. 3, pp. 55–71.

———(1991), "Transition démocratique en Afrique," *Afrique 2000,* no. 4, January–March, pp. 55–70.

Touraine, Alain (1992), *Critique de la modernité,* Paris, Fayard.

Touré, Abdou, and Yacouba Konaté (1990), *Sacrifices dans la ville—Le citadin et le devin en Côte d'Ivoire,* Abidjan, Editions Douga.

Tylor, Edward Burnett (1958), *Primitive Culture,* New York, Harper (first published in 1871).

Vail, Leroy (1989), ed., *The Creation of Tribalism in Southern Africa,* Berkeley, University of California Press.

Vargas Llosa, Mario (1993), "Cuba, éternel crépuscule," *Le Monde,* January 28, p. 2.

Varshney, A. (1993), "Introduction: Urban Bias in Perspective," in: A. Varshney (ed.), *Beyond Urban Bias,* special issue of *The Journal of Development Studies,* vol. 29, no. 4, pp. 3–22.

Vattimo, G. (1987), *La fin de la modernité. Nihilisme et herméneutique dans la culture post-moderne,* Paris, Seuil.

Verba, Sidney, Kay Lehman Schlozman, Henry Brady, and Norman Nie (1993), "Citizen Activity: Who Participates? What Do They Say?" *American Political Science Review,* vol. 87, no. 2, June, pp. 303–318.

Veyne, Paul (1984), *Comment on écrit l'histoire,* Paris, Seuil.

Wade, R. (1990), *Governing the Market: Economic Theory and the Role of Government in East Asian Industrialization,* Princeton, Princeton University Press.

Wald, K. D. (1992), *Religion and Politics in the United States,* Washington, D.C., CQ Press.

Weatherford, M. S. (1992), "Measuring Political Legitimacy," *American Political Science Review,* vol. 86, no. 1, March, pp. 149–166.

West, Cornel (1990), "The New Cultural Politics of Difference," in: Russell Ferguson et al. (eds.), *Out There: Marginalization and Contemporary Cultures,* New York and Cambridge, The New Museum of Contemporary Art and MIT Press, pp. 19–36.

———(1993), *Race Matters,* Boston, Beacon Press.

White, Louise (1988), "Domestic Labor in a Colonial City: Prostitution in Nairobi, 1900–1952," in: Sharon Strichter and Jane L. Papart (eds.), *Patriarchy and Class: African Women in the Home and the Workforce,* Boulder, Colo., Westview Press.

Widner, Jennifer (1993), "The Origins of Agricultural Policy in Ivory Coast 1960–86," *The Journal of Development Studies,* vol. 29, no. 4, pp. 25–59.

———(1994), "Introduction," in: J. A. Widner (ed.), *Economic Change and Political Liberation in Sub-Saharan Africa,* Baltimore, Johns Hopkins University Press. See also her chapter "Political Reform in Anglophone and Francophone African Countries."

Willame, Jean-Claude (1995), "Aux sources de l'hécatombe rwandais," *Cahiers afrcain,* No. 14, Paris/Bruxelles, L'Harmattan/Afrika Studies.

Williams, D. C. (1992), "Accommodation in the Midst of Crisis? Assessing Governance in Nigeria," in: G. Hyden and M. Bratton (eds.), *Governance and Politics in Africa,* Boulder, Colo., Lynne Rienner Publishers, pp. 97–119.

Willis, R. G. (1970), "Instant Millennium: The Sociology of African Witch-Cleansing Cults," in: M. Douglas (ed.), *Witchcraft: Confessions and Accusations,* London, Tavistock Publications, pp. 129–139.

Wiredu, K. (1980), *Philosophy and African Culture,* Cambridge, Cambridge University Press.

Wittman, Donald (1989), "Why Democracies Produce Efficient Results," *Journal of Political Economy,* vol. 97, no. 6, pp. 1395–1424.

Wolfinger, Raymond E., David P. Glass, and Peveril Squire (1990), "Predictions of Electoral Turnout: An International Comparison," *Policy Studies Review,* vol. 9, pp. 551–574.

Woodall, Pam (1995), "Who's in the Driving Seat?" *The Economist, A Survey of the World Economy,* October 7, pp. 3–5.

Woodward, Bob (1994), *The Agenda: Inside the Clinton White House,* New York: Simon and Schuster.

World Bank (1994), *Adjustment in Africa: Lessons from Country Case Studies,* Washington, D.C., World Bank.

Young, Crawford (1994), "Evolving Modes of Consciousness and Ideology: Nationalism and Ethnicity," in: D. E. Apter and C. G. Rosberg (eds.), *Political Development and the New Realism in Sub-Saharan Africa,* Charlottesville, University Press of Virginia, pp. 61–86.

Young, Tom (1993), "Elections and Electoral Politics in Africa," *Africa,* vol. 63, no. 3, pp. 299–312.

Zakaria, Fareed (1995), "Bigger than the Family, Smaller than the State," *New York Times Book Review,* August 13.

Zartman, I. William, and J. Aurik (1991), "Power Strategies in De-escalation": in: L. Kriesberg and S. J. Thorson(1991), pp. 152–181.

Zghal, A. (1991), "Le concept de société civile et la transition vers le multipartisme," in Michel Camau (ed.), *Changements politiques au Magreb,* Paris, Editions du CNRS, pp. 191–205.

Index

About the Book

Many scholars have argued that the ongoing democratization process in Africa is doomed to fail because the political reforms have been essentially imposed by external donors. Others have challenged the very roots of the current changes, alleging that Africa needs cultural and economic adjustments before being ready for sustainable democracy.

Célestin Monga argues that both views are wrong. African peoples, he demonstrates, have been trying for decades to challenge authoritarianism, but their patterns of behavior could not be captured by the classical tools used for measuring political participation and political culture. *The Anthropology of Anger* sheds light on the continent's long tradition of an indigenous form of activism.

Analyzing social changes from a grassroots perspective, Monga shows that the quest for freedom in Africa is deeply entrenched. He goes beyond discussions of anger, ethnic conflicts, and despair to provide new frameworks for understanding Africa's internal social dynamics, and to reveal how Africa—an unusual political "market" with highly creative political entrepreneurs—is renewing democratic theory.

CÉLESTIN MONGA is Sloan Fellow at the Massachusetts Institute of Technology and visiting professor of economics and political science at Boston University and the University of Bordeaux. The author of numerous books and articles, he has been involved in the political process in his native country, Cameroon, as one of the leaders of its civil society.